Exploration and Irony in Studies of Siam over Forty Years

Cornell University

Benedict R. O'G. Anderson

Exploration and Irony in Studies of Siam over Forty Years

SOUTHEAST ASIA PROGRAM PUBLICATIONS
Southeast Asia Program
Cornell University
Ithaca, New York
2014

Cornell Southeast Asia Program Publications
640 Stewart Avenue, Ithaca, NY 14850-3857

Studies on Southeast Asia Series No. 63

Printed in the United States of America

ISBN: hc 978-0-87727-793-4
ISBN: pb 978-0-87727-763-7

Cover: designed by Kat Dalton
Illustration: designed by Stephen Mark Perina

TABLE OF CONTENTS

AUTHOR'S PREFACE

A collection of articles and essays written over four decades forces both the author and the editor to make some uncomfortable decisions. The first and most important is whether or not to tamper with the original texts, specially the earlier ones, which are most likely to contain foolish predictions, outdated "theories," missing significant evidence, writing in primitive academic prose, and so on.

In my experience, academics don't like to confess anything like "I was badly wrong" or "I was a real fool." So usually they rely on a kind of face-lift, which is often declared to be "updating." But like mainstream cosmetic treatment, the updating doesn't last long before another and yet another face-lift is necessary. My preference is not to meddle with the texts, and instead to let them gradually age. Furthermore, young readers will discover in the essays and articles the *Weltgeist* of the 1960s, 1970s, 1980s, and so on, and will also be invited to consider how the elderly professor's outlook, talents, and obsessions shift over time. There is nothing better for them than the author's confessions of being "wrong." It is perfectly justified for the old person to insert some intellectual improvements so long as these are italicized and dated, and the originals are not erased.

Second is how to spell. There are two kinds of problems exemplified by the cases of Indonesia and Siam. From around 1947 to 1974, Indonesians used the excellent Romanized Soewandi orthography, clear and simple, which also gently fixed the rather chaotic spellings of the late colonial era. In 1974, dictator Suharto imposed what was called the New Spelling, which, alas, lives on till today. The obvious, but never confessed, political purpose was to make anything written in the Soewandi style belong to the wretched past, outdated, often radical and revolutionary—youngsters would never read them, thought the tyrant. I see no reason to lose Soewandi, and have consistently written in his version up to now. Thus in footnotes, identifying sources, I look at the original publication date, and mark these sources as either pre-dictatorship or from the thirty-three years of the Suharto regime and its ugly aftermath. The case of Siam is the opposite. No government has ever succeeded in any dictatorial imposition that determines how to turn Thai letters into Romanized form. In my earliest texts, I used a rather pompous., school-boyish style marking the tones taken from mainstream Thai writing, and uncertainly following either the elaborate spelling in Thai or the nearest version tailed to the actual sounds of everyday speech. In this collection, I have deleted the tone markers, which help almost no one, and tried to stick to oral sounds, even if this manner is irritating to upperclass Thais. (The "proper" way to spell the last name of an upperclass prime minister is officially Pramoj, which no English ordinary reader would figure out; the oral way is Pramote.)

Finally, this is the place to express my deep gratitude to the Thais who taught me so much and so amusingly. They belonged or still belong to four "generations" as follows: 1. Three youngsters who got their PhDs in the United States just before the fall of the Sarit–Thanom–Prapat regime: Charnvit Kasetsiri above all, Thak

Chaloemtiarana, Nidhi Iosiwong, plus Suchart Sawatsi, the great second editor of *Sangkhomsat Parithat*, the liberal-left intellectual journal of the time. Kavi..... 2. The Revolutionaries of the 70s: Thanet Apornsuwan, Kasian Tejapira, Seksan Prasetkun, Thongchai Winichakul, And Chusak.... and Supot. 3. The Star Women of the 90s and till now: Idaroong (na Ayutthaya) editor of *Aan*, a journal that supercedes all previous intellectual journals in Siam, and far ahead of comparables in the rest of Southeast Asia; May Adadol Ingawanij, brilliant film critic, and Mukhom Wongthet, Thailand's top satirist. Plus the great filmmakers Apichatpong Wirasethakun, and Anocha ..... 4. The youngsters of today: Siriwut.... Pokpong.... And ?

I will never forget the debt to two terrific American women. Tamara Loos, who has written a great introduction for this book. Introductions in academia tend to be like advertisements, shallow and overly friendly. But "Tam" has not hesitated to be critical and has produced a penetrating account of my changing attachment to Siam, which I would never have thought of myself. Deborah Homsher has edited all Cornell Southeast Asian productions for the past twenty years with a keen eye, a great heart, and a huge sense of humor. She and I worked for two decades together, and we perfectly complemented each other: I the Bad Cop, and She the Good Cop.

— Benedict R. O'G. Anderson

LIFE COMMITMENTS: BEN ANDERSON'S SCHOLARSHIP ON THAILAND

Tamara Loos

October 2013 marks the fortieth "anniversary" of the first of two bloody crackdowns perpetrated by military and parastate units on unarmed demonstrators gathered on the campus grounds of Thammasat University in Bangkok.[1] The first occurred on October 14, 1973, and is perhaps more worthy of celebrating in anniversary style. It catalyzed the most open political atmosphere of Thailand's modern history. The second, on October 6, 1976, has not yet found its narrative closure. It refuses compliant incorporation into Thai history. Four decades hence, SEAP Publications has decided to republish the essays about Thailand written by Professor Ben Anderson, who wrote incisively about the political upheaval and possibilities of the 1970s and beyond.

Ben Anderson's sharp critiques of Thai society and its most powerful institutions came easily, or so it appears from his incisive argumentation and all-encompassing analysis. Perhaps that is because he is at once an insider and an outsider to that country, and to all the countries that he may claim as places to which he is deeply attached—Ireland, the United States, Indonesia, and the Philippines. It is tempting to scour his personal history for a genesis of this capacity for intellectual distancing and a simultaneous sense of belonging. Though this is pure speculation, it might help us understand how a man born in Kunming, China, in the mid-1930s to a British mother and an Anglo-Irish father changed the way the world thinks about nationalism.

---

[1] These crackdowns and coups were not the last interventions into politics by the Thai military. In 1991, a military coup organized by Sarit-style conservative generals overthrew the corrupt Chatichai government of "turn-the-battlefields-into-marketplaces" fame. Delayed civilian demonstrations against the military regime arose in May 1992 that provoked a violent response (known as "Bloody May"). The king negotiated a compromise, which has been criticized as a crucial turning point in the monarch's political power: it became more directly interventionist. The military staged another coup in 2006, ousting Prime Minister Thaksin Shinawat. A standoff between the mostly pro-Thaksin Red Shirts and the appointed (not elected) government of British-born Prime Minister Abhisit Vejjajiva provoked another military intervention in April and May 2010. Nearly one hundred people were killed and two thousand injured.

Ben could not take for granted his affiliation with any single country, and in fact he applied to become an Irish citizen in 1964, at age twenty-seven. At that point, he abandoned his UK passport in quiet protest against the waning British empire's repellent role in its former colonies that were then seeking independence.[2] His was a political decision as much for Ireland as against Britain. In fact, it took some effort to prove to the Irish state that he was eligible for Irish citizenship: his father's birthplace was Penang, his grandfather's was Singapore, and one grandmother's was Wales.[3] Although two of his grandparents were born in Ireland, their birth certificates were destroyed in the 1916 Easter Uprising in Dublin. His ability to assert a critical distance from, rather than reflexively assume patriotic attachment to, a national "home" is the benefit of his multinational upbringing. The downside was being viewed as an outsider wherever he went: "[I]n English schools we were marked as 'Irish', as we had been 'American' in Waterford [Ireland] and 'English' in California … [W]e were odd fowl there [in Waterford] too: the only family for hundreds of miles around who ate rice regularly."[4] He turned this into an advantage over time. Still, Ireland felt like home even though he and his younger brother were mostly educated in England. A year after his father died at the too-young age of fifty-three in 1946, Ben's mother sent him to an elementary school that specialized in prepping bright kids for entry into the very top high schools.[5] Living on her husband's pension, she made it clear that both Ben and his brother, Perry, had to rely on their wits to obtain scholarships. They both earned one of the few annually awarded scholarships to Eton, an elite, all-boys' public school in England.[6] In all, the brothers were away from home and their mother for nine months per year while attending elementary and high school, both of which were boarding schools and only for boys.

By the age of ten, Ben had spent time in Kunming, Shanghai, California, Colorado, London, and Waterford, among other places. This was not the superficial skating through delimited spaces that constrains tourists, but involved family life in southern China where his father worked for the multinational Imperial Maritime Customs Service. It also entailed being marooned in the United States for the duration of World War II—no civilians were allowed to sail to Europe. There the family moved from California to Colorado. In time the family returned to Ireland; he remembers racing his bike through the gauntlet of local Catholic bullies standing between school and home.[7] Like his father and paternal grandfather before him, who spoke Chinese and Pushtu, respectively, Ben absorbed languages. He also read voraciously, and as a ten-year-old began studying Latin, then Classical Greek in elementary school, and French, Russian, and some German at Eton.[8] Ben won a scholarship to attend Cambridge, where he read Classics, not government or politics.

---

[2] Benedict O'G. Anderson, "Selective Kinship," *The Dublin Review* 10 (Spring 2003), pp. 11, 9. This is an essay in which he reflects on his Irish and British ancestry. For another essay about his ancestry and father's life in particular, see Perry Anderson, "An Anglo-Irishman in China: J. C. O'G. Anderson," *Spectrum* (London: Verso, 2005), pp. 343–88.

[3] Anderson, "Selective Kinship," p. 11.

[4] Ibid., p. 9.

[5] See also P. Anderson, "An Anglo-Irishman in China," p. 343.

[6] Benedict Anderson, personal communication, August 24, 2013.

[7] Anderson, "Selective Kinship," pp. 7–8.

[8] Benedict Anderson, "Bot Songthai" [Epilogue], in *Nai Krajok* [In the Mirror] (Bangkok: Aan Publications, 2010), p. 362; Benedict Anderson, personal communication, August 24, 2013.

His essays about Thailand reveal a breadth of understanding about language, art, and literature that reflects his earlier linguistic pursuits and moves beyond the surface level of politics.

Ben's fondness for languages and keen insights into how everyday people use them was established early on. The specific focus on Southeast Asia was happenstance or a "fluke" as he remembers it.[9] Unclear about what he wanted to do after graduating from Cambridge, Ben received a letter from a friend who invited him to study, casually, for a year at Cornell University and serve as a teaching assistant. By this point, Ben knew he wanted to be a scholar, rather than a businessman, politician, diplomat, or other professional, and he knew, too, that the social context in the United States provided a sort of personal freedom that the UK or Ireland did not. A nudge from his brother, Perry, tipped the balance, and he came to Cornell in 1958 to study Indonesian politics with Professor George Kahin.

By the late 1950s, when Ben arrived in Ithaca, Cornell's fledgling Southeast Asia Program already included students from Indonesia, Thailand, Burma, Vietnam, and elsewhere. Thanks to anthropologist and founder of the Southeast Asia Program, Lauriston Sharp, the program's initial strength was in Thai Studies, with Indonesian Studies under Kahin running a close second. So, when Ben began teaching at Cornell in 1967, he found himself in the company of many sharp Thai graduate students who had recently arrived in Ithaca. They were the beneficiaries of economic development policies in Thailand that led to, among other changes, an increase in tertiary student enrollments from fewer than 20,000 to over 100,000 in the 1960s.[10] Many of them went abroad for a university education, including to Cornell. Many members of this almost exclusively male coterie at Cornell became intellectual luminaries. In the late 1960s and early 1970s, they included, among others, Charnvit Kasetsiri, Warin Wongharnchao, Bunsanong Punyodhayana, Akin Rabibhadana, Thak Chaloemtiarana, Chalatchai Ramitanon, and Prani Jiaraditarporn, trailed by her non-matriculating suitor, Sujit Wongthet.[11] Other now well-known Thais visited Cornell, for the good company, no doubt, but also to use the library's outstanding Southeast Asia collection, such as Thanet Aphornsuvan, Nidhi Aeosiwong, and Surin Phitsuwan, all of whom were studying elsewhere in the United States.[12] A particularly strong camaraderie developed between Ben and Nidhi, whose PhD dissertation from the University of Michigan focused on Indonesian novels and novelists in the final decades of Dutch rule, from the 1920s till the early 1940s.[13]

This generation of Thai intellectuals came to Ithaca just as circumstances were forcing Ben to rethink his choice of countries to study. If we may use romance as a vehicle for describing intellectual commitments, then Indonesia was Ben's first love. It should be noted that even as Ben published what became classics on Thailand, nationalism, and the Philippines, he never stopped writing about Indonesia, where

---

[9] Anderson, "Selective Kinship," p. 9.

[10] Pasuk Phongphaichit and Chris Baker, *A History of Thailand* (Cambridge: Cambridge University Press, 2005), p. 185.

[11] In addition to Prani Jiaraditarporn, Wirada Somsawat and Yupha Klangsuwan also studied at Cornell, but on average there were many more Thai male students than females.

[12] Thanet earned his PhD at Binghamton, Nidhi at the University of Michigan, and Surin at Harvard.

[13] Nidhi Aeosiwong, "Fiction as History: A Study of Pre-war Indonesian Novels and Novelists (1920–1942)" (PhD dissertation, History Department, University of Michigan, 1976).

he spent 1961 to 1964 conducting field research: "It was simply that I fell in love with the country, its people, its cultures, its food, its awesome landscapes, even its smells. It was also that Indonesia was politically saturated ..."[14] He found Indonesia infinitely rich to experience, not just study, which made it all the more painful to watch, as he did from Ithaca, the massacre of somewhere between a half a million to over a million people in the wake of a coup attempt in 1965. The massacres in Indonesia—the place where he could hang out with street vendors and ex-ministers with equal ease—had provoked in Ben a deep sense of bewilderment laced with betrayal, "like discovering that a loved one is a murderer."[15] Along with Professor Ruth McVey and fellow graduate student Frederick Bunnell, Ben co-authored a "preliminary analysis" of the coup, which earned him the lasting enmity of General Suharto, whose government banned Ben from Indonesia from 1972 until the fall of the authoritarian ruler in 1998.[16]

Cinematically, a combination of world events telescoped to this moment: Thailand sent a cohort of mostly progressive Thai intellectuals to Cornell at about the same time that Ben realized that his days in Indonesia were numbered. He was in search of a new country to study and considering Sri Lanka.[17] In 1967, he had just turned in his doctoral thesis on the 1945 Indonesian revolution, after which he began teaching as an assistant professor in the government department at Cornell.[18] Charnvit Kasetsiri remembers traveling with Ben in the summer of 1968 on the latter's first trip to Thailand. On a train ride from Bangkok to the north, Charnvit spoke with obvious pride about his country, the land of smiles. "I was still romanticizing about my great country ... But Ben said your country is changing" and referenced population growth, forest depletion, and changes in land use that would put an end to Thailand's abundance.[19]

According to his own account, Ben decided on Thailand for two reasons. The events of October 14, 1973, were welcome to him because of the possibilities offered for the advancement of progressive politics in Thailand after the fall of the military dictatorship. He has written elsewhere that the "euphoria resulting from the restoration of basic freedoms was infectious."[20] But just as important were the Thai

---

[14] Anderson, "Selective Kinship," p. 10.

[15] Benedict R. O'G. Anderson, *Language and Power: Exploring Political Cultures in Indonesia* (Ithaca, NY: Cornell University Press, 1990), p. 7.

[16] Benedict R. O'G. Anderson, Ruth McVey, and Frederick P. Bunnell, *A Preliminary Analysis of the October 1, 1965, Coup in Indonesia* (Ithaca, NY: Cornell Modern Indonesia Project, 1971). They finished the analysis by early 1966. For a partial history of the botched attempt to keep this document confidential, a failure that led to Anderson's being blacklisted from Indonesia, see Benedict R. O'G. Anderson, "Scholarship on Indonesia and Raison d'Etat: Personal Experience," *Indonesia* 62 (1996): 1–18.

[17] Anderson, "Bot Songthai," p. 362.

[18] The dissertation was later published as *Java in a Time of Revolution* (Ithaca, NY: Cornell University Press, 1972).

[19] Charnvit Kasetsiri, personal communication, August 13, 2013. Statistics collected later supported Anderson's comments: forests that had covered two-thirds of the country in the 1940s had dwindled to one-third by the 1970s, a result of the pillaging that masqueraded as economic development. It also served the purpose of eliminating cover for the communists who had been waging guerrilla warfare against the military dictatorship since the 1960s, by which point Thailand had become a crucial US ally in the Cold War, and served as a base for US troops during the US–Vietnam War. See Pasuk and Baker, *A History of Thailand*, p. 157.

[20] Anderson, *Language and Power*, p. 8.

students involved in the movement who had studied at Cornell.[21] His conversations with this group prepared him for a research trip to Bangkok between 1974 and 1975 to study the Thai language and the political situation as it unfolded. However, the events of October 6, 1976, caused a shift in Ben's perspective, as it dawned on him that here, too, as in Indonesia, his political critiques might cause his expulsion. The massacre of unarmed protesters led to the return of a military-backed government, the cessation of open politics and political parties, and severe repression of left-wing activists, who fled in great numbers. Almost simultaneously, the Indonesian military invaded East Timor, after which Ben split his time between his work on Thailand and testifying before US congressional committees and the United Nations on Suharto's domestic Gulag and the murders in Timor.[22]

Although over thirty-five years have passed since he wrote the first of the articles in this collection, Ben's essays continue to be read and assigned to students because they established the tone and framework for understanding the American Era (late 1950s to the early 1970s) in Thailand. Others have enhanced this understanding in important ways by including the views from outside Bangkok and from classes other than the bourgeoisie and student radicals. For example, Tyrell Haberkorn has questioned the scholarship's Bangkok-centric focus on students in her exceptional work on radical farmers from the north. Pasuk Phongphaichit and Chris Baker have provided precision and detail in their analyses of domestic capitalism, business interests, and the entanglements between economic and political processes. Katherine Bowie has considered the development of the rural, right-wing Village Scout movement. And Thongchai Winichakul has offered a fearless first-person account and analysis based on memories of the bloody crackdown on students in 1973 and 1976.[23] Even so, these scholars build off Ben's scholarship rather than fundamentally challenging it.

Two contexts, then, are important to a reading of the first three essays in this collection: "Studies of the Thai State: The State of Thai Studies" (1978); "Withdrawal Symptoms" (1977); and the excerpted introduction to *In the Mirror* (1985), a collection of Thai short stories. The first is the political context of Thailand. The second is the intellectual milieu of Thai-studies scholars in the United States.

Under the penumbra of US Cold War policies and funding, Thailand's economy grew exponentially, a condition that had ramifications for the Thai political and social order, including the development of an educated middle class. The period witnessed a powerful alignment of interests among the recently revived monarchy,

---

[21] Anderson, "Bot Songthai," p. 362.

[22] See, for instance, Benedict Anderson, "Prepared Testimony on the Question of Human Rights in Indonesia," in *Human Rights in Indonesia and the Philippines* (Washington, DC: US Government Printing Office, 1976), pp. 72–80. Another appalling parallel occurred in late 1991 with the Santa Cruz massacre in Dili and Bloody May a few months later in Bangkok. Prodded by Charnvit Kasetsiri, Anderson wrote about both incidents in "Two Massacres: Dili–Bangkok," *Southeast Asian Network Bulletin* 1 (December 1992), pp. 19–20.

[23] Tyrell Haberkorn, *Revolution Interrupted* (Madison, WI: University of Wisconsin Press, 2010); Pasuk and Baker, *A History of Thailand*; Thongchai Winichakul, "Remembering/ Silencing the Traumatic Past: The Ambivalent Memories of the October 1976 Massacre in Bangkok," in *Cultural Crisis and Social Memory: Modernity and Identity in Thailand and Laos,* ed. Shigeharu Tanabe and Charles Keyes (Honolulu, HI: University of Hawaii Press, 2002), pp. 243–86; Katherine Bowie, *Rituals of National Loyalty* (New York, NY: Columbia University Press, 1997).

the Thai military, and big business.[24] Their unstable unity fragmented by the early 1970s, however, because people grew increasingly critical of the unremitting exploitation by business interests and the military elite's flagrant corruption. Protests arose from many corners—not just students in Bangkok protesting the government's slavish subordination to American policy, but factory and farm workers fed up with poor working conditions and exploitative land policies, Buddhist monks critical of crass materialism and the Americanization of Thai culture, and villagers challenging the increased penetration and exploitation by the state.

Urban and rural dissent was on the rise, and folks such as those Thai graduate students at Cornell were reporting home about US university campuses ablaze with protests against the US–Vietnam War. In fact, nearly all of SEAP's Thai graduate students published in the left-leaning, critical journal *Sangkhomsat Parithat* (Social Science Review). Founded in 1963 by Sulak Siviraksa, the journal had become bolder and more influential under the editorship of Suchat Sawatsri in the late 1960s and 1970s, until it was closed by the Social Science Association in early 1977.[25] The journal provided an outlet for Thai graduate students in the United States to expose the Thai government's nefarious role in Laos and Vietnam during the US–Vietnam War. In addition, even some Thai Members of Parliament (MPs) were agitating for change, and the Communist Party of Thailand (CPT) was at last successfully recruiting members. Over half a million people gathered in Bangkok on October 13, 1973, to demand a constitution, which was granted. However, as the soldiers dispersed the remaining demonstrators on October 14, they killed nearly eighty and injured over eight hundred unarmed civilians. This action undermined all remaining authority of the military regime, sending the leaders into exile. It also initiated a stunning period of open politics, with near-daily demonstrations, democratic elections, labor strikes, organized agitation by farmers, and a decrease in censorship. It must have been exhilarating to experience, especially for a certain young political scientist and his Thai peers.

However, many in Thailand—especially those who had benefited from the military regime and its lucrative links to the United States—grew wary of the economic and social instability that characterized the period between 1973 and 1976. Domestic and global factors contributed to a polarization of politics. During the same short few years, the US withdrew from Vietnam; communist states were established in Vietnam, Laos, and Cambodia; economic crises struck Thailand as a consequence of the continuous strikes and the global economic downturn; and extremist right-wing propaganda whipped the newly organized rural and vocational youths into frenzy. The match that lit this incendiary mix was a faked newspaper photo of a Thammasat protest skit about the very real murderous assault and hanging of two workers who had put up posters decrying the return of the former dictator, Thanom Kittikachorn. The image of the two hanged protestors depicted in the play had been

---

[24] The classic study of this period and process is still Thak Chaloemtiarana's *Thailand: The Politics of Despotic Paternalism* (Ithaca, NY: Cornell Southeast Asia Program Publications, 2007 [1979]).

[25] The first issue honors its royal benefactors but contains articles by the Dalai Lama, Sulak Sivaraksa, Prince Dhani Nivat, Phya Anuman Rajadhon, and respected but more gentile academics. By contrast, the last issue, published in early 1976, boasts an editorial board filled with left-leaning academics such as Charnvit Kasetsiri, Thak Chaloemtiarana, Banthon Ondam, and others. See *Sangkhomsat Parithat* 1,1 (June 1963) and *Sangkhomsat Parithat* 14,1–2 (January–March 1976).

tampered with, likely by military intelligence, to suggest an image of the Crown Prince hanging in effigy. Purposefully misrepresented as an attack on the royal family, the photograph served to catalyze lynch mobs and justify the military to take over on October 6, 1976. The Thai Border Patrol Police (BPP), an agency created with US assistance, was the key organizer of the mob and paid some thugs handsomely for their participation.[26] Over 200,000 members of the BPP (in mufti), regular police, Village Scouts, and other right-wing groups, such as Nawaphon and the Red Guars, surrounded Thammasat University and began firing rockets, handguns, and anti-tank missiles at the ten thousand unarmed protestors.[27] At least forty-three were killed, over eight thousand arrested, and thousands of students, workers, writers, and farmer activists fled cities for the jungle and abroad.

This, for Ben, marked a turning point in Thai politics. On October 6, the military government had orchestrated mob violence—that is, it had drawn on segments of the population as allies to help crack down on leftist activists. A coup then returned to power the military, the bureaucratic elite, and the monarchy, which was now on the side of the military regime. Books were burned, journals closed, and political meetings outlawed. An instructive example is the journal *Sangkhomsat Parithat*, which was shut down by its parent institution, the Social Science Association, in 1977. The reasons for its closing were profoundly political even though the post-1976 regime did not directly order the journal's termination or arrest its editor, Suchat Sawatsri, who had gone into hiding because of the journal's political alignment with the Thai leftist students. In the last issue of *SP*, published in 1976, the editorial note critically commented on Thailand's new Dark Age and the violent potential of disunifying slogans, such as "right kill left." Suchat fully expected to return to work once the political situation normalized, but, instead, was provided six months salary and a letter of dismissal signed by the Social Science Association's acting president, Dr. Somsak Xuto, and executive director, Dr. Sombat Chantornwong.[28] The reasons given: the journal was not financially solvent nor was it considered sufficiently scholarly.[29] Unilaterally and without discussion among the members of the association's executive board, the journal was shut down.[30]

---

[26] Daniel Fineman, *A Special Relationship: The United States and Military Government in Thailand, 1947–1958* (Honolulu, HI: University of Hawaii Press, 1997), pp. 182–83.

[27] The Village Scout paramilitary movement was founded by the Border Patrol Police in the 1970s to counter communist insurgency and pro-democracy groups. Wattana Kiewvimol, with the support of the Ministry of the Interior and ISOC (Internal Security Operations Command), established the right-wing parastate group Nawaphon. Wattana claimed to have developed close ties to US intelligence agencies when he studied in the United States. Another right-wing organization, the Red Gaurs, consisted of hired vigilantes recruited and organized by two ISOC officers. Lured by promises of alcohol, prostitutes, and high pay rather than driven by ideology, this group was filled with unemployed students, high school dropouts, and thugs. See Bowie, *Rituals of National Loyalty*, pp. 105–6; and Pasuk and Baker, *A History of Thailand*, p. 192.

[28] Thanet Aphornsuvan, personal communication, November 4, 2013.

[29] Thak Chaloemtiarana, personal communication, October 31, 2013.

[30] Intriguingly, some of the same members of *SP*'s editorial board joined with Sombat to form a new English-language journal, also called *The Social Science Review*, which began publication in March 1976. It included articles by authors who were or became prominent in their fields: Chatthip Nartsupha, Thamsook Numnonda, Thak Chaloemtiarana, Sombat Chantornwong, Ammar Siamwalla, and others. The close relationship between the two journals reveals the insidious ways that political tension seeped in to fracture relationships among progressives, not just between leftists and rightists.

The National Administrative Reform Council (NARC), which staged the coup, submitted a list of names to the king in the hopes that he would select a military man as prime minister. However, the king did not want a military officer leading the government, and selected a civilian who had no political experience in government. The generals complied, and by October 9 the rabidly anti-communist former supreme court judge, Thanin Kraiwichian, was appointed as prime minister. A year later, however, in 1977, a group of young military officers known as the Young Turks supported a coup that replaced Thanin with General Kriangsak Chomanand. Much to the dismay of the king, Kriangsak literally cooked up a media event by freeing the "Bangkok 18"—left-wing activists jailed after the 1976 crackdown—and inviting them to his home to eat noodles (and be photographed by the press). Kriangsak's government gutted the CPT of its radical student population by offering a general amnesty, which most of the students came out of the jungles to accept. By the mid-1980s, the CPT had dissolved.

Although he never lingers on the monarchy, Ben has a way of naturally inserting it in his essays where it is culpable. He points out in "Withdrawal Symptoms" that "[t]he essential point to bear in mind is that the pivot on which this whole right-wing offensive turned was the monarchy" (this volume, p. 74). Key to this influence was the monarch's initial tentative support, if not for the students, then at least for limiting the violence committed by the military and police in 1973. However, the press made undeniable the king's about-face, as he was pictured in the *New York Times* as early as October 10, 1976, signing the decree that named the head of the new military regime.[31] He is pictured again a few days later signing a draft of a new, eviscerated "constitution with no specific guarantees of civil or human rights."[32] The US government and public, if they were paying attention, were well aware of the role of the United States in abetting the return to a military dictatorship in Thailand and indirectly supporting, through CIA funding of security organizations in Thailand, the vocational student vigilante group that perpetrated some of the most inhumane acts of violence and desecration against the student activists in October 1976.[33]

Closely observing these events from Cornell, Ben was compelled to take action. He wrote a letter to the *New York Times* denouncing the killers and the hypocritical stance of the US State Department. However, Thai specialists in the United States contacted by Ben refused to sign this open letter.[34] In fact, the Cornell campus and Southeast Asia Program faculty split in the 1970s not just over the US war in Vietnam, but also over the US government's role in Thailand. Radical student and professorial groups accused some of Cornell's Thailand specialists of assisting the US government's counterinsurgency efforts in Thailand, thereby embroiling them in the

---

[31] David A. Andelman, "Coup Driving Leftist Leaders in Thailand into Hiding," *New York Times*, October 10, 1976, p. 3.

[32] David A. Andelman, "King of Thailand Gives Approval to New Rightist–Military Regime," *New York Times*, October 23, 1976, p. 2.

[33] David Morell and Susan Morell, "Thailand and the US," *New York Times*, November 22, 1976, p. 25.

[34] The letter was signed by Anderson, Indonesia and Vietnam specialist George McT. Kahin, Indonesianist Dan Lev, and China specialist Jerome A. Cohen. Benedict R. O'G. Anderson, et al., "Thailand: The New Dictators," *New York Times*, November 2, 1976, p. 26.

"Thailand Controversy" that played out on several campuses nationwide.[35] For Ben, the lack of support for his letter to the *Times* among these specialists was infuriating and disheartening. It also helps explain what he calls his "Rottweiler" methods in "Studies of the Thai State," a *tour de force* that took Thai Studies scholars writing in English to task for their uncritical treatment of Thai history and politics.

He presented his critical review of the extant English-language scholarship about Thailand at a specially convened Council on Thai Studies conference held in conjunction with the annual meeting of the Association for Asian Studies, in Chicago in March 1978.[36] Present were all the major scholars of Thailand: Herbert Phillips, David Wilson, Sulak Sivaraksa, Michael Moerman, Piriya Krairiksh, Lucien Hanks, Clark Neher, Charles Keyes, and others. One can only imagine the tension in that room full of established Thai scholars as one young upstart courageously sketched in pointed detail the conservative political implications of their work. Eliezer Ayal, the conference convener, noted that "The one [paper] that aroused the most reaction at the conference was Ben's, because he challenged many long-accepted ideas."[37] The resulting article's breadth of vision and mastery of the scholarship set the tone for much of the critical scholarship written about Thailand after it was published in 1978. Ben is intellectually omnivorous and able to consume texts in multiple languages, yet little had been published about Thailand when he first began his foray into that country's history, politics, and culture. A glance at his footnotes reveals that he read all the scholarship available, including unpublished dissertations, and bitingly utilized the same data to support vastly different, gutsy conclusions about Thailand.

He revealed the poverty of political studies about Thailand, and listed the copious topics that had *not* been studied—a boon (still!) to those PhD students in need of a topic. A single sentence about what needed examination catalyzed a number of studies that turned into dissertations, then books. No mere pedantic taxonomy of the scholarship, this essay exposed the field for the political implications underlying its blind spots, and reassembled its denuded pieces in a way that starkly bared the politics of Thai Studies. He proposed four counterintuitive "scandalous hypotheses," which argued that Thailand was unfortunate because it had been indirectly colonized, it was the last *national* state in Southeast Asia, it was a modernizing state in the same manner that typifies "modernizing" colonial regimes rather than independent nationalist states, and its leaders were inflexible and the state was notoriously unstable, rather than flexible and stable, as much of the scholarship understood them to be. These shifts in perspective caused, no doubt, consternation among scholars who saw their work in a new and unflattering light, but it also pried open the conformist lid on Thai studies. It forced Western scholars into a critical posture *vis-à-vis* the Thai state and monarchy. This was revolutionary,

---

[35] Eric Wakin, *Anthropology Goes to War: Professional Ethics and Counterinsurgency in Thailand* (Madison, WI: University of Wisconsin Center for Southeast Asian Studies, Monograph 7, 1992).

[36] I am grateful to Robyn Jones, the conference manager for the Association for Asian Studies, for tracking down information about the Thai Studies conference held in conjunction with the AAS in 1978. Eliezer B. Ayal, *The Study of Thailand: Analysis of Knowledge, Approaches, and Prospects in Anthropology, Art History, Economics, History, and Political Science* (Athens, OH: Ohio University, Center for International Studies, Southeast Asia Series No. 54, 1978).

[37] Ibid., p. ix.

if one can apply that concept to intellectual work. Now it is safe to say that these scandalous hypotheses are taken as axiomatic.

"Withdrawal Symptoms" (1977) and Ben's introduction to *In the Mirror* (1985) were written in the same tone as "The State of Thai Studies" (1978). Published first, "Withdrawal Symptoms" launched Ben as a scholar of Thailand. Here, too, he overturned normative assumptions about the meaning of the 1976 coup as unique and revolutionary among the otherwise ubiquitous coups and countercoups that characterized Thailand's modern history. Although the arguments about the intra-class divisions and interclass alliances can seem tortured, the article maintains that the development of a petty bourgeoisie and a middle class provided old ruling elites with new, "popular" allies. This "popular" involvement in the bloody crushing of students in 1976 reveals the ambivalent nature of the political and economic changes affecting Thai society during the Cold War period.

If "Withdrawal Symptoms" offered an analysis of the violence perpetrated by the right, the editor's introduction to *In the Mirror* provided a parallel piece about the sociocultural history and literary work of the Thai left.[38] The excerpt from that book's introduction reproduced here traces the history of the short story in Thailand, beginning in the 1880s and leading up to the American Era. The short stories selected for translation reflect transformations wrought during the latter period. Based on his conversations with his Thai intellectual comrades, nearly all of whom were male, and his reading of *Sangkhomsat Parithat*, Ben believed that the military regime would continue its efforts to eradicate from public memory and the education system all texts and personalities that advocated fundamental social change. Publishing the translations by writers from this generation, the majority of whom were born outside Bangkok and politically conscious by the 1970s, would both liberate and preserve their voices from suppression by the Sarit and post-Sarit regimes. It also would give non-Thai readers access to "the real Siam."

By the 1990s, the underlying tenor of Ben's scholarship on Thailand had shifted: less anguish and anger, more irony. "Murder and Progress in Modern Siam," published in 1990, charts the history of political assassination in Thailand. It is the first time he analyzes a film, *Mue Puen* (The Gunmen, 1983), which triggered the counterintuitive idea that the increase in assassinations of MPs in the 1980s was a sign of political progress. Politically located between military conservatives prone to staging coups and the Left, the emergent bourgeoisie gained confidence after the 1970s eradication of any threat from the Left: the CPT had been vanquished and left-leaning political parties had disappeared. Out of this *nouveau riche* arose MPs whose economic and social base in the provinces helped elect them to national office, where they finally had a say in political affairs. Ben proposed that bourgeois power was being consolidated to the point that it not only challenged longstanding military–bureaucratic authority, but it also gave the position of MP market value: it was literally worth killing for. This ironic little insight turned on its head assumptions about the staid power of the military–bureaucratic government that exercised real authority. A twisted argument to be sure, but a compelling one.

"Radicalism after Communism in Thailand and Indonesia," published in 1993, reminds us that Ben never stopped thinking comparatively about communism or

---

[38] Anderson's reflections about the context within which he edited *In the Mirror* and wrote the introduction inform my review of his work and its contexts. Anderson, "Bot Songthai," pp. 361–73.

Indonesia as he studied Thailand. The essay contrasts the radically distinct histories and trajectories of communists in Indonesia and Thailand who shared little in terms of class, education, nationality, ethnic identity, or political experience. The consequences of their communist affiliations were also radically different. Ben writes that "Radically minded thinkers in Thailand were, in the 1980s and early 1990s, living freely and usually comfortably in a buoyant, crassly rich, thoroughly corrupt, bourgeois semi-democracy, unlike their Indonesian comrades terrorized by a merciless military regime" (p. 124). He articulates the questions he believes members of the Thai October generation must be asking themselves about the ultimate meaning or meaninglessness of their dalliance with communism. For the Thai leftists who considered him their mentor, even if they never formally or directly worked with Ben, this article may have given them pause. Perhaps not surprisingly, the three Thai former activists whose work he singles out for praise were all educated in the West, all male, and still (as of 2013) productive scholars. As in *Imagined Communities*,[39] nationalism (which ultimately motivated the political lifework of these artists and intellectuals he singled out in "Radicalism after Communism") was a male endeavor par excellence.

Between 1990 and 2006, Ben published *Language and Power: Exploring Political Cultures in Indonesia* (1990), *The Spectre of Comparisons* (1998), and *Under Three Flags* (2005),[40] but nothing on Thailand. He was busy writing and lobbying for the independence and freedom of the people of East Timor. He also continued to teach, edit, mentor, review the work of other scholars, give talks, and travel. His workload in combination with the intensity of his connection to all things political had taken its toll on his health, so he shifted gears, slid into semi-retirement, and sidelined political analysis in favor of the study of cultures. By the time he began publishing again on Thailand in 2006, Ben had entered his sixth decade and had been engaged with Thai politics for nearly forty years. The angry, hard-hitting, and ironic tone of the earlier articles gave way to mischievous playfulness. Still, all his pieces are provocative.

For example, in 2006 he published an article about film director Aphichatpong Weerasethakul's feature *Sat pralaat* (Tropical Malady) called "Sat Pralaat Wa!" or "What in the Heck is this Strange Beast?!"[41] In his article, which was written in Thai and directed at *Sinlapa Watthanatham*'s Bangkokian, majority Sino-Thai middle-class readership, Ben asks his educated, cosmopolitan audience why they don't understand *Strange Beast* but rural Thais do.[42] The film, which won the Special Jury

---

[39] Benedict R. O'G. Anderson, *Imagined Communities* (London and New York, NY: Verso, 1983).

[40] Benedict R. O'G. Anderson, *Language and Power: Exploring Political Cultures in Indonesia* (Ithaca, NY: Cornell University Press, 1990); Benedict R. O'G. Anderson, *The Spectre of Comparisons: Nationalism, Southeast Asia, and the World* (London and New York, NY: Verso, 1998); and Benedict R. O'G. Anderson, *Under Three Flags: Anarchism and the Anti-colonial Imagination* (London and New York, NY: Verso, 2005).

[41] Benedict Anderson, "Sat Pralaat Wa!" *Sinlapa-Watthanatham* 27,9 (July 2006): 141–53. This essay was translated from the English into Thai by Mukhom Wongthet. Three years later, a revised version was published in English as "The Strange Story of a Strange Beast: Receptions in Thailand of Apichatpong Weerasethakul's *Sat pralaat*" (included in this volume, pp. 131–46). For the original English version, see Benedict Anderson, "The Strange Story of a Strange Beast: Receptions in Thailand of Apichatpong Weerasethakul's *Sat pralaat*," in *Aphichatpong Weerasethakul*, ed. James Quandt (Vienna: Synema, 2009), pp. 158–77.

[42] Lysa Hong has written indirectly about the shift in consumer market for *Sinlapa Wattahanatham*, which originally published articles that challenged the monolithic narrative of

Prize at the 2004 Cannes International Film Festival, follows the relationship between two young men, one a lower-class soldier and the other a poor country boy, who are in love. The film shows them meandering together through various rural settings where time moves slowly and myth blends with reality, until the country boy morphs into a tiger haunting the soldier in the jungle.

Middle-class Sino-Thais dismiss the film as too abstract and aimed at Westerners, yet the fact that it won one of the most prestigious international awards puts them in a bind. They want the film to be recognized as world-class and as a reflection of how great the Thai are, but they don't understand the film, which is in any case not about Bangkok, heterosexuals, or the middle class, but is instead focused on a romance between two lower-class men from the provinces. By contrast, rural Thais, whom the middle class routinely dismiss as ignorant, see the relationship between the two men as so normal it is almost unworthy of comment. In short, Ben argues that only authentic rural Thai "get it," which he proves anecdotally thorough a few interviews with villagers who saw the film. Because many middle-class readers and intellectuals have come to revere Ben and identify with the politics of his critical scholarship, this essay's indecorous flip of social hierarchies provokes in them a mental scramble to retreat from their initial response to the film. In this way, his playful teasing is productive off the page. It also rejects the uninvited idolization of him and his ideas.

Unlike his earlier work on Thailand, the later pieces in this collection consider sexuality, gender, artistic production, monuments, and ephemera. Because Ben is the type of scholar whose work is profoundly grounded in the interests of the company he keeps, it makes sense that a shift in his comradely communities and scholarly focus would occur simultaneously, as they did in his articles about Thailand published after the millennium.

His conversations and friendships with a new, younger generation of publishers, intellectuals, and artists, many of whom are openly gay and/or female, clearly inform his work. Oblique critiques of capitalism, the persistent, seemingly incidental indictments of the monarchy, and dogged diagnoses of various middle-class afflictions gambol alongside his analysis of art and life. His writing remains refreshingly free of jargon, and he increasingly writes or makes the pieces available first in Thai rather than in English. Ben has always emphasized the significance of the translation of Southeast Asian literature, speeches, memoirs, and so on into English, even when his political scientist colleagues found this baffling because it would never advance his career in that field. However, in his later scholarship, he began to move in the opposite direction—to write *for* the young audiences from the countries like Thailand, Indonesia, Japan, and the Philippines to which he is attached, rather than for Anglo-Americans. This meant writing in or having his work translated into the dominant languages of those countries.

In addition, there is a quirky freedom in these Thai-language pieces, published in the politically defiant, cultural and literary journal *Aan*, edited by feminist Ida Aroonwong. In his articles, Ben's simple observations can bloom into profound political commentary as easily as they can sprout batty but entertaining insights. For example, his short and snappy "Two Unsendable Letters," published in 2011,

---

official Thai history, but for financial reasons had to target a more conformist middle class readership. Hong Lysa, "Of Consorts and Harlots in Thai Popular History," *The Journal of Asian Studies* 57,2 (May 1988): 337–38.

ironically jabs at Thai regimes over the years for their unethical political activities and inability to express an inkling of remorse for raiding the lands and pillaging the monuments of their neighbors. "Billboards, Statues, T-Shirts: Revolving Ironies" muses on the subject matter reified in ephemera like T-shirts, amulets, billboards, and statuary. His observations about comparable objects in Japan and the Philippines provide open-ended commentary about the jumbling contrasts between disorderly street consumerism and the orderly state organization of object worship. Thailand and Japan's constitutional monarchies impede the creation of statues or billboards honoring or featuring commoner heroes, whose images instead can only be found in the local towns where they were born. But in the republican Philippines, nearly every small town has built statues of national heroes. A difference exists in the ways consumerism surfaces in billboards in Thailand versus the Philippines. In the latter, one won't see representations of Catholicism on billboards, but will be bombarded by chiseled, sexy bodies selling just about everything else. By contrast, in Thailand—a country known for its sensory delights—billboards do not reflect this aspect of its capitalist culture. Instead, they reveal Buddhist abbots greedily peddling amulets, purveyors who have apparently chucked the idea of impermanence in favor of offering the promise of an array of this-worldly gains. Ben published the article in the same year (2012) and ironic vein as his consideration of the curious cement Buddhist hell amusement parks in *The Fate of Rural Hell: Asceticism and Desire in Buddhist Thailand* (London: Seagull Books, 2012).

In this collection's final essay on Anocha Suwichakonpong's film *Mundane History* (Jao nok krajok), the content within the film's frame takes center stage rather than the political economic context of the film's production and reception. Ben uses it to reflect on the presentation of masculinity, marginality, and the monarchy. He points out that the film may be interpreted as a political allegory of the decaying bourgeoisie, or as a parable of the decline of the monarchy. The film might be a commentary on the multivalent meanings of the father–son relationship in the high-anxiety political context of a dying monarch who has been neurotically and relentlessly symbolized as father to the nation. But for Ben, the film's core strength lies in its representation of masculinity and men as meandering, directionless, and angst-ridden, especially in contrast to productive, purposeful Thai women. "The unwritten text in this wonderful film is the anxiety, fragility, and perhaps, in the end, attachment/violence inside the ranks of those millions of human beings who don't remember being born, don't know when they will die, and ... can't give birth to babies" (p. 166).

The shift in his analysis from politics to culture, from military regimes and male leftists to film and masculinity, from the primacy of English to Thai language publications, reveals more than Ben's omnivorous intellectual appetite. It also suggests the reciprocal influence of Thai colleagues from two generations: the October generation from the 1970s and what might be called the "Lost" or May (1992) generation. These friendships inform his stance on Thai politics and culture, so the distinct compositions of these friendships—nearly all men in the 1970s generation, and mostly gender non-conforming female intellectuals and gays in the 1990s—are relevant. The student leaders Ben befriended and championed in his early publications returned, after Kriangsak's amnesty, to lead very different lives. Most were absorbed into academia, family or personal business ventures, NGOs, writerly occupations, or electoral politics. Most astonishing perhaps, given their iconoclasm of the 1970s, was their post-1976 political afterlife. As forty- and fifty-year-olds, many of these former activists joined the government(s) of Sino-Thai capitalist Thaksin Shinawat or the Red Shirts; and a few even joined the rightwing, royalist yellow shirts, the PAD (People's Alliance for Democracy).[43] Moreover, today in Thailand, unlike the 1970s, there is no clear progressive political ground to stand on or party to join. For left-leaning intellectuals of the 1990s cohort, Thai politics offers no moral compass. In this sense, they are, for now, a "lost" generation. Ben's capacity to unflinchingly assess the Octoberists has opened a space for members of the younger cohort to express their political and social aspirations and critiques, even of the much vaunted October generation. The strength of Ben's social, political, and intellectual camaraderie with both groups provides a bridge between the two.

It is a bridge planked by long, hot afternoons of blazing tropical sun and equally heated conversation. The happy outcome is this collection. Few people have had, in a mere handful of essays, such a lasting and catalyzing effect on Thai Studies as Ben Anderson. And Thai intellectuals over the generations have had as profound an impact on his understanding of his home away from home. The articles reproduced here map out, at once, an intellectual and personal journey that reflects the friendships and ethical commitments of a scholar who has dedicated his life to the politics, art, and culture of Southeast Asia.

---

[43] "Epilogue," pp. 369–73, treats the political afterlife of the 1970s generation.

STUDIES OF THE THAI STATE: THE STATE OF THAI STUDIES[1]

"What damn good is this country—you can't compare it with anything!"
attributed to David Wilson[2]

The world of English-language writing about Thai politics is a strange one. Consider only the following oddities: (1) No country in Southeast Asia, except perhaps the Philippines, has been more continuously open to Western scholars, yet there are only half a dozen serious published monographs about modern Thai political life—Coast, Darling, Riggs, Siffin, Skinner, and Wilson.[3]

(2) All the major studies were done in the 1950s. We have nothing satisfactory in English on the Sarit dictatorship, except an unpublished dissertation by a Thai, Thak Chaloemtiarana;[4] nothing on the Praphat–Thanom era; and nothing on the "democracy" of 1973–76. (3) While the military and the monarchy have quite clearly

---

[1] This essay originally appeared in *The Study of Thailand: Analyses of Knowledge, Approaches, and Prospects in Anthropology, Art History, Economics, History, and Political Science*, ed. Eliezer B. Ayal (Athens, OH: Ohio University Center for International Studies, 1978), pp. 193–247. Reprinted with permission.

[2] Herbert P. Phillips, "Some Premises of American Scholarship on Thailand," in *Modern Thai Politics: From Village to Nation*, ed. Clark D. Neher (Cambridge, MA: Schenkman Publishing Co., 1976), p. 452; orig. pub. in *Foreign Values and Southeast Asian Scholarship*, ed. Joseph Fischer (Berkeley, CA: University of California Center for South and Southeast Asian Studies, Research Monograph 11, 1973). So far, the only serious published critique of American scholarship on Siam.

[3] See: John Coast, *Some Aspects of Siamese Politics* (New York, NY: Institute of Pacific Relations, 1953). Frank C. Darling, *Thailand and the United States* (Washington, DC: Public Affairs Press, 1965) is the best available account of US–Thai relations, but is now dated; a traditional liberal critique of US backing for Thai militarism. Fred W. Riggs, *Thailand: The Modernization of a Bureaucratic Polity* (Honolulu, HI: East-West Center Press, 1966) is an early attempt at developing a political science framework for understanding modern Siamese politics. It contains very useful data on the economic activities and interrelationships of the Thai military politicians of the 1950s. William J. Siffin, *The Thai Bureaucracy: Institutional Change and Development* (Honolulu, HI: East-West Center Press, 1966) is a discussion of bureaucratic change in Siam from the late nineteenth century to the 1950s from a straightforward "public administration" perspective. G. William Skinner, *Leadership and Power in the Chinese Community of Thailand* (Ithaca, NY: Cornell University Press, 1958) is a systematic study of the power structure of the Chinese community in the 1950s, and of its relations with the Thai political elite. David A. Wilson's *Politics in Thailand* (Ithaca, NY: Cornell University Press, 1962) is now badly out of date, but still the best general political science book in English on Thai politics.

[4] Thak Chaloemtiarana, "The Sarit Regime, 1957–1963: The Formative Years of Modern Thai Politics" (PhD dissertation, Cornell University, 1974). Far and away the best treatment of the Sarit regime. Includes innovative analysis of Thai ideologies and of the politics of the Thai monarchy in the post-World War II period.

been the two most important political institutions in twentieth-century Thai politics, few in-depth studies exist of either.[5] There are no substantial works on political parties, on legislative behavior, on leftwing movements, or—aside from Skinner's outstanding work on the Chinese—on the political experience of the country's minorities.[6]

Indeed, the list of topic areas *not studied* could be expanded indefinitely. (4) I cannot think of a single political biography to put alongside the very useful books available to Southeast Asianists on, for example, Ho Chi Minh, U Nu, Sukarno, or Magsaysay.[7] (5) In Neher's helpful recent compilation, *Modern Thai Politics*, published in 1976, half the texts were written over a decade ago and only a third were authored by political scientists.[8] (6) Finally, and perhaps most interestingly, with the exception of Phillips's "Some Premises of American Scholarship on Thailand," written in 1973, there is, to my knowledge, no self-conscious or self-critical literature about the larger problems of approach or method—not to say paradigm—in Western (or American) writing about modern Thai history and politics. One has no sense that Phillips's text, interesting as it is, aroused any significant response or discussion among Thai specialists; indeed, I think it is fair to say that the piece itself was a response less to theoretical problems within his own or parallel fields than to the general politico-moral crisis produced among Southeast Asianists by the Vietnam war.

---

[5] With regard to the monarchy, two significant unpublished studies exist: Stephen Greene, "Thai Government and Administration in the Reign of Rama VI (1910–1925)" (PhD dissertation, University of London, 1971). This is a conventional but careful account of court politics under the controversial monarch, which includes good material on the royal favorites. Benjamin A. Batson, "The End of the Absolute Monarchy in Siam" (PhD dissertation, Cornell University, 1977). This is a valuable, clear-eyed account of Rama VII's reign, and a sophisticated revisionist rehabilitation of this monarch at the expense of the 1932 coup leadership. Walter Vella's 1978 book reached me too late for inclusion in the present discussion. See Walter F. Vella, *Chaiyo! King Vajiravudh and the Development of Thai Nationalism* (Honolulu, HI: University Press of Hawaii, 1978). On the military, Wilson, von der Mehden, and Lissak are skimpy. See David A. Wilson, "The Military in Thai Politics," in *The Role of the Military in Underdeveloped Countries*, ed. John J. Johnson (Princeton, NJ: Princeton University Press, 1962), pp. 253–75; Fred R. Von der Mehden, "The Military and Development in Thailand," *Journal of Comparative Administration* 2,3 (1970): 323–40; and Moshe Lissak, *Military Roles in Modernization: Civil–Military Relations in Thailand and Burma* (Beverly Hills, CA: Sage Publications, 1976). These works do not compare in depth of knowledge or sophistication of analysis with the work on the Indonesian military by scholars such as Harold Crouch, Herbert Feith, Daniel Lev, Ruth McVey, and Ulf Sundhaussen.

[6] G. William Skinner, *Chinese Society in Thailand: An Analytic History* (Ithaca, NY: Cornell University Press, 1957) (arguably the best single book on modern Siam), and Skinner, *Leadership and Power in the Chinese Community of Thailand*. Richard Coughlin's *Double Identity: The Chinese in Modern Thailand* (Hong Kong: Hong Kong University Press, 1960) is less satisfactory. Peter A. Poole's *The Vietnamese in Thailand* (Ithaca, NY: Cornell University Press, 1970), on the Vietnamese in Thailand, is a counter-insurgency tract whose weaknesses are clearly demonstrated in E. Thadeus Flood, "The Vietnamese Refugees in Thailand: Minority Manipulation, and Counterinsurgency," *Bulletin of Concerned Asian Scholars* 9,3 (1977): 31–47 (much the best discussion of the political fate of the Vietnamese minority in modern times).

[7] See: Jean Lacouture, *Ho Chi Minh: A Political Biography* (New York, NY: Random House, 1968); Richard Butwell, *U Nu of Burma* (Stanford, CA: Stanford University Press, 1963); John D. Legge, *Sukarno: A Political Biography* (New York, NY: Praeger, 1972); and Frances L. Starner, *Magsaysay and the Philippine Peasantry* (Berkeley, CA: University of California Press, 1961).

[8] Neher, *Modern Thai Politics*. Contributing political scientists were: Thawatt Mokarapong, Donald Hindley (visiting Indonesianist), David Wilson, James Scott (visiting Malayanist), Clark Neher, William Siffin, Fred Riggs, and Vicharat Vichit-Vadakan.

Various explanations for this strange situation present themselves; I would like to offer some of them for consideration, in ascending order of their interest for the purposes of this essay (and also of their intrinsic complexity).

(1) The small number of Western Thai specialists, and their homogeneous cultural and class background, have certainly been important factors. Most of the relevant work has been done in America, and by middle-class white male Americans. Thai political studies have not benefited as, say, Indonesian political studies have done, from a world-wide proliferation of alternative study centers. In the field of Indonesian politics, for instance, American scholars must pay careful attention to work being done in Australia, England, France, Holland, and Japan. Indonesian studies in America have also been cross-fertilized by a sizable number of non-Americans (to name only some of the better known: Herbert Feith, Justus Maria van der Kroef, Claire Holt, Guy Pauker, and Harry Benda) who, however parochial their particular perspectives, nonetheless, coming from different "parishes," often forced Americans into self-awareness by posing non-American questions. It is instructive, for example, that the first shots in the continuing theoretical debate about approaches to understanding Indonesia were fired between a Jewish-Austrian-Australian political scientist and a Jewish-Czech-American historian (see Feith's 1962 book, Benda's 1964 review of it, and Feith's 1965 reply to Benda).[9]

(2) If it is true—and it may not be entirely so—that the Thai were advantaged in not being directly colonized by a Western power, Western scholars have been seriously disadvantaged. It is difficult to imagine what modern scholarship on Burma, Indonesia, Vietnam, and the Philippines would be like today, did it not rest on the magisterial work of colonial civil-servant scholars like D. G. E. Hall, J. S. Furnivall, G. H. Luce, Bertram Schrieke, Jacob C. van Leur, Willem Frederik Stutterheim, Theodoor G. T. Pigeaud, Christiaan Snouck Hurgronje, Pierre Gourou, Yves Henry, Paul Mus, J. Ralston Hayden, and many others.

But (and this suggests an ironical perspective on the relation between good Western scholars and the fate of the peoples they study) this scholarship was made possible only by the colonial dictatorship itself. Such scholars were not limited by twelve- or eighteen-month grants, fragmentary data, politically turbulent field conditions, and so forth. They lived for years in the countries they studied, usually acquired a deep knowledge of the languages and cultures, had excellent bureaucratic access, were able to use the colonial administration to gather data, and worked in the total (if soporific) calm of late colonial domination. Modern Thai studies had to start largely from scratch, not only in terms of data and analysis but even—as will be noted below—of fundamental perspectives.[10]

---

[9] Herbert Feith, *The Decline of Constitutional Democracy in Indonesia* (Ithaca, NY: Cornell University Press, 1962); Harry J. Benda, "Democracy in Indonesia," *Journal of Asian Studies* 23,3 (May 1964): 449–56; and Herbert Feith, "History, Theory, and Indonesian Politics: A Reply to Harry J. Benda," *Journal of Asian Studies* 24,2 (February 1965): 305–12.

[10] I am, of course, referring to *scholarly* works, as opposed to travel reports, memoirs, and so forth. The most important pre-World War II scholarly works on Siam are, in order of their appearance: H. G. Quaritch Wales, *Ancient Siamese Government and Administration* (London: Quaritch, 1931); Kenneth P. Landon, *Siam in Transition* (Chicago, IL: University of Chicago Press, 1939)—possibly the earliest American account of twentieth-century Thai politics and still well worth reading; and Virginia Thompson, *Thailand: The New Siam* (New York, NY: Macmillan, 1941). Useful as these works are, they are not in the same class as the products of the colonial authors mentioned above.

(3) An important corollary of this condition is that in London, Paris, Leiden, The Hague, and various places in the United States, voluminous archival materials on the inner workings of politics in the colonial territories lie accumulated—on the whole well-organized and well-catalogued, mostly written in Western languages, and increasingly open to the interested scholar. That the Thai escaped direct colonialization has meant that nothing comparable exists for students of early modern Thai history. Not only are most of the essential comparable materials written in Thai, but they have been jealously guarded by the Thai rulers and ruling class.

(4) Much of the more valuable post-World War II scholarship on the newly independent states of Southeast Asia was informed or stimulated by anti-colonial sympathies. Needless to say, these sympathies did not in the least *of themselves* guarantee work of any interest or stature. But they did, in combination with the actually existing political situation, force modern scholars into a critical posture. This compulsion operated on two distinct levels, though in differing degrees for different territories. On the political level, insofar as the US government at various times and to varying degrees aided or supported dying colonial regimes, many scholars had to distance themselves from US policy right from the start, and to get used to the idea that policy and scholarship might have different values and objectives.

On the intellectual level, something more interesting happened. Since much of the best writing on the colonial countries was done by colonial officials and much of the best data came from colonial sources, liberal post-war scholars were automatically put in a beneficial adversary relationship with the intellectual-conceptual milieu in which they started working. They had to think out their positions vis-à-vis the colonial giants, if they were to challenge them successfully; they had to interrogate colonial materials in an inquisitorial mood if they were to penetrate to native reality through white documentation.

Precisely because the Thai were not directly colonized, however, all these processes worked in contrary motion for the Thai specialists. On the political level, if the Truman Administration hurried to abandon Pridi for Phibun, the implications of choosing between the two Thai leaders were far less serious than those of choosing between Sukarno and Hubertus van Mook, or Thierry d'Argenlieu and Ho Chi Minh. One might be critical of Truman's policy, as many of the senior Thai specialists were; but one continued to have cordial relations with the Phibun government in a way that it was difficult to have them with Van Mook's or d'Argenlieu's.

Much more importantly, however, Thai specialists were not confronted by a formidable body of colonial scholarship. Coming of age at a time when all their Southeast Asianist colleagues were imbued with pro-indigenous sympathies, they approached Thai, Thai governments, and Thai history in the same tender spirit. Rama VI and Phibunsongkhram were placed within the same conceptual category as Ba Maw, Sukarno, Phan Boi Chau, or José Rizal—rather than that of Francis Burton Harrison, B. C. De Jonge, Sir Reginald Craddock, or Albert Sarraut. In the name of nationalism the scholars were generally protective and, as a result, were inhibited from critical confrontation with the objects and materials of their study. It is only one of the ironies of the Thai/West relationship that precisely the same forces that tended to create a critical scholarly atmosphere in the study of the rest of Southeast Asia reinforced a timid—not to say conformist—outlook among the Thai specialists.

There is one further involution of this paradox that may be worth emphasizing. Because Indonesia, Burma, Vietnam, and the Philippines were ex-colonies, they fitted easily into a general conceptual category—that of "new states." They were seen as instances, or examples, of a *general* problem or situation. A great many superficial (and a few intelligent) works were written in the 1950s and 1960s from a global comparative perspective to show that however unique ex-colonial countries might imagine themselves to be, in fact for most serious purposes they were similar to one another and had similar relations with the industrial West. Southeast Asia specialists, confronted with the disciplinary prestige of this comparativism, had to struggle—for good intellectual (and often bad personal) reasons—to validate and explicate the *uniqueness* of their country of study. Much of the best work on ex-colonial Southeast Asia after World War II was done in this vein.[11]

Siam, however, not being ex-colonial, was taken as *ipso facto* "unique." And this "uniqueness" was typically celebrated, rather than studied or concretely demonstrated. Again, the general influence of Southeast Asianism was deleterious to Thai studies. Where everyone else was struggling to represent Burmese, Indonesian, or Vietnamese uniqueness, Thai specialists could—and did—proudly *assume* Thai uniqueness. Precisely in the case of Siam, a critical stance would have raised the comparative question and brought Barrington Moore, Jr., Shmuel N. Eisenstadt, and Samir Amin into play, to allow a penetrating assessment of what was really unique in the Thai experience, and what was not. It would have rejected the alibi offered by the general stance of other Southeast Asianists, who were facing very different perspectival and methodological problems.

The end product of these four constraints was, I think, a placid consensus among scholars (with rare but important exceptions, such as Norman Jacobs and E. Thadeus Flood) on a set of axioms about modern Siam, which I shall sketch out below. Only the events since October 6, 1976, have begun to shake the unconscious hold these axioms have maintained over the Thai specialists. One could, however, draw an analogy between Thai studies and the development of astronomy in the late fifteenth century. In that era, astronomers discovered growing discrepancies between what they observed and the axioms of Ptolemaic cosmology, and were led to increasingly strained and involved extrapolations from those axioms to "save the phenomena." But once the essential simplification and axial twist was made—that the earth revolved around the sun—it turned out that many conventional astronomical questions no longer needed to be asked, while many fruitful new ones became imaginable. Similarly, in Thai studies, I think, research done in the late 1960s and early 1970s was producing concrete data that could be explained, within the framework of the old axioms, only by elaborating qualifications and theoretical "subletting."

But before proceeding further, let me outline what I believe some of these axioms were—at the same time noting that they were actually constructed (so incapable are we of imaging the unique) on a set of implicit comparisons:

(1) Non-colonization was an unqualified blessing, which marked Siam as unique in nineteenth- and early twentieth-century Southeast Asian history.

(2) Accordingly, Siam was, in effect, the first independent modern nation-state in Southeast Asia.

(3) The Jakri dynasty's historical role was "modernizing" and "national."

---

[11] In a parallel vein, McVey's superb *The Rise of Indonesian Communism* was intended to demonstrate the autonomy and idiosyncrasy of early Indonesian communism against the "comparative" stereotype of Third World communist parties as faithful replicas and tools of the Kremlin; see Ruth T. McVey, *The Rise of Indonesian Communism* (Ithaca, NY: Cornell University Press, 1965).

(4) Siam's success was due mainly to the basic "stability" of Thai society and to the famous "flexibility" of its patriotic leaders.

If these are the central axioms, let me suggest two types of largely implicit comparisons that make them plausible. One sort—which underlies Axioms 3 and 4—is that the dynasty's historical role is to be understood as analogous to that of the nationalist leaders in the rest of Southeast Asia, starting with the Filipinos of Rizal's generation. That is, the Jakri were, whether they understood it or not, nationalist patriots.[12] The second sort—which underlies Axioms 1 and 2—is that the history of modern Siam is to be seen as fundamentally comparable to Japan's; in both cases, as it were, astute monarchical regimes made the necessary flexible adaptations to Western expansionism to escape colonization and to modernize "traditional" society.[13]

It hardly needs to be said that the facts that scholars are uncovering make both of these analogies more and more difficult to defend. Rather than finding further qualifications and elaborations to "save the phenomena," let us consider the following doubtlessly scandalous hypotheses:

(I) In certain important respects Siam was unfortunate, not so much in being colonized, as in being indirectly colonized.

(II) In certain important respects, Siam was almost the last to become an independent *national* state in Southeast Asia.

(III) The role of the Jakri dynasty, if modernizing, was modernizing only in the special sense that the regimes of colonial governors were modernizing.

(IV) Siam's "success/failure" is to be understood primarily as a result of the European imperialist pacification of Southeast Asia; Thai leaders have, in fact, been comparatively inflexible, and Thai political life has been (at least since the 1930s) an exemplary case of instability.

No less than their antecedents, these hypotheses rest on a comparative basis. But the relevant comparisons now are not with Sukarno and Ho Chi Minh or with the

---

[12] This perception clearly underlies the best book so far on Chulalongkorn's reign, Wyatt's *The Politics of Reform in Thailand*. It is explicit in the following sentence in the book's conclusion: "The king's task was, first, to seize power from his father's generation, and then so to use it as to bring *the nation* to a point at which it could accept his dreams and make them its own." David K. Wyatt, *The Politics of Reform in Thailand* (New Haven, CT: Yale University Press, 1969), p. 378; emphasis added. This book is a valuable study of changing educational policies in the broader context of politics during the reign of Rama V.

[13] Even the generally iconoclastic Jacobs accepted this analogy. In *Modernization without Development*, he wrote: "The Siamese or Thai case is of particular interest for a study of development because of the great similarity between Siam and Japan during the mid-nineteenth century at the time that the challenge of modern development first presented itself to both societies. Both societies were independent, both were largely homogeneous in culture, both had a strong sense of national identity, both had creative and often brilliant elites who were strategically located in decision-making positions from which they could innovate constructively, both had bureaucratic staffs able and willing to implement elite decisions, both were realistic about foreigners' (particularly Europeans') intentions and power and sensed the need for social innovation rather than verbalization to meet the threat, and both had the key, cash crops, to use as the means by which to implement productive change—to mention only some of the key factors often discussed as crucial to successfully achieving modern development. *Yet, Japan developed but Siam did not* ... " See Norman Jacobs, *Modernization without Development: Thailand as an Asian Case Study* (New York, NY: Praeger, 1971), pp. 3–4, emphasis added. This is an iconoclastic study of Thai society and politics in terms of a neo-Weberian patrimonial model. It views Thai "modernization" as a superficial adaptation to external pressures that leaves traditional power structures essentially unchanged.

Meiji reformers but rather, in different ways, with the indirectly ruled principalities of Southeast Asia (e.g., Brunei, the Javanese Vorstenlanden, and the unfederated Malay states) and with the "modernizing" regimes of colonial Southeast Asia.[14] (Simply from the point of view of world-historical time, these comparisons seem rather more plausible: Chulalongkorn's reforms correspond temporally with the "new" colonial policies of the Netherlands Indies and British Burma rather than with the Meiji reforms.[15] All of them precede by a generation the nationalist movements of Indonesia, Burma, and Vietnam.)

It will immediately be apparent that these hypotheses call into question the accepted view of the modern Thai monarchy and, still more important, the relationship between that monarchy and the modern Siamese nation. Rather than assuming a harmonious lineal descent from one to the other, they suggest contradictions between them. In fact, it is tempting to argue that it has been the identification of the two that has, on the scholarly level, systematically distorted understanding of twentieth-century Thai politics and, on the political level, retarded the development of the Siamese nation—leaving it, in some important respects, "behind" its directly colonized neighbors. The remainder of this essay will be devoted to an elaboration of this argument. For I believe that it may help supply a sort of "axial twist" that will both simplify and clarify some of the "problems" of the contemporary political historiography of Siam.

* * *

Few things illuminate the role of the Thai monarchy in the nineteenth century and early twentieth century better than a consideration of the "modernization" of the Thai armed forces. (In addition, one cannot, I think, comprehend the modern political role of the Thai military without clearly understanding its historical origins.) Nothing shows more clearly the *non-parallelism* of the Chulalongkorn regime with that of the Meiji oligarchs and the *parallelism* with the indirectly ruled states of nineteenth-century Southeast Asia.

---

[14] Batson, generally admiring of the Jakri, makes the latter analogy with great lucidity. "The late nineteenth-century Thai government, with its goals of technological development, rationalization of the administration, and expansion of central government control to areas remote from the center, was in many respects similar to colonial regimes in neighboring countries, and the Thai official sent from Bangkok to supervise the administration in Chiengmai or Ubon was *only somewhat less foreign* than the British district officer in Malaya or the French *résident* in Indochina" (Batson, "The End of the Absolute Monarchy in Siam," p. 18; emphasis added).

[15] Noel Battye shows that the purpose of the young Chulalongkorn's visits to colonial Singapore and Batavia in 1870 and British India in 1872 was, in Chulalongkorn's own words, "selecting what may be safe models." See: Noel A. Battye, "The Military, Government, and Society in Siam, 1868–1910: Politics and Military Reform during the Reign of King Chulalongkorn" (PhD dissertation, Cornell University, 1974), p. 118. Battye's is the only full-length study of relations between the crown and the military in modern Thai history. Very rich in data; theoretically, a bit diffuse. As Battye wryly notes, "There was both *enticement* and instruction in these colonies which throve on order maintained by small but efficient military establishments" (p. 120; emphasis added). It is instructive that the young sovereign never made a comparable trip to Japan. Later on, in a pattern followed by many of the more advanced Southeast Asian "protected" rulers, he sent his heir to be educated in the metropole (in this case, England).

The Meiji oligarchs came to power in 1868 by coup d'état. Taking advantage of Western-style military organization, tactics, and munitions, they defeated the obsolete levies of the Bakufu and proceeded immediately to establish what was essentially a military dictatorship in the name of the restored monarch. Residual feudal military forces were liquidated—not only on the basis of borrowed technical instrumentalities but by nationally conceived and administered conscription (1873). Already in 1872, a program of mass education had been initiated in order to provide the popular basis for a large standing army and a *national* polity. The army (and navy) were basically intended for external use, and within a generation they had proved their capacities in successful wars with China and Imperial Russia.

By contrast, while Chulalongkorn came to the throne in the year of the Meiji oligarchs' coup, a Thai Ministry of War was not set up till 1894, the year prior to the Sino–Japanese war. Conscription was not introduced until 1905, a whole generation later than in Japan.[16] Furthermore, no attempt was made to tie educational development to military requirements; indeed, modern primary education was not even made formally compulsory till the reign of Rama VI.[17]

The key fact—which provides the framework for understanding the entire evolution of the Thai monarchy and the Thai military—is that between roughly 1840 and 1940 the state ceased not only to engage in warfare but even to seriously contemplate doing so.[18] Long before the French and British annexations (which

---

[16] Ibid., p. 429.

[17] By the beginning of this century, virtually all Japanese children were in primary school, and a national pyramid of secondary and tertiary educational institutions run by Japanese was in good working order. By contrast, the Thai government was happy to announce in 1957 that in fourteen of seventy-one provinces more than half the population had completed primary education. See Harvey H. Smith et al., *Area Handbook for Thailand* (Washington, DC: US Government Printing Office, 1968), p. 161. As late as 1974, the average number of years spent in school by Thai nationals was 5.56, only slightly more than a lower primary education stretch. See Bevars D. Mabry, "The Development of Labor Institutions in Thailand" (1977), to be published as Cornell University Data Paper 112, Southeast Asia Program Publications, 1979, p. 11. The first full-fledged university (Chulalongkorn University) was set up in 1917, four decades after the Imperial University in Tokyo. And as Wilson observes, "Until World War II, the best secondary schools were administered by Europeans, and university deans were often Europeans" (Wilson, *Politics in Thailand*, p. 62).

If this discrepancy between Siamese and Japanese progress escaped the eye of the Thai monarchs, it was evidently obvious to some of their subjects. Greene notes that the ringleaders of the 1912 attempted coup against Rama VI cited Japan as their model in demanding changes in the state educational system, cuts in government expenditures in certain fields, and democratization. Otherwise, they felt, Siam would *"continue* to fall behind the rest of the world and *continue* to receive the disrespect of all the advanced nations" (Greene, "Thai Government and Administration in the Reign of Rama VI [1910–1925]," p. 133, emphasis added).

[18] As Battye notes, "Mongkut [Rama IV] was the first Chakri king who never led an army into battle and [Sisuryawong] the Great Minister had campaigned only once, and then unsuccessfully" (Battye, "The Military, Government, and Society in Siam, 1868–1910," p. 66). Skinner observes: "Rama III's successors were able to avoid 'shooting' wars altogether" (Skinner, *Chinese Society in Thailand,* p. 30).

It should perhaps be added that the term "Thai military" is essentially anachronistic. Battye ("The Military, Government, and Society in Siam, 1868–1910," pp. 20–22) shows that the armed units serving the Jakri rulers in the nineteenth century were anything but Thai (just as the eighteenth-century Prussian army was anything but Prussian). Most of these units were manned by Vietnamese, Khmer, Mon, and Lao—either descendants of war captives or immigrant adventurers who offered their services to the king. "Under Rama III and IV non-Siamese—who had long since manned the Second and Third Foot Guards—bore the brunt of

occurred between 1885 and 1909), the real external security of the Thai monarchical state had been guaranteed by the European imperial powers. All of the Thai rulers' traditional rivals—Burmese, Khmer, Lao, and Vietnamese—were demilitarized by being subjected to European colonialism.[19] (In precisely the same way, all the surviving monarchs of Southeast Asia had their external relations "pacified" by one or another of the colonial powers.)

As a result, the "modern Thai" army (and navy) had no serious external defense function, and indeed virtually never fought except against "domestic" forces (compare Japan!). The Thai military was mainly a means for *internal* royalist consolidation;[20] it was, in addition, an emblem of modernity for the outside world.[21]

---

calls for new military formations." Under Rama III, Vietnamese were recruited for training as "sepoy" artillery, Mon for "sepoy" infantry. In 1852, Khmer and Bangkok Lao were formed into new units of King's Guards. Non-Siamese were especially overrepresented in "the more technical and up-to-date" units. The crews of the "Thai" navy were predominantly Cham and Malay.

[19] The Thai rulers were fully conscious of the advantages they derived in this respect from European imperialism. As late as 1930, the year of the Nghe An and Ha Tinh peasant insurrections and the Yen Bay military uprising in Vietnam, Rama VII observed: "As long as French rule continues in Vietnam it is a 'safeguard' for Siam. No matter how much we sympathize with the Vietnamese, when one thinks of the danger that might arise, one has to hope that the Vietnamese will not easily escape from the power of the French. Aside from the necessity of maintaining good relations with the French, I believe it is the direct interest of Siam not to give protection to Vietnamese rebels or in any way to aid the Vietnamese in freeing themselves from French rule." See Batson, "The End of the Absolute Monarchy in Siam," p. 183. Needless to say, it is hard to imagine such thoughts occurring to Ho Chi Minh, Sukarno, or Aung San at that time.

[20] Though he himself largely overlooks it, this point is thoroughly demonstrated by Battye's data (Battye, "The Military, Government, and Society in Siam, 1868–1910"; all references in this footnote are from that work). He notes that at the beginning of Mongkut's reign, the royal armies had been outgunned by the Lord of Keng Tung. But this situation soon changed as "Bangkok began to gather new strength, *for new weapons could be speedily dispatched by Western sail and steam*" (p. 76; emphasis added). When the young Chulalongkorn came of political age, one of the first "reforms" he undertook was the formation of a special royal bodyguard, which "formed a most important base of support for the king's 'party' or faction in the lively politics of his first regnal year" (p. 133). But the young king's ambitions soon expanded. "The king had not forgotten the link between the armies of the [British] Raj and the [Dutch] Kumpeni and effective government and prosperity ... He wanted an adequate force 'to put down unlawful persons within the country ...'" (p. 132). He wrote to the Governor-General of India in March 1874 that "we must make an effort to constrain the provinces"; and he duly sent a royal commissioner to Chiengmai accompanied by a military garrison (p. 146). Battye adds, "There is no reason to disbelieve the report of the British Consul that the ["modern"] army, a novelty on the Siamese scene, was created for 'internal political rather than external military purposes'"(p. 226).

After a military success in Isan in 1885, made possible by imported land mines (whose novelty terrified the local opposition), Chulalongkorn for the first time, in his Birthday Speech of 1886, began to speak of his Lao "provinces" (pp. 251ff). In the late 1880s and early 1890s, "before he turned to major reform of his government, King Chulalongkorn carried out a series of military reforms which bear all the marks of internal political safeguards" (p. 268). Finally, Battye shows that military conscription, decreed in 1905, was prompted by the so-called Holy Man and Shan rebellions of 1902, which in turn were "reactions to the extension and intensification of Siamese government into former tributary states ... Confidence in internal security [sic] was shaken ... The argument for a national conscript army as *an essential instrument of internal governance* ... unexpectedly gathered strength" (pp. 429–30; emphasis added).

In this light we may better understand the status panic of the Thai military at Rama VI's creation of a second, rival toy soldiery in the Wild Tigers.[22] Had the Thai military had a credible external role to play, this panic would certainly never have arisen.

Wholly ineffective as far as defense was concerned, the Thai military nonetheless (or rather, precisely *because* it had no external function) eventually came to dominate the domestic political process, turning on the rulers who created it[23] in a pattern that has been more recently replicated in Libya, Egypt, Ethiopia, Iraq, and Cambodia. (It is instructive in this light to reflect on the parallels between Rama VII and Idrus, Farouk, Haile Selassie, Faisal, and Sihanouk.)

Yet in many basic respects the coup of 1932 did nothing to change the basic role, outlook, and habits of the Thai military.[24] Indeed, these habits, rigidly maintained (Thai "flexibility" notwithstanding), help to explain the less-than-glorious role of the military since the century of European imperialist pacification came to an end and

---

[21] "Most foreigners saw Siam's armed forces as too large for purposes of maintaining internal order and yet far too small in the event of a conflict with a major European power, which in any case now (1920s) seemed an extremely remote possibility. As Siam's only territorial neighbors were British or French colonial possessions, it was not clear what enemy the Thai military was designed to fight ... Many Thai, however, felt that a substantial military establishment was necessary for national prestige" (Batson, "The End of the Absolute Monarchy in Siam," p. 51). Sir Edward Cook, Financial Adviser to the royal government, noted in 1925 that 23.3 percent of the budget was spent on "defense," a proportion higher than in the budgets of Japan, the Netherlands, Spain, etc. (ibid., p. 29). An instructive early example of dangerous overspending on "prestige."

[22] For useful material on the Wild Tigers, see Greene, "Thai Government and Administration in the Reign of Rama VI (1910–1925)," pp. 103–13 in particular. He suggests that, in forming this corps, Rama VI was doing exactly what his father, Rama V, had done in 1873/74: creating a loyal military force to consolidate a shaky political position and to challenge an entrenched political "old guard." That the Wild Tigers were basically "toy soldiers" is, I think, widely accepted; but the term may seem inappropriate when applied to the Thai armed forces.

Once again, material in Battye ("The Military, Government, and Society in Siam, 1868–1910") is illuminating. With regard to the Franco–Siamese crisis of 1893, he comments that the Thai fleet "was more familiar with picknicking and the logistics of royal vacations than with combat maneuvers" (p. 325). He also cites (p. 326) these words of Henry Norman in the *Contemporary Review* (1893): "A couple of hostile British and French gunboats, and a thousand soldiers on shore, and the whole structure of Siam would fall like a house of cards ..." Such views cannot be written off as colonial-minded prejudice. Rama V's Finance Minister, Prince Mahit, wrote acidly in 1906 that Siam should "stop playing soldiers" (p. 463). And an expert French military observer noted calmly in 1908 that *"cette force navale est, pour ainsi dire, nulle"* (p. 533).

[23] Two vignettes illustrative of the Thai military and its domestic political role are offered by Battye and Batson. Battye (ibid., pp. 263ff.) remarks that in the mid-1880s, young reformers with European education—while dismissing any hope of external defense against the West—still strongly supported modernizing the military in order to push through domestic reforms against conservative opposition and the provinces. Batson ("The End of the Absolute Monarchy in Siam," p. 202) brings to our attention a memorandum written in 1928 by Prince Boworadet to Rama VII. In this memorandum, the Prince, then Minister of War, criticized Thai officers for their "slackness and general apathy," "intriguing mentality," and "money-making bent," adding that "Actually, the spirit of the officers is deplorable, and if left may even become a source of danger, for it must be recollected that we live in times in which subversive propaganda is likely to become prevalent." In reply, Rama VII said that the military cadet school was in such bad shape that at one time he believed the only thing to do was to close it down and "let the bad examples be forgotten and start afresh."

[24] See Jacobs, *Modernization without Development: Thailand as an Asian Case Study*, esp. 43ff.

the Thai found themselves once again up against Khmer, Vietnamese, Burmese, and the rest. In the 1950–76 era, Siam's defense continued to be guaranteed by foreigners (in this case, American and Chinese troops), present in numbers never before seen on Thai soil.[25] The Thai military's external role in Korea, South Vietnam, and Laos was little more than economic. Burdened with its ancestry, it remains today—like its half-forgotten cousin, the Wild Tigers—a cluster of self-absorbed, status-conscious, privileged bureaucratic factions. (We need only compare the intra-Southeast Asian prowess of the "Thai" armies of pre-1840 with those of post-1940.)

At the same time, the coup of 1932 assumes, within this perspective, a meaning that shows precisely the superficiality of any comparison between Meiji Japan and Jakri Siam. For a "1932" never occurred in Japan, and the Japanese military in modern times never turned against the Japanese monarchy. The reason is simple but instructive. While the able, lower samurai "oligarchs" claimed to be restoring the centrality of the monarchy against Bakufu usurpation, in fact they never permitted the monarch to play an active political role. Drawing popular legitimacy from the monarch and exploiting his sacral prestige, the oligarchs abolished the samurai as a politico-military caste and engaged in fierce political competition among themselves as, in some sense, "citizens."

To an important extent, real power in Meiji Japan lay in "commoner" hands and flowed in "meritocratic" channels. The ruler remained the "object," not the "subject," of politics. In Siam, the Jakri dynasty—like other nineteenth-century Southeast Asian royalties—continued till very late in the day to play "subject" rather than "object."[26] The pool of available political and military talent remained arbitrarily narrow for precisely this reason. "Merit" versus "blood" accordingly became a political issue in a way that was inconceivable in Japan.[27]

---

[25] In 1968, there were at least 46,000 American troops alone on Thai soil—almost three times the number of colonial troops in the Netherlands Indies in the 1930s. (For the 1968 figure, see *New York Times*, April 14, 1968.)

[26] It is almost with a sense of time-warp that one reads in Wyatt that Rama V, like his father before him, bought "property abroad for use in the event that abdication and exile became necessary" (Wyatt, *The Politics of Reform in Thailand*, p. 61). Is it possible that these men were the first Southeast Asian political figures to take out *this kind* of political life insurance? It is difficult to imagine the Emperor Meiji doing the same thing. How aware the Siamese royalty were of the difference between their own role and that of the Japanese emperors is revealed by Rama VI's remark, to his cabinet in 1925, that he had no intention of being pushed aside "like the Mikado in Japan" (see Batson, "The End of the Absolute Monarchy in Siam," p. 30).

[27] It is sometimes thought that this became a real problem only in the reign of Rama VII. However, Battye's work ("The Military, Government, and Society in Siam, 1868–1910," from which comes all the material in this note) shows conclusively how Chulalongkorn's military policies ran flatly against professional, meritocratic standards. For example, when conscription was finally enacted, civil servants who were conscripted were given military ranks equivalent to those they had previously held in the civil service, regardless of their military talents and qualifications (pp. 454–56). In 1906, the rules for entry into the Military Academy were changed: henceforth, candidates had to be children of "reputable" parents and to be sponsored and guaranteed by a commissioned government official (p. 494).

In 1909, entrance to the three preparatory grades of the Military Academy was limited exclusively to scions of the royal family, the maternal family of Bang Chang, and sons of military officers. In addition, a special class was created for sons of royalty with the rank of Serene Highness and above, and sons of military officers with commissioned or warrant rank: no examinations were required for this class (p. 495). In 1910, the year of Chulalongkorn's death, only members of the royal family held the ranks of General and Lieutenant-General; six out of thirteen Major-Generals were also of royal birth. The upper echelons of the War

We may note one further fact of decisive comparative significance. Royal succession in Japan was able to continue calmly in the old vein, in spite of the combination of inbreeding and the modern etiquette of monogamy, because the monarchy served only symbolic functions. If some of the Japanese royal children happened to be feeble-minded or homosexual, it was not a matter of political importance.[28] In Siam, however, as in other parts of indirectly ruled Southeast Asia, the controlling presence of the Europeans and the prestige of European ideas about monarchical succession and functions[29] had a signally deleterious impact just *because* the monarchy remained a political "subject." The ending of royal polygyny began to reduce drastically the pool of capable royalty in the younger generation and to increase the likelihood of dangerous inbreeding within the royal circle.[30]

Succession determined in European-style legal-genealogical terms permitted the accession of monarchs like Rama VI and VII, who—whatever their personal merits— would surely have been barred from succession a century earlier on grounds of political incapacity or sexual orientation.[31] (Such "ossification" of traditional

---

Ministry were more heavily royal than those of any other department; five of the nine Divisional Commanders, including the commanders of the First Division (Bangkok) and the Second (Nakhon Chaisi), were also royalty—most of them very young indeed. "Twenty-year-old generals were common" (p. 519).

Whatever the gifts of Chulalongkorn's brothers, sons, and nephews in other fields of government, there is no convincing evidence that any were *militarily* competent, precisely because the Thai military did no serious fighting in which such talent could manifest itself. Hence the packing of the War Ministry with royal adolescents must have seemed particularly egregious and unprofessional favoritism.

[28] In fact, the Taishō Emperor (father of Hirohito) was insane for prolonged periods; but this made absolutely no difference to the conduct of the Japanese government. Such a situation is unimaginable in modern Siam.

[29] This trend started very early. Riggs notes that Rama IV already created "secular" royal ceremonies on the English model, such as for the King's Birthday and his Coronation Anniversary (Riggs, *Thailand: The Modernization of a Bureaucratic Polity*, p. 105). In 1887, Rama V made his nine-year-old son the *legal* heir to the throne, rather than Upparat ("Second King" or Ruler of the Front Palace); indeed, the traditional office of Upparat was abolished. By this "the king brought Siam into line with the 'civilized' monarchies of Europe" (Battye, "The Military, Government, and Society in Siam, 1868–1910," pp. 270ff.). By the time Rama VI ascended the throne, things had become "civilized" to the point that Western and other foreign royalty— including princes or dukes from Britain, Russia, Greece, Sweden, Denmark, and Japan— attended the public coronation ceremonies (Greene, "Thai Government and Administration in the Reign of Rama VI [1910–1925]," p. 92).

[30] Royal monogamy rather spectacularly reduced the total production of royal children in any one generation. In addition, since only one royal consort was now permitted, her social rank had to be of "unblemished" quality. As principalities with which Thai rulers had earlier had marital links declined or disappeared, royal marriages necessarily became more and more endogamous. A culmination of this process can be seen in the recent marriage of Crown Prince Vajralongkorn to his own first cousin (on his mother's side).

[31] The policies, style, mistakes, and problems of Rama VI's reign cannot be understood without acknowledging the ruler's homosexuality. (Yet it is striking that Greene's dissertation on Rama VI's reign, completed as recently as 1971, tiptoes silently around this fact. Needless to say, in this discretion he follows virtually all published work on modern Siamese history and politics.) When rulers spent time and money on female sexual partners, these women— however powerful they might become behind the scenes—were nonetheless barred from holding public office and thus offered no political competition to the usual princely and noble candidates. Male sexual partners, on the other hand, were eligible for public office; and Rama VI aroused great enmity within the Bangkok establishment by making such appointments.

leaderships as a result of European pacification, European etiquette of succession, and European prejudices against polygyny is characteristic of most colonial zones.) The 1932 coup was thus the product of a failure either to maintain the pool of royal talent or to remove royalty from active politics.

Yet even the coup did not achieve a real resolution of this contradiction. For a short time, the coup leaders came close to abolishing the monarchy; but in the end they lost their nerve.[32] Unlike the monarchies of Libya and Ethiopia, the Thai monarchy has survived; but it has never made the full modern transition to the Japanese or European twentieth-century monarchical style. "Royalism," in the sense of an active quest for real power in the political system *by the royal family*—i.e., the role of political "subject"—persists in a curiously antique form in contemporary Siam.[33]

If the external pacification of Siam's borders and the "Europeanization" of Thai monarchical etiquette strongly indicate that some of the relevant comparisons are not with Meiji Japan but with the indirectly ruled principalities of Southeast Asia, such comparisons seem all the more pertinent when we turn to the economic and juridical spheres. The Bowring "treaty" of 1855 essentially deprived the Thai sovereigns of a key element of their sovereignty (i.e., control over foreign trade) as well as of the royal commercial monopolies. As Bowring himself observed: "It was clear that my success involved a total revolution in all the financial machinery of the government [,] ... that it took a large proportion of the existing sources of revenue."[34] Siffin comments that "The Thai role in this economic relationship [with the imperial West] *somewhat resembled that of a colony*, but there was a significant political difference—the nation was not brought completely within the sphere of interest of any single Western nation."[35] Whether or not a multiplicity of Western "interests" really made that much of a difference is, it seems to me, a moot point—if we remember that seventy-five years later, on the eve of the 1932 coup, 95 percent of the Thai export economy remained in the hands of foreigners and Chinese.[36]

Nothing in all this reminds us of Japan; everything recalls Johor or Kelantan. On the juridical level, it should suffice to note that *extraterritoriality* is in essence simply another term for the privileged supra-legal status that white colonials enjoyed elsewhere in indirectly ruled Asia under different nomenclature. Without perceiving

---

One is reminded that the English rulers Richard II and Edward II both were overthrown and murdered in part because of the political consequences of their homosexual inclinations.

[32] "The revolution of 1932 might well have led to the establishment of a republic, as it seemed determined to do in the first flush of victory" (Riggs, *Thailand: The Modernization of a Bureaucratic Polity*, p. 94). Batson describes how the coup leaders told Rama VII that if he did not accept a constitution, he would be replaced by a relative or a republic would be established (Batson, "The End of the Absolute Monarchy in Siam," p. 283).

[33] This is all the odder since the present ruler's accession to the throne was the product purely of formal lineage and accident and should therefore have made him an ideal political "object." As neither Rama VI nor Rama VII had male heirs, as Rama VII abdicated while in self-imposed exile, and as Rama VIII—the present king's elder brother—died of a mysterious gunshot wound while still a minor, the element of accident is apparent; Rama IX ascended the throne as a politically untutored adolescent simply because of his close blood tie to his predecessor.

[34] John Bowring, *The Kingdom and People of Siam* (London: Parker and Son, 1857), II, p. 227.

[35] Siffin, *The Thai Bureaucracy: Institutional Change and Development*, p. 48; emphasis added. Note that, for Siffin, the Siam of 1855 is a "nation."

[36] Darling, *Thailand and the United States*, p. 29.

this connection, Wilson nonetheless correctly notes that it was not until 1938 that "Thailand's long struggle for *complete autonomy* [sic] was finally achieved," and "Thailand [gained] control over all legal and fiscal aspects of its administration."[37]

The material presented thus far plainly points to a semi-colonial, indirectly ruled condition wholly incompatible with the "national"—not to say "nationalist"—terminology typically applied in most Western scholarship on Siam. What then has made such terminology plausible?

I would suggest that the answer is a myopic interpretation of the rationalization and centralization policies of Rama IV, Rama V, and Rama VI, which reads the internal consolidation of the dynastic state as identical with the development of the nation. Yet the most elementary comparisons reveal the dubiousness of such a reading. For example, the rationalization and centralization of the Austro-Hungarian Empire under the later Habsburgs was precisely *discontinuous* and *non-identical* with the formation of the modern nations of Hungary, Austria, Czechoslovakia, Rumania, and so forth—all of which are republics, and most of which were born in resistance to the Habsburgs, not in succession to them.

It is important to remember that while the later Jakri were carrying out their reforms (under strong foreign guidance), analogous centralizations of state bureaucracies were being carried out both in neighboring indirectly ruled territories by "native rulers" and in directly ruled zones by white administrators.[38] Everywhere, centralization was accelerating as a result of the demands made by, and the opportunities derived from, the expanding global capitalist system.[39] The role of Dutch colonial bureaucratic centralization in creating the embryo of the modern Indonesian *state* is quite clear—this state is surely unimaginable in its present form without it—but who would identify the colonial bureaucratic state with the modern Indonesian nation?

If Rama V should be understood as performing much the same historical role as Muhammad II of Kelantan and the European pro-consuls of late nineteenth-century colonial administrations, this role does not obviously identify him with the development of the modern Siamese *nation*. Indeed, the argument runs in a diametrically contrary direction. It is rather that because the construction of the centralizing "colonial"-style late nineteenth-century state was effected by the monarchy, the growth of an authentic popular Siamese nationalism was stunted; and this, in turn, has been the central reason for the failure to achieve modern national political integration of "minorities" and to create a stable, legitimate political order. Furthermore, the conceptual identification of monarchy and nation has no less seriously stunted Western scholarly investigation of these problems.

---

[37] Wilson, *Politics in Thailand*, p. 18; emphasis added. Note that, for Wilson, the "subject" of this long struggle is an eternal Thailand.

[38] Compare Kelantan in the 1838–86 reign of Sultan Muhammad ("Mulat Merah") II (see Clive S. Kessler, *Islam and Politics in a Malay State—Kelantan 1838–1969* [Ithaca, NY: Cornell University Press, 1978], pp. 41–44) and Johor in the 1862–95 reign of Abubakar (see Carl A. Trocki, *Prince of Pirates: The Temenggongs and the Development of Johor and Singapore, 1784–1885* [Singapore: University of Singapore Press, 1978], chapters 5–6).

[39] The idea of "opportunities" is important. It helps to explain why, in the words of Siffin, the provisions of the Bowring treaty obtained "willing enforcement over the years by King Mongkut and his successor" (Siffin, *The Thai Bureaucracy: Institutional Change and Development*, p. 48). Siffin is less successful in explaining why a national patriot should have *willingly* enforced the provisions.

Minorities and National Integration. Although Siam comprises considerable numbers of non-Thai peoples—Malays, Karens, "Hill Tribes," Vietnamese, Khmer, Chinese, and so forth—little in-depth work has been done on their political history and experience (with the exception of Skinner's rewarding texts on the Chinese). Nothing illustrates this neglect more strikingly than the fact that the indices to Wilson's *Politics in Thailand*, Siffin's *The Thai Bureaucracy*, and Neher's *Modern Thai Politics* contain no single entry for "minorities" in general, or for any particular minority beyond the Chinese; Riggs's *Thailand: The Modernization of a Bureaucratic Polity* has a single reference (to two pages) for "minorities." This relative lack of concern compares sharply with scholarly interest in, say, Burmese, Indonesian, or Filipino "minorities." My suspicion is that this comparative neglect reflects an axiomatic view of Siam as "Thai-land," in direct succession to the Old Thai kingdoms. This perspective itself mirrors the outlook of the Bangkok elite, an outlook that does much to account for their historic failures in dealing with the "minorities" (especially "indigenous minorities"), indeed in ever really comprehending the problems posed by these groups.

Like Burma, and unlike Indonesia and the Philippines, the modern Siamese state in some sense does territorially correspond to a "pre-colonial" kingdom based on a wet-rice agricultural core area dominated by a single ethnic group. The historical movement from the kingdom of Burma to the nation of Burma might perhaps have followed a Siamese path had not the monarchy been liquidated by the British who interposed, for about sixty years, something called British Burma or Colonial Burma. A state emerged—named Burma, but by no means ruled by Burmans. Precisely this development necessitated a clear politico-cultural distinction between nation and ethnocultural group, signaled in the British period and afterwards by the semantic distinction (and, to be sure, at times also confusion) between "Burmese" and "Burmans," terms that in different times and different places denoted ethnic group and national community.

In this sense, the ethnic Burmans were forced to confront their own "minority-ness" within the Burmese nation. Modern Burmese nationalism has been deeply conscious of and concerned by the whole complex question of "national identity" and "national integration." At independence, elaborate constitutional mechanisms were worked out to handle the problem.[40] Even today, the Rangoon military leaders talk and think about national identity and national integration with an energy and anxiety wholly missing from the preoccupations of their opposite numbers in Bangkok.

In spite of the potential advantage to the Thai of having as the name of the Old Monarchy's realm (Siam) an appellation quite distinct from the name of any ethnic group, a Burma-style evolution of political consciousness, clearly differentiating ethnic group from modern nation, has still, in my view, not been fully achieved. There is no word for the Thai that prevents them from semantically monopolizing the nation. "Thailand," the term for the contemporary state ruled from Bangkok—product of the opportunist chauvinism of the Phibunsongkhram–Luang Wichit

---

[40] The 1948 Constitution established a two-chamber parliament, one chamber of which was called the Chamber of Nationalities. The new state was formally entitled the Union of Burma, a federal republic composed of a number of ethnically defined (sub-) states, for some of which the option of secession was constitutionally guaranteed. See Josef Silverstein, *Burma: Military Rule and the Politics of Stagnation* (Ithaca, NY: Cornell University Press, 1977), esp. pp. 54–59.

ideological duumvirate of the late 1930s—is symptomatic. Western scholars have tended (mistakenly, I believe) to regard this formulation as expressing Thai nationalism.[41]

It is striking that the progressive and genuinely nationalist regime of Pridi Phanomyong (1945–47) restored the old name Siam—not out of nostalgia for a monarchical past, but because the name symbolically marked the possibility for a new nation that would *not* be the monopoly of the ethnic Thai. In subsequent generations, it has been the Thai left which has worked hardest at this redefinition of the state. We may note, for example, that the thrust of the late Jit Phumisak's last work was precisely to combat ethnic Thai chauvinism by showing the heterogeneous ethnic origins of the "Thai" themselves and their close interaction with non-"Thai" groups.[42]

But we must be clear about the basic historical reason for the prevailing "minorities" crisis: the conceptual conflation of monarchy and nation. In Old Siam, as indeed in all traditional kingdoms, the state was defined by its center, not by its boundaries—not by its populations, but by its ruler. For this reason, it was relatively easy for Mon, Lao, Persians, Chinese, or Malays to be loyal to the monarch; they were, after all, in common his *subjects*. Their ethnic identity in no way determined the degree of their access to him. Traditional monarchs, including "Thai" monarchs, usually worked hard at integrating their kingdoms—and indeed expanding them— by multi-ethnic polygyny.[43]

---

[41] It is perhaps symptomatic that Wilson refers to Phibunsongkhram's repression of the Chinese minority in the late 1930s and early 1940s as an "intensely nationalist policy" (Wilson, *Politics in Thailand*, p. 120). Given this view, it is not surprising that he characterizes the "first Phibun era from 1938 to 1943" as one of "extreme nationalism" (p. 19). There are good reasons for thinking that Jacobs is nearer the mark when he observes that "True to patrimonial principles ... anti-Chinese political actions were not regularized but appear to be immediate responses to the arbitrary and capricious personal predilections of whoever was in power" (Jacobs, *Modernization without Development: Thailand as an Asian Case Study*, p. 75).

In other words, the anti-Chinese repression was a matter more of extortion than of nationalism. Coughlin points out that *no* administrative controls were placed on Chinese immigration until May 1947, when the liberal and nationalist Pridi regime was in power (Coughlin, *Double Identity: The Chinese in Modern Thailand*, pp. 24–25). In other words, for all the "extreme nationalism" of the first Phibun era, nothing was done to limit the influx of golden-egg-laying geese.

Skinner is sufficiently a victim of conventional thinking that he can write, in reference to the post-1948 era: "In one of the most intriguing paradoxes of Thai history, militant economic nationalism has resulted not in the defeat of the [Chinese] enemy, but in cooperation between the antagonists" (Skinner, *Chinese Society in Thailand*, p. 360). In fact, the pattern is clearly reminiscent of, say, Czarist policies towards the Jews, in which racist propaganda and periodic pogroms combined with close economic ties built on extortion and corruption—policies few would claim to be in any sense "nationalist." We should perhaps not be surprised that in July 1938, Luang Wichit (then Director of the Fine Arts Department) "gave an address in which he compared the Jewish problem in Germany to the Chinese problem in Thailand and implied that the Nazi solution might be applicable" (ibid., p. 261). This episode is ignored in Wilson's text.

[42] Jit Phumisak, *Khwampenma khong kham sayam thai lao lae khom lae laksana thang sangkhom khong chu chongchat* (Bangkok: Samakhom Sangkhomsat haeng Prathet Thai, 1976). See also Flood, "The Vietnamese Refugees in Thailand."

[43] "Some measure of control was exercised over the vassal states and over the distant provinces with hereditary governorships, however, through a system of marriage alliances. It was the policy of the Thai kings to acquire the daughters of heads of dependencies to fill the

In a paradoxical formation—which may remind us that there has not been an ethnically English king of England since the eleventh century—traditional rulers were the *least* "ethnic–national" people in their realms. Study of the physiognomies of the Thai ruling family (as of royalty elsewhere in Southeast Asia) shows clear atypicality produced by complex inter-ethnic mixes.[44] All these rulers are mixed-bloods, for mixed blood was once a political advantage. However, though a Malay chieftain could be loyal to a ruler in Ayutthaya or even in early Bangkok, there is no reason to suppose that this loyalty could or would be sustained towards rulers who, in modern times, were gradually transformed ideologically into *Thai* monarchs, symbols of the ethnic Thai monopoly of a new would-be nation-state.[45]

In just the same way, the Hungarians of one generation could be loyal to the Habsburgs *as* Habsburgs, while the next generation rejected them because they had come to be seen as Germans or Austrians. Precisely because much of the Bangkok ("Thai") elite—and many Western scholars—have never really thought about this transformation[46] and have assumed a continuity that in fact does not exist ("Thai" rulers as Ur-Thai, rather than as mixed-breeds), they have been unable to comprehend the *real* crisis of the minorities and the need for a radical redefinition of the modern state. Policies have thus varied among indifference, condescension, and

---

royal harem. These women formed a permanent bond between the Bangkok government and the leaders of vassal states and provinces." Walter F. Vella, *The Impact of the West on Government in Thailand* (Berkeley, CA: University of California Press, 1955), p. 327.

[44] We can illustrate this point with one important component of the Jakri ethnic mix: Chinese ancestry. Skinner's genealogical analysis is illuminating (Skinner, *Chinese Society in Thailand*, pp. 19, 26). He begins by reminding us that "We have King Mongkut's word for it that the bride of his great-grandfather was a beautiful daughter of one of the richest Chinese families in Ayutthaya." In other words, Rama I was half Chinese. Assuming that the mothers of Rama II and III were "pure Thai," these rulers would have been, respectively, one-quarter and one-eighth Chinese. Since his mother was the daughter of Rama I's sister and a rich Chinese, Rama IV would have been half Chinese. Rama V's mother was a granddaughter of Rama II (and thus at least one-sixteenth Chinese), so Chulalongkorn was more than one-quarter Chinese. Queen Saowapha, mother of Rama VI and VII, was the daughter of a "pure Chinese" concubine of Mongkut; thus, these two sovereigns were over half Chinese in ancestry. It is curious, but not altogether surprising, that the strongly anti-Chinese Wachirawut should have had more Chinese than Thai "blood."

[45] Keyes makes instructive reading in this respect (Charles F. Keyes, *Isan: Regionalism in Northeastern Thailand*, Cornell Data Paper 65, Southeast Asia Program Publications, 1967; a still-valuable monograph, especially useful for its historical overview of Isan's incorporation into the contemporary Thai state). On the whole, he is clear that the people of Isan are a Lao minority; he gives an excellent description of long-standing attempts by Bangkok rulers to incorporate them into a Bangkok-controlled state; he is sympathetic to the difficulties these Lao have thereby suffered. But the thrust of his argument is that Lao loyalty to the Jakri is proving to be the mediating mechanism for the development of loyalty to the modern nation-state; if they dislike the government, at least they love the monarch. As will be clear from my own argument to this point, this "love" has very little to do with the nation-state and is in fact retrogressive, preventing a modern incorporation into an authentic national polity. This weakness is unconsciously stressed by Riggs's formulation: "For the perpetuation of this [Thai] sense of nationhood the survival of the monarchy would appear to be necessary" (Riggs, *Thailand: The Modernization of a Bureaucratic Polity*, p. 106). One can agree with Riggs, provided one understands "this sense of nationhood" to mean something stunted and archaic.

[46] A splendid example is Tambiah, who manages to spend 375 pages on the people of Isan without once referring to them as Lao. His fieldwork site is blissfully entitled "our remote and humble Thai village." S. J. Tambiah, *Buddhism and the Spirit Cults in North-east Thailand* (Cambridge: Cambridge University Press, 1970), p. 372.

repression—not so much because of the malice of governments as because of their politico-cultural backwardness. Moreover, this backwardness originates in and depends on a fundamental mystification about the nature and origins of the modern Thai state and the role and meaning of the monarchy within it.

Stability and Instability. If neglect of the problem of minorities and nationalism is one tell-tale sign of this mystification, the intellectual confusion over the much-discussed issues of "stability" and "instability" is another. Let me offer two well-known instances for consideration. The later Jakri monarchs are regularly described in the literature as farsighted, patriotic, dynamic, and modernizing rulers.[47] (Writers in this vein tend to overlook the fact that competitive examinations for government posts were instituted only four years before the overthrow of the "absolute monarchy,"[48] long after the neighboring colonial regimes had instituted such systems for their populations.) Yet here is the conservative Wilson's judgment (emphases in original) of the Siam he studied in the 1950s: "The society of Thailand today is, *as it was a century ago*, predominantly preindustrial—almost pre-commercial—*economically*; more or less neolithic *technologically*; and residually feudal *socially*. I would like to quote here from Ingram's *Economic Change in Thailand* in reference to the past century of world history:

> The Thai population has largely remained in agriculture, and has neither improved techniques nor increased the proportion of capital to labor. Moreover, most changes in the economy as a whole have been in volume rather than kind. New methods have not been used, new products have not been developed. No product of any importance (besides rubber) is exported today which was not exported in 1850.[49]

This quotation illustrates the truly striking fact that between 1850 and 1950, a century of revolutionary upheaval in the world, Thailand in very substantial ways remained very much the same.[50]

One naturally asks where all that modernizing dynamism went. Why was it that, after a century of modernizing rulers, a "uniquely independent" Southeast Asian state remained so backward? Why did its export economy look like a retrograde version of the neighboring colonial economies (indeed, closely resemble the economies especially of *indirectly ruled* colonial territories)?

Our second instance is the image of Thai politics made popular by the work of Riggs—i.e., the "bureaucratic polity," a polity described as immensely stable, impervious to appeals or pressures from outside or below.[51] Yet, if we compare the

---

[47] This is a commonplace in the literature. See, e.g., Wilson, *Politics in Thailand*, pp. 97–112; or Siffin, *The Thai Bureaucracy*, pp. 51–63.

[48] On the Civil Service Act of 1928, see Siffin, *The Thai Bureaucracy*, pp. 211–13.

[49] James C. Ingram, *Economic Change in Thailand since 1850* (Stanford, CA: Stanford University Press, 1955). An updated version was published in 1971, as *Economic Change in Thailand, 1850-1970*, same press.

[50] David A. Wilson, "Political Tradition and Political Change in Thailand," in *Modern Thai Politics*, ed. Neher, p. 333.

[51] " ... cabinet politicians have shown themselves more responsive to the interests and demands of their bureaucratic subordinates than to the concerns of interest groups, political

years 1782–1932 (in which seven monarchs and one regent held power—roughly 18.8 years per power-holder) with the years 1932–73 (heyday of the "bureaucratic polity"—with twelve different men in the Prime Ministership, an average of 3.3 years per person, and no less than eight successful and many more unsuccessful coups carried out), a picture of great *instability* emerges.[52] By contrast, Indonesia in the post-independence period has had only two presidents in thirty-three years, though no one, till very recently, would have called Indonesia a bureaucratic polity.[53]

I draw attention to both longitudinal and latitudinal comparisons precisely to focus attention on the peculiarity of modern Thai political instability and to explore the reasons for its scholarly devaluation. Here, it seems to me, the original—for their time—speculations of Hanks may have played an important role. (See his seminal 1962 text, elaborated in his 1975 article.[54]) His discussion of the dialectic of "merit and power" and his model of the "entourage" have been especially attractive because they incorporated instability within stability: a ceaseless "karmic" quest for patrons and followers, which never crystallized into stable institutions but at the same time never turned into anything new or different.[55]

It was easy to take the *model* for a timeless *reality*, and hypostasize it as "uniquely Thai."[56] With history abandoned, it was tempting to perceive the bureaucratic polity as both "natural" in its instability (i.e., culturally rooted) and as national (after all, it was "uniquely Thai").[57] Instability was thus frequently read, comfortingly, to mean "Thai-style stability"—rather than as an indicator of the crisis of the Thai state.

---

parties, or legislative bodies outside the state apparatus" (Riggs, *Thailand: The Modernization of a Bureaucratic Polity*, p. 312).

[52] Riggs recognized this obliquely. Of the 1930s he wrote: "Both the People's Party and the parliamentary system proved unable to control the dynamism of intrabureaucratic conflict which broke out as the monarchical control system was dislodged" (Riggs, *Thailand: The Modernization of a Bureaucratic Polity*, p. 178). "The resultant system of government, which I have termed a 'bureaucratic polity,' is in a sense a nameless system. It is nameless because no one dares to ascribe to it a basis of political legitimacy which corresponds to the facts of effective control" (ibid., p. 323).

[53] Karl D. Jackson, "Bureaucratic Polity: A Theoretical Framework for the Analysis of Power and Communications in Indonesia," in *Political Power and Communications in Indonesia*, ed. Karl D. Jackson and Lucian W. Pye (Berkeley, CA: University of California Press, 1978), pp. 3–22.

[54] Lucien Hanks, "Merit and Power in the Thai Social Order," *American Anthropologist* LXIV (1962): 1247–61; reprinted in Neher, *Modern Thai Politics*, pp. 107–23; and also elaborated on in: Lucien Hanks, "The Thai Social Order as Entourage and Circle," in *Change and Persistence in Thai Society: Essays in Honor of Lauriston Sharp*, ed. G. William Skinner and A. Thomas Kirsch (Ithaca, NY: Cornell University Press, 1975), pp. 197–218. This is an influential article on the "anthropology" of Thai politics, stressing patron–client ties.

[55] "I emphasize persons *moving* in their *fixed* setting, like players with their rules and tactics on a football field" (Hanks, "Merit and Power in the Thai Social Order," p. 107; emphasis added).

[56] Hanks (ibid.) warned his readers that "This paper treats the scene ahistorically, though it refers to the period from the beginning of the nineteenth century to the present." Yet he has on occasion ignored his own warnings. I suspect, in addition, that there are irremediable intellectual problems with all ahistorical models that "refer to" specific historical periods.

[57] It is interesting that Riggs initially tried to disassociate his "bureaucratic polity" model from any "Thai cultural" explanation. He attacked Phillips's and Wilson's 1964 Memorandum for trying to account for the bureaucratic polity by "alleged traits of the Siamese 'race'" (Riggs, *Thailand: The Modernization of a Bureaucratic Polity*, pp. 320ff). But, in the end, he reverted to a "cultural" explanation of the Thai population's acceptance of the bureaucratic polity, even to the point of uncritically accepting Phillips's and Wilson's conclusion that "villagers actually enjoy making known to those in power their willingness to be ruled. Indeed, this is to them

It should be clear, I think, that the instability was (and is) real, important, and historically rooted. The roots lie, I would argue, in a stunted and incomplete transition from kingdom to modern nation-state—a transition whose problematic nature is glossed over by the axiom that "Thailand" started "modernizing" in the 1850s under Mongkut and has continued to do so ever since.[58]

This conceptual framework is strikingly evidenced in Akin Rabibhadana's 1969 work, arguably the most brilliant English-language text on modern Siam by a Thai.[59] Akin proposes the following general model of the dynamics of dynastic rule in Old Siam: A dynasty typically begins after some major calamity— energetic, reintegrative leadership being provided by a parvenu statesman-general. Precisely because this figure emerges at a time of crisis, when existing structures are in disintegration, he is able to summon the most able men in the kingdom to his side. The first reign is thus classically a period of unusual social mobility, in which exceptional *homines novi* can make their mark. Taking advantage of his savior role, the new sovereign is able to subject most of society directly to his command. Above all, the numbers of *phrai luang* (commoners liable to state corvée) are at their height.

The hero's successors, however, who come to power by descent rather than by coup or conquest, find themselves increasingly entangled in complex rivalries with and dependencies on fellow-members of the established royal family, prominent nobles, and so forth, whom they have to "take care of" by assigning them *phrai som* ("private" corvée laborers). The services required by princes and nobles are so much less onerous than those demanded by the state that there is a steady leakage from *phrai luang* to *phrai som*—slowly draining the sovereign's manpower resources until the dynasty is too weak to survive a major challenge. A new dynasty then arises, and the cycle begins all over. This very rough sketch of Akin's model does not do justice to the subtlety and learning with which it is elaborated, but it perhaps suffices for raising some interesting questions of perspective.

First of all, if we ignore for the moment "Thai uniqueness," it is clear that Akin's model closely approximates the general Weberian model of patrimonialism, in which the central tension is between the natural drive to centralization and the localizing, fissiparous tendencies represented by provincial notables, noblemen, and royal princelings. In other words—and this is important—centralizing, "absolutizing" tendencies have nothing intrinsically to do with *modernization* and everything to do with the inherent dynamics of a certain type of state system. We should thus already be warned to be cautious about interpreting Jakri centralization in modernizing terms, rather than in terms of the patrimonial model.

---

one of the major pleasures of being a citizen" (ibid., p. 324). Riggs evidently saw no inconsistency between acceptance of this gem and his own description of the bureaucratic polity as a "nameless" political system *without legitimacy*. See fn. 52, above.

[58] Here lies the central weakness of Jacob's stimulating work (Jacobs, *Modernization without Development*). He is so determined to undermine the conventional myths about the "development" of Siam that he finds it difficult to admit that any substantial changes have taken place at all in modern Thai history. Mongkut's Siam and Sarit's Thailand—everything is a timeless "patrimonialism." In fact, as I shall argue below, the "patrimonial model" can be very useful for the study of Thai political history, but it cannot be used to explain everything; and it is a *model* for analyzing historical reality, not that reality itself.

[59] Akin Rabibhadana, "The Organization of Thai Society in the Early Bangkok Period, 1782–1873," Cornell Data Paper 74, Southeast Asia Program Publications, 1969.

Secondly, Akin appears to face an uncomfortable paradox. He posits as the "great men" of Thai history those dynasts who are most capable of cornering the manpower market—implicitly belittling those latter-day sovereigns who seem incapable of organizing the peasantry for state corvée. In his view, "Thailand" is great only when these state corvées are working optimally. On the other hand, the silent migration of the population from *phrai luang* to *phrai som* status shows clearly that the Thai people much preferred service under *anyone but the sovereign*. In a sense, then, it is the Thai people who undermine their own chances for national glory. This paradox is tenable only if one sees the sovereign—as Akin tends to do—not so much as a dynastic power-politician following patrimonial imperatives but as Ur-Thai national hero; then the suffering and sacrifices imposed on Thai commoners can be glossed as analogous to tax-paying, military conscription, and all the other obligations that *citizens* of national republics properly owe *their* state. Avoiding royal corvée then appears as heinous as dodging the draft!

If we accept Akin's argument that there were basic instabilities built into the Thai patrimonial state, but emphasize that they involved conflicts of interest (not only between sovereign and nobility, but also between ruler and subject), we can proceed to the next step in analyzing modern Thai political instability: theoretical reconsideration of Jakri policy towards the Chinese. Two small but important points should be made before turning to the basic questions raised by this policy. First, the policy of encouraging in-migration of Chinese (especially Chinese as mobile, single, male manual laborers) *precisely* parallels the policies of the British and Dutch colonial regimes, and of petty Malay sultanates like Johor and Perak—in terms both of the policy itself, and of the world-historical epoch in which it was enacted.[60]

Second, it was a policy that absolutely cannot be made to fit with the Thai-monarchs-as-national-heroes trope. For one thing, it is inconceivable that a nationalist leadership would pursue such a policy. For another, it is anti-Chinese sentiment that Western scholars see as one of the first signs of "Thai nationalism."[61]

---

[60] Skinner writes: "It may seem strange that the Chinese outnumbered the Thai in the Thai capital city, but most nineteenth century observers attest the fact" (Skinner, *Chinese Society in Thailand*, p. 82). "More and more *towns* in the interior of Thailand, too, took on a Chinese cast during the latter half of the nineteenth century" (ibid., p. 88; emphasis added). Exactly the same phenomenon of alien immigrants demographically dominating urban areas occurred in British Burma for exactly the same reasons. See John Furnivall, *Colonial Policy and Practice* (New York, NY: New York University Press, 1956), pp. 44, 53, 116–23. Comparable tendencies are observable in the Netherlands Indies and in British Malaya in the late nineteenth and early twentieth centuries.

[61] "Rama VI ... was in effect the founder of intellectual nationalism among the educated Thai. He wrote a number of articles in the press under various pen names which expounded the subject of love of nation and also attacked the developing separateness of the Chinese community in the country" (Wilson, *Politics in Thailand*, pp. 9–10). Wilson's readers are not informed that this "vivacious" founder of Thai intellectual nationalism was the pseudonymous author of a celebrated near-racist pamphlet attacking the Chinese, entitled *The Jews of the East*. Victor Purcell's *The Chinese in Southeast Asia* (London: Oxford University Press, 1951), p. 155, contains useful material on the Chinese community in Siam, and its relations with Thai governments and China.

There is, in fact, good reason to argue that the anti-Sinicism of Rama VI (himself more Chinese than Thai by ancestry) had little to do with any putative nationalism. Skinner, for example, stresses that Wachirawut's anti-Chinese sentiments were largely derivative of the prevailing racist prejudices of the British whom he so deeply admired (see Skinner, *Chinese Society in Thailand*, p. 160, also pp. 248–49). In addition, after the overthrow of the Manchus in 1911, Thai rulers feared that Chinese immigrants could bring with them republican ideas that

(So serious is this sentiment, by the way, that—in a remarkable manifestation of "uniquely Thai" flexibility—Thai rulers from 1911 right through to 1946 consistently refused to entertain official relations with *any* Chinese national leadership.[62]) It is thus clear that the Chinese immigration policy has to be understood in terms of dynastic, rather than national, needs. For if it helped in the short run to "stabilize" dynastic power (as it clearly did), it generated long-term instabilities and contradictions in Thai society—just as the immigration policies of the British and Dutch and of the Sultans of Perak and Johor did for contemporary Indonesia and Malaysia.

Systematic importation of Chinese labor first became a major element of state policy under Rama III.[63] But it was "the expansion of the Thai economy after 1855 [the Bowring 'Treaty,' that] greatly increased the demand for manual workers and eventually led to the recruitment of Chinese peasants for 'coolie labor' in Siam and to the mass migration which began in the 1880s."[64] What were the reasons for this policy, and what was the structural relationship between the immigrant labor force and Jakri absolutism?

The answer is two-fold: (1) Manifesting themselves as laborers *looking for work* (rather than as Thai peasants *seeking to evade work*), the Chinese immigrants presented the Thai rulers with a directly exploitable labor force outside the Siamese political system—i.e., not subject to the classical slippage from *phrai luang* to *phrai som*. (2) The Thai rulers quickly discovered, as did the British colonial authorities in Malaya (and, to a lesser degree, the Dutch in the Netherlands Indies), that this labor force could be managed in such a way as to pay not only for its own exploitation but for the general expansion of the state itself.

Let us look briefly at each part of the answer in turn. The enormous advantage of the Chinese immigrants, in relation to the rulers' manpower needs, was that they were vulnerable, ignorant, youthful, single, and mobile. Provided funds could be found to pay them wages, they could be used for a far greater variety of tasks than could the Thai peasantry. Furthermore, "wage labor came to be recognized as more efficient than conscripted labor."[65] Chinese coolie labor was thus "used extensively in canal and railroad building, tin-mining, stevedoring and other port work, rice-milling, saw-milling, and on Chinese commercial plantations."[66] Skinner indeed

---

might infect the Thai (Batson, "The End of the Absolute Monarchy in Siam," p. 89). Greene comments that Wachirawut decided that many of the leaders of the abortive 1912 coup were of "mixed Thai-Chinese stock" and believed this to be "highly relevant in the light of the recent political unrest in China" (Greene, "Thai Government and Administration in the Reign of Rama VI [1910–1925]," p. 125).

[62] Purcell describes the Siamese–Chinese Amity Agreement of 1946, negotiated in the brief interregnum of civilian rule between the two Phibunsongkhram dictatorships (Purcell, *The Chinese in Southeast Asia*, pp. 192–94). After Mao's victory in 1949, successive Thai military regimes provided a further splendid example of "uniquely Thai" realism and flexibility by maintaining diplomatic relations with Taipei for the next quarter of a century. It took the civilian Kukrit Pramote government to open relations with Peking in 1976.

[63] But, as Skinner observes, "The first two Jakkri kings developed state trading and royal monopolies to an unprecedented degree. In order to increase the production of Siam's exports and provide crews for their royal ships, they encouraged Chinese immigration" (Skinner, *Chinese Society in Thailand*, pp. 24ff.).

[64] Ibid., p. 109.

[65] Ibid., p. 114.

[66] Mabry, "The Development of Labor Institutions in Thailand," p. 43.

suggests that the construction of Siam's railroad system, which began in 1892 and was essential to the maturation of Rama V's centralization policies, "would, from all accounts, have been impossible without Chinese labor."[67] And Chinese deaths: "It is no exaggeration to say that thousands of Chinese lost their lives prior to 1910 on railway construction in Siam."[68]

Nonetheless, Skinner is also correct in pointing out that, since the Chinese were so essential to royal plans, "they had to be given *freedom unthinkable for the Thai masses of the time.*"[69] "Instead of corvée … [they] were charged a head tax large enough to be a sizable source of revenue, but not so large as to discourage immigration."[70] Furthermore, "In the 1860s, Werner attempted an exhaustive list of the commercial crafts in which any Thai were to be found … He concluded that *practically the entire industry of Siam* had [*by then*] passed into Chinese hands."[71] Is it superfluous to reiterate that such policies are absolutely irreconcilable with the conventional "far-sighted patriot" images of the nineteenth- and early twentieth-century monarchs?

With regard to the financing not only of this system of state-paid wage-labor but also of the absolutizing state itself, Skinner demonstrates that the Jakri rulers (with the assistance of a few extremely wealthy Chinese leaders, on whom they showered honors[72]) astutely established the following highly utilitarian structure: (a) head taxes were kept very low to encourage Chinese immigrants to stay in Siam;[73] (b) opium addiction, gambling, prostitution, and alcoholism were encouraged within the immigrant community,[74] to ensure that the Chinese laborers stayed put and spent their wages locally rather than remitting them to their families in China.[75]

The facts speak for themselves: "It is significant that four of the most lucrative [revenue] farms—*together providing between 40 percent and 50 percent of the total state*

---

[67] Skinner, *Chinese Society in Thailand*, p. 114.

[68] Ibid., p. 115.

[69] Ibid., p. 97; emphasis added. In exactly comparable vein, British and Dutch colonial regimes in other parts of Southeast Asia gave immigrant Chinese (or Indians) "freedom unthinkable for the [local indigenous] masses."

[70] Ibid. This head tax amounted to 4.5 baht paid once every three years. It did not change from 1828 to 1909. When compulsory male corvée labor was finally abolished for the Thai in 1899, it was replaced by a head tax amounting to four to six baht every year. Skinner was rather puzzled by this "inequity," but viewed it as part of "the favoritism [*sic*] shown the Chinese by the Thai government in the nineteenth century." Needless to say, the simple explanation for the discrepancy is that the tax on Chinese had to be kept fairly low not to discourage them from immigrating; as for the Thai, why not impose a stiff tax, since they had nowhere to escape to? On all this, see ibid., pp. 97, 162, 123.

[71] Ibid., p. 97; emphasis added.

[72] "It was also government policy to give titles to most of the Chinese holding revenue monopolies. In the third reign, both the lottery and gambling farmers were automatically given the title Khun; *by the fifth reign the rank had been raised* to Luang. The opium farmer was also given noble rank … " (ibid., p. 153; emphasis added).

[73] Skinner explicitly makes this case (ibid., p. 125).

[74] This may seem harsh, but Virginia Thompson reports a League of Nations survey in the 1920s which found that in Siam "the average Chinese coolie spent fifty percent of his earnings on opium, but not one out of fifty among them was an opium smoker" *before* arrival in Siam. See: Thompson, *Thailand: The New Siam*, p. 609.

[75] The policy was extremely successful. Skinner concludes that "in all probability, by far the greater part of the money income of the Chinese remained in Thailand" (Skinner, *Chinese Society in Thailand*, p. 227).

revenues during most of the second half of the nineteenth century—were based on Chinese consumption. These were the opium, gambling, lottery, and spirit farms."[76] In 1905–06, revenue from the opium farm netted Rama V over 10,000,000 baht, about 15–20 percent of government revenue.[77] In 1903–04, the gambling farm produced 5,700,000 baht, the lottery 2,100,000 baht, and alcohol 4,200,000 baht. (By contrast, the head tax never produced even 1,000,000 baht a year at any time.[78])

It is revelatory of "late Ptolemaic" thinking that Skinner should have observed that "for a period of at least fifty years, during which Siam achieved a modern government, a thriving economy, and entered the world economy and family of nations, almost half of the government's revenues was derived directly or indirectly from the comparatively small Chinese minority," and yet have found this conclusion "anomalous."[79] In fact, it is common sense, provided one abandons conventional mythologies.

In effect, under conditions of externally imposed peace,[80] the sovereign could essentially forget about defending the state militarily against external enemies and could devote himself full-time to internal aggrandizement ("centralization"), for which a free-floating, politically impotent alien population was decidedly advantageous. It is in this light that one is to understand the abolition of slavery in 1874[81]—an act that today is often glossed as an enlightened, liberating move but that should really be understood as a logical extension of the policies outlined above. The important thing to remember is that slaves were traditionally exempt from state corvée and were thus outside the reach of the sovereign's grasp. "It became apparent to the reforming kings that, by freeing the slaves, the supply of peasant farmers would be increased, and the basis of the government would simultaneously be enlarged."[82]

We can now proceed to reconsider, in this light, the general thrust of Jakri policies in the late nineteenth and early twentieth centuries—policies that have been studied in different ways by scholars such as Wyatt, Keyes, Siffin, Wilson, and others. It is well known that these policies involved (a) the sizeable employment of foreign advisers;[83] (b) the extension of Bangkok administration over Isan, Chiengmai,

---

[76] Ibid., p. 120; emphasis added.

[77] Ibid., p. 121. The opium-farm system was abolished in 1908–09 but then became a state-controlled monopoly. Skinner tells us that in the period 1910–38, government revenue from opium varied from 8 to 23 million baht a year, averaging 14,900,000. In precisely the same way, the British colonial government in Malaya avoided taxing British enterprises by growing fat on drug-peddling to the immigrant Chinese community (ibid., p. 226). To a lesser extent, the same is true of the Dutch colonial government in the Indies.

[78] Ibid., p. 123.

[79] Ibid., p. 125.

[80] Battye says that Chinese were exempted from military conscription—a rather insubstantial privilege after the 1840s (Battye, "The Military, Government and Society in Siam, 1868–1910," p. 22).

[81] In fact, the measure did not emancipate those already burdened with the status of slave; it merely forbade the creation of new slaves. Final, formal abolition of all slavery had to wait a generation, until 1905 (Mabry, "The Development of Labor Institutions in Thailand," p. 42).

[82] Riggs, *Thailand: The Modernization of a Bureaucratic Polity*, p. 58.

[83] On this, Siffin is, as usual, illuminating as to the facts, Ptolemaic as to interpretation. He notes that in 1909, the last year of Rama V's reign, more than three hundred foreigners were employed by the government (Siffin, *The Thai Bureaucracy: Institutional Change and Development* p. 97). They included a dozen "general advisers," thirteen director-generals of departments or

and the South[84]—considerably aided, towards the end, by the expansion of imported rails, telegraphs, telephones, and, ultimately, motorized transportation;[85] and (c) attempted direct subordination of the ecclesiastical hierarchy to the state, and its manipulation for state purposes (i.e., the post-Mongkut role of the Dhammayut sect under strong royal patronage—notably the appointment of Chulalongkorn's brother Prince Wachirayan as Supreme Patriarch and his function in harnessing the Sangha to the sovereign's overall administrative and educational policies[86]).

In important respects, many of these policies follow—on a small scale—the patterns of European absolutism symbolized by the immortal words of Louis XIV, "L'état c'est moi." Indeed, they are/were, on the whole, in the short run, "rational" from the perspective of the *moi*-state. Yet there is a difference. The European *moi*-states were profoundly unstable and destabilizing precisely because they were so strong. Bourbon, Romanov, and Stuart absolutism all collapsed before massive popular revolutions generated in reaction to the transforming policies of entrenched absolutism itself. In the Thai case, however, the depth and duration of absolutism were insufficient to precipitate such a social upheaval; what emerged instead was the partial, mystified revolt, signaled by the coup of 1932, of absolutism's own engine, the functionalized bureaucracy. The real political problem in Siam was—and is—

---

equivalent, twenty-three assistant-director-generals or equivalent, and sixty-nine "foreigners engaged in administrative work at the level immediately below departmental management." (We are a long way from late Meiji Japan, and very close to late Abubakar Johor.) On the next page, however, he says *both* that these advisers "were not to have final control over major policies of the nation" *and* that "foreign advisers did not formally control major policy, but their influence sometimes verged on control." (!) Elsewhere (ibid., p. 96) we learn that these advisers' "contribution to the central values of the new bureaucracy defies description." Greene's description of the situation under Rama VI is less schizophrenic: " ... England had a tremendous amount of influence within the Thai government in the form of her many foreign advisors. Out of a total number of approximately 208 foreign advisors, 133 of them were English. Moreover, the English, more than any other nationality, *were spread throughout the bureaucracy.* They were represented in every department which in some way exploited the natural resources of the nation in addition to being in every financial department" (Greene, "Thai Government and Administration in the Reign of Rama VI [1910–1925]," p. 261; emphasis added).

[84] For example, see Keyes, *Isan: Regionalism in Northeastern Thailand,* chap. 3; and Siffin, *The Thai Bureaucracy: Institutional Change and Development,* chap. 4. Siffin suggests that the total number of salaried bureaucrats in 1892, just prior to the "radical reforms" of Rama V, was about 12,000 (ibid., pp. 94, 80). By 1899, this number had doubled; by 1905, it had doubled again. By 1910, the number in the Ministry of the Interior alone (15,000) exceeded the total salaried bureaucracy of pre-1892.

[85] By 1907, Siam had more than seven thousand miles of telegraph lines linking sixty-seven administrative and commercial centers. About 550 miles of railway were in operation (Siffin, *The Thai Bureaucracy: Institutional Change and Development,* p. 122).

[86] See Wyatt, *The Politics of Reform in Thailand,* chaps. 7–9; also see Craig J. Reynolds, "The Buddhist Monkhood in Nineteenth-Century Thailand" (PhD dissertation, Cornell University, 1972), esp. chaps. 3–5 and 7 (this is an important pioneering study, focusing on the reign of Rama V's brother, Prince Wachirayan, as Supreme Patriarch). Actually, this process may go back to Mongkut himself, if Jacobs is to be believed. He writes: "Rama IV, in a frank moment, admitted that one of the motives he had in introducing the dharma reform movement was to compete with and thwart millennium movements which might arise during the dislocation accompanying his forthcoming modernization program" (Jacobs, *Modernization without Development,* p. 260). (Somehow, this does not sound quite like Mongkut talking.)

precisely this: that there was no decisive popular break with "absolutism" fueled by social radicalism and indeed mass nationalism.[87]

The bureaucratic engine of absolutism was incapable by itself of breaking with the perspectives and traditions of absolutism; yet, by its heterogeneity and functional specialization, it was also incapable of generating the temporal legitimacy that monarchical absolutism had previously had. Riggs's "bureaucratic polity" was, in fact, the absolutist *moi*-state manqué. Suspended between royalist absolutism and popular nationalism, the modern "bureaucratic polity" was both deeply conservative and highly unstable—not because it was "uniquely Thai," but because it contained within itself no real foundation of or criteria for internal or external legitimation.[88]

The suspension began to come to an end only in the early 1960s—and then largely by inadvertence, when American military power and giant corporate capitalism imposed themselves on a stagnant political order. (Sarit's "absolutism," like that of the Jakri, was made possible only by external pacification and external support.) This massive penetration generated extremely rapid social changes (planned and unplanned) in Thai society, which the bureaucracy itself was incapable of imagining—let alone generating—for all its "modernizing" protocol. Out of these changes, in turn, developed the popular Thai nationalism that is, I believe, the most significant feature of the contemporary scene.[89]

Culture and Politics. It will be apparent that much of the criticism of existing studies of Thai politics sketched out thus far is, at bottom, criticism of a certain reification of Thai culture. Ambiguous rubrics like "uniquely Thai values," anachronisms such as (nineteenth-century) "Thai nationalism," and questionable axioms such as "The monarchy is essential to the Thai national identity" encourage us to base our thinking on a wholly imaginary eternal Thai essence. Barrington Moore has warned students of politics against "culturalist" explanations precisely because, in his view, they are intrinsically conservative, ahistorical, and uncritical.[90] I think that his argument is, in general, exaggerated—indeed, often unfair. But in the case of Thai studies, there is a good deal to be said for it.

---

[87] Batson puts it gently thus: " ... elsewhere in the region the period [of the early twentieth century] was characterized by the growth of disparate nationalist movements whose one common aim was the achievement of political independence. In Siam, *this focal point was absent* ... " (Batson, "The End of the Absolute Monarchy in Siam," p. 18; emphasis added). That the seeds for such popular nationalism in fact existed is suggested by the "Ai Kan" uprising in Saraburi in 1925; its leader, attacking foreign oppression, said he would take care of it himself if the king did not do something about it in seven days (ibid., p. 174).

It is likely in any case that the stunted form of twentieth-century Thai nationalism is not wholly unique in Southeast Asia. A comparable case is Malaya, where till very recently there has also been only a stunted and mystified nationalism, manifested in anti-Chinese racism and slavish admiration for the imperial British. Large numbers of "nationalist" Malays, clinging with pride to their sultans, totally ignore the fact that these very sultans (or their immediate ancestors) were, along with the British, primarily responsible for bringing the hated Chinese into Malaya in the first place.

[88] Riggs himself recognized this: see note 52, above.

[89] See my "Withdrawal Symptoms: Social and Cultural Aspects of the October 6 Coup," in this volume, especially the section "Ideological Upheaval" and following (pp. 47–76, esp. pp. 66ff).

[90] Barrington Moore, Jr., *The Social Origins of Dictatorship and Democracy* (Boston, MA: Beacon Press, 1966), pp. 483–87.

The irony is that for all the importance attached, in analyses of Thai politics, to the idea of "uniquely Thai culture," this culture has very rarely been studied in a critical and dispassionate spirit. Nor is its dynamic relation to Thai social and political life concretely explored. Let me suggest two sorts of reasons for this undesirable situation. First, there has been a tendency among political scientists who pride themselves on being area specialists to defend that title by indiscriminate raids on the work of anthropologists (especially those influenced by the "culture and personality" school), in search of a "uniquely Thai" cultural matrix. The anthropologists' experimental models and hypotheses have too easily been reified by non-anthropologists as the axiomatic, fundamental reality of Thai society.[91]

Second, since most of the political scientists have unconsciously been committed to the modernizing-monarchs = patriotic-national-heroes axiom, it has been easy to assume (especially for those not much interested in culture in any case) that late Jakri "high culture" represented Thai national culture.[92]

Once again, it is comparison—longitudinal and latitudinal— that is required. We can start by comparisons with an earlier Siam. Nothing strikes one more vividly than the lack of visual distinction in the plastic arts of the Jakri period. The Buddha images are lifeless imitations of the strikingly individual imagery of Sukhothai and early Ayutthaya. Similarly, much of the religious and secular architecture of the nineteenth and twentieth centuries has an exhausted, fussy air about it. This is not just my personal view. Here is the judgment of the *Area Handbook for Thailand*:

> The establishment of Bangkok in 1782 marked the beginning of the fifth school of traditional Thai art, the Ratanakosin (Jakri). It was a period of little accomplishment, in which the decadence of the late Ayutthaya era continued ... By 1868 traditional Thai sculpture, architecture, painting, music, ornamentation, and handicrafts were stagnant ... Traditional Thai sculpture had almost disappeared.[93]

It is perhaps of more than symbolic significance that the *Handbook*'s dating of this stagnation is the year that Chulalongkorn ascended the throne. The Fifth and Sixth reigns show the final disintegration of any real idea of Thai architecture.[94] The royal

---

[91] This tendency may have been encouraged by the predominance of anthropologists among the first generation of post-World War II Thai-ologists and their general "culture and personality" orientation. It is significant that the "loosely structured society" model continued to be used by political scientists long after most anthropologists had abandoned it, in whole or in part. (Note that the whole "loosely structured society" debate—aside from a certain basic triviality—concerned a supposed "inherent," "given" *essence* of Thai society, wholly divorced from history.)

[92] Hence a mythologizing of late Jakri upper-class life as "Old Siam." The cynic might offer more personal reasons for this nostalgic identification. For in talk and texts, "Old Siam" manifests itself as a typical blend of comfort and exoticism. Steam-powered river transport, modern tropical medicine, a stable currency, and easy communications with the Western world combine with colorful ceremonies, picturesque sights and sounds, piquant cooking, cheap antiques, plentiful servants, and a "relaxed" attitude on sexual matters. Needless to say, this "Old Siam" does not date further back than about 1900.

[93] Smith et al., *Area Handbook for Thailand*, pp. 182–83.

[94] May part of the reason be that these monuments and buildings were more and more constructed by immigrant Chinese rather than by native Thai craftsmen, thanks to the policies of the Jakri rulers? Skinner records that Chinese built the structures for the cremation of Rama

complex at Bang Pe In expresses this melancholy process perfectly. An incoherent jumble of miniature replicas of "typically Thai" palaces and garish "overseas Chinese"-style dwellings, it prefigures nothing so much as the suburban villas of post-independence elites in other parts of Southeast Asia.[95]

It is my strong impression that the lively arts have suffered much the same fate. An almost unbroken succession of conservative regimes, ostensibly committed to Thai culture and values, parallels a steady decline in "classical" music, dance, and drama to the point of near-extinction.[96] Old teachers die without successors. The classics are occasionally revived, but in an academic context, and they breed no children. All these arts tend to become museum pieces, more for the entertainment of foreign tourists who have never seen them before than for living Thai society itself.

Similarly in literature: it seems of more than symbolic significance that the fall from favor of the last classical Thai poet of consequence, Sunthǫn Phu, coincided with the accession to the throne of the Chinese-importing Rama III. What figures of comparable stature grace the reigns of the later Jakri? What vigorous literary styles were created? Is there not simply a kind of Victorianization?[97] A narrow, cramped ideal of gentility everywhere smothering vitality? A museumized culture which found its institutionalization in the Siam Society of former times? Not until the 1960s—and then removed from court and Siam Society—did Thai literary culture regain a creative élan.

Surely this widely acknowledged cultural decline, considered in juxtaposition to the "modernization" of the realm, raises serious questions about the character of modern Thai history and politics. The solution to the paradox cannot be found in the nature of absolutism itself; the royal absolutists of Europe—Louis XIV par excellence—presided over brilliant efflorescences in literature and the arts. But part of the answer may be found if we remember that Jakri absolutism was a dependent absolutism, at bottom a byproduct of European pacification and penetration.[98]

II in 1824 and that they had long been accustomed to erecting Thai-style temples (Skinner, *Chinese Society in Thailand*, pp. 113–14). We may also recall Werner's description (mentioned above; as cited in ibid., p. 117) of the nineteenth-century collapse of Thai craft industries at the hands of Jakri-imported Chinese.

[95] For a comparative discussion of the political meaning of such miniaturization and replication, with reference to Indonesia and Cambodia, see my 1978 article, "Cartoons and Monuments: The Evolution of Political Communication under the New Order," in *Political Power and Communications in Indonesia*, ed. Karl D. Jackson and Lucian W. Pye (Berkeley, CA: University of California Press, 1978), pp. 282–321.

[96] On occasion, one hears the view expressed that the decline in court arts is to be blamed on the leaders of the 1932 coup. While this view is intrinsically implausible, it is pleasant to find Wachirawut starting a *khǫn* (dance drama) school around 1908 because he was worried that "this most highly developed of all Thai art forms was withering away due to lack of support" (Greene, "Thai Government and Administration in the Reign of Rama VI [1910–1925]," p. 30).

[97] Herbert Phillips reports an informant telling him that the classical erotic literature written at the court during the seventeenth through nineteenth (early nineteenth?) centuries was "Thailand's only original contribution to the great literature of the world." Such literature re-emerged from the underground only in the last fifteen years or so. See: Herbert P. Phillips, "The Culture of Siamese Intellectuals" (a most pioneering study) in *Change and Persistence in Thai Society: Essays in Honor of Lauriston Sharp*, ed. G. William Skinner and A. Thomas Kirsch (Ithaca, NY: Cornell University Press, 1975), p. 332.

[98] This point brings to mind one of the most obvious gaps in the study of the modern history of Siam: a synoptic analysis of Anglo–Thai relations. Here are a few items for consideration:

Latitudinal comparisons are no less illuminating. Coming from the study of neighboring Southeast Asian countries, one cannot but be struck with the relative narrowness of twentieth-century Siamese (in comparison with modern Vietnamese, Indonesian, or Filipino) literature. The "springtime" of this literature also manifested itself at least one, and probably two, whole generations after its regional companions. These comparisons are made not with the intention of disparaging Thai achievements but to remind ourselves of the inescapable interrelation between cultural and political life. It is clear that the growth of a creative modern literature in the other countries mentioned, starting with the extraordinary novels of José Rizal, is intimately connected with the nationalist movement. The crampedness of Thai literature is, I would suggest, symptomatic precisely of the incomplete transition from absolutist kingdom to nation-state.[99]

Finally, we turn briefly to the largest and most complex cultural institution of all: the Sangha. It is certainly likely that from early times Thai rulers "used" Buddhism to cement their legitimacy and increase their manpower resource base. One function of traditional Buddhist monument construction was certainly to "attract" followers. Buddhist missionary activities were certainly encouraged, in part, for *raisons d'état*. Nonetheless, one must remember—as when studying the politics of the Middle Ages in Europe—that only one cosmology was then available, and even the most cynical, Macchiavellian rulers could not stand outside it. Such traditional Thai rulers were subject to Buddhism no less than, though in different ways from, their subjects. What seems to have happened in the late nineteenth century was the onset of a slow secularization of the Thai ruling class. Fewer and fewer boys from these milieus entered the monkhood at all (let alone for good); and increasingly, when they did, the act was perfunctory.[100]

(i) Battye reminds us that England strongly supported Rama V's attempt to develop an army. In 1884, the English Minister Resident wrote to London that he was "convinced that in strengthening the king and the throne lies the only hope for the future of Siam and *for its possible utility to ourselves*" (Battye, "The Military, Government and Society in Siam, 1868–1910, p. 269; emphasis added).

(ii) "England exercised a virtual stranglehold on the Thai economy. Not only could England close her two entrepôt ports of Singapore and Hong Kong, which handled the bulk of Thailand's export trade, but she could also blockade the nation's primary port" (Greene, "Thai Government and Administration in the Reign of Rama VI [1910–1925]," p. 261).

(iii) In reference to the reign of Rama VI: "On most international questions, the Prince [Devavong] usually adhered to the policy line established by Great Britain. Sir Herbert Dering, England's diplomatic representative in Bangkok, was on exceptionally friendly terms with Devavong. In fact, he conferred with Devavong so often that in many Thais' eyes he was, in effect, the Ministry's Foreign Advisor, usurping the power of the American hired for that post" (ibid., p. 264).

(iv) As late as the mid-1920s, six times as many Thai students were studying in England as in any other country (Batson, "The End of the Absolute Monarchy in Siam," p. 72).

[99] Greene's analysis of Rama VI's stance is very apt: "Whenever opposition arose he sought to surmount it by intensifying his call for loyalty to the king and nation. By so closely identifying the monarchy with nationalism and by maintaining a virtual monopoly on the leadership of the movement, Wachirawut impaired its effectiveness. His concept of nationalism was suspect because it was the King, himself, who so ardently preached loyalty to the monarchy." Greene, "Thai Government and Administration in the Reign of Rama VI (1910–1925)," p. 426.

[100] Batson records that the magazine of the Thai students in England in the 1930s contained numerous articles on the growing indifference to religion among the younger generation of Thai. Batson, "The End of the Absolute Monarchy in Siam," p. 79.

Thus, to the extent that it was possible to stand outside it, it became possible to "use" Buddhism for political purposes in a more drastic and cold-blooded way.[101] (There are clear analogies here with the manipulation, by certain power-groups, of Islam in contemporary Malaysia and Indonesia, and of Buddhism in Burma. In all cases, the policies are reflections of cosmological separations between ruler and ruled.) Under conditions where rulers no longer really believe in the ideology/religion they propagate to the ruled, such "faiths" rapidly petrify in their official institutional manifestations. Does this help to explain the contemporary paradox of a Sangha hierarchy in obvious decay (despite official affirmations to the contrary), and the wide lateral spread—to left and right, as it were—of lay Buddhist activism?

CONCLUSION

I have tried to indicate what seem to me the weaknesses of English-language writing about modern Thai political life, and to suggest some of the material, political, and conceptual reasons for those weaknesses. Rather than repeating or even recapitulating what has been said so far, let me try here to offer a brief synthesis.

Reflecting on the corpus of available writing on modern Thai society, one is struck by the many apparently contradictory motifs: loose structure/rigid bureaucratic hierarchy, Buddhist activism/decline of the Sangha, dynamic rule/unchanging society, stability/instability, conservatism/decay. Each of the elements of these pairs (and many others) has been the subject of useful study—by anthropologists, students of religion, political scientists, historians, economists, and others.

Yet awareness of these apparent contradictions has not, on the whole, encouraged scholars to go beyond either (a) insisting that one element in the pair is the real, the important, or the preponderant one; or (b) insisting, with a certain complaisance, that such "dualities" are simply "natural givens" of a complex and uniquely Thai society. What is badly needed is a perspective that seriously studies the interrelations, not only within each dualism but also of the general configuration that contains them all. In other words, we need to dare to think carefully about Thai society, history, and culture *as a totality*.

In this regard, it is very important to assess dispassionately the situation of the "Thai specialists" in the American (Western) academic marketplace. All are both area-specialists and members of formal disciplines. The prestige and plausibility of area studies—perhaps never very high, and nationally significant only in the context of American expansion into the Third World after World War II—has been on the decline for a decade. Many area specialists feel vulnerable to the charge of being methodologically backward and theoretically unsophisticated in terms of their disciplines. (On the whole, these disciplines have only a modest appreciation of the concrete, as well as the theoretical and methodological, difficulties facing their members working in places like Siam: language difficulties, data difficulties, access difficulties, cultural difficulties, political difficulties, etc.)

Nonetheless, it strikes me that the responses of the area specialists often reflect a kind of failure of nerve. Two polar types of response seem only too frequent. One

---

[101] This process reached an apogee of sorts in the brutal manipulations of the Sangha by the late dictator Sarit Thanarat.

consists of mindlessly trying to "catch up" with the discipline's latest methodological or theoretical fads—applying them randomly and without reflection to the data, in the hope of making respectable showings at the discipline's annual conventions. The other consists in defiantly crawling deeper into an "area-ist" shell, insisting—in a defensive, ideological way—on the uniqueness and incomparability of the area of specialization, and engaging in the study of ever more narrowly defined and esoteric topics. ("Humanistic studies" can often be a useful shield for this maneuver.) Yet how often the defiant country specialist in fact submits him/herself to the fancied boundaries of the discipline. How easy it can be to snuggle down within the limits of *both* discipline *and* country.

It seems to me that being an area specialist is actually nothing to be ashamed of, but we must have the energy and self-confidence to undertake the task implicit in that to-be-honored title: in other words, propose as our task the study of that area or country *as an area* or, as I put it earlier, *as a totality*. This means not only reading the work of fellow area specialists in disciplines other than our own but allowing these works to interrogate ours. It means precisely *not* raiding these works for evidence to support existing conceptions or hypotheses, or citing them simply to add a cross-disciplinary, "humanistic" patina to our writings.

With all its obvious shortcomings and probable errors, this survey is meant to contribute to what I conceive to be the real purpose of this conference—to give some genuine meaning to the idea of "Thai Studies."

.

WITHDRAWAL SYMPTOMS: SOCIAL AND CULTURAL ASPECTS OF THE OCTOBER 6 COUP[1]

> ... And in those days all men and beasts
> Shall surely be in mortal danger
> For when the Monarch shall betray
> The Ten Virtues of the Throne
> Calamity will strike, the omens
> Sixteen monstrous apparitions:
> Moon, stars, earth, sky shall lose their course
> Misfortune shall spread everywhere
> Pitch-black the thundercloud shall blaze
> With Kali's fatal conflagration
> Strange signs shall be observed throughout
> The land, the Chao Phraya shall boil
> Red as the heart's-blood of a bird
> Madness shall seize the Earth's wide breast
> Yellow the color of the leadening sky
> The forest spirits race to haunt
> The city, while to the forest flee
> The city spirits seeking refuge ...
> The enamel tile shall rise and float
> The light gourd sink down to the depths.

Prophetic Lament for Sri Ayutthaya (c. 17th century)

INTRODUCTION

In themselves, military coups are nothing new in modern (or ancient) Thai history. There have been at least eight successful, and many more unsuccessful, coups since the one that overthrew the absolute monarchy in 1932.[2] It is therefore not altogether surprising that some Western journalists and academics have depicted the events of October 6, 1976, as "typical" of Thai politics, and even as a certain "return to normalcy" after three years of unsuitable flirtation with democracy.[3] In fact,

---

[1] This essay originally appeared in *Bulletin of Concerned Asian Scholars* 9,3 (July–September 1977): 13–30. Reprinted with permission. See www.criticalasianstudies.org

[2] See, for example, David Wilson, *Politics in Thailand* (Ithaca, NY: Cornell University Press, 1967), chapter IX; Fred W. Riggs, *Thailand: The Modernization of a Bureaucratic Polity* (Honolulu, HI: East-West Center Press, 1966), Appendix B.

[3] A liberal variant of this approach is to describe October 6 in Sisyphean terms, as yet another in an endless series of frustrating failures to bring democratic government to Siam. For a nice

however, October 6 marks a clear turning point in Thai history for at least two quite different reasons. First, most of the important leaders of the legal left-wing opposition of 1973–76, rather than languishing in jail or in exile like their historical predecessors, have joined the increasingly bold and successful maquis. Second, the coup was not a sudden intra-elite *coup de main*, but rather was the culmination of a two-year-long right-wing campaign of public intimidation, assault, and assassination best symbolized by the orchestrated mob violence of October 6 itself.[4]

Political murders by the ruling cliques have been a regular feature of modern Thai politics—whether under Marshal Phibunsongkhram's dictatorship in the late 1930s, under the Phibunsongkhram–Phao Siyanon–Sarit Thanarat triumvirate of the late 1940s and 1950s,[5] or the Sarit Thanarat–Thanom Kittikajon–Praphat Jarusathien regime of the 1960s and early 1970s.[6] But these murders, sometimes accompanied by torture, were typically "administrative" in character, carried out by the formal instrumentalities of the state, very often in secret. The public knew little of what had occurred, and certainly did not participate in any significant way. What is striking about the brutalities of the 1974–76 period is their nonadministrative, public, and

---

example of this, see Frank C. Darling, "Thailand in 1976: Another Defeat for Constitutional Democracy," *Asian Survey* XVII,2 (February 1977): 116–32.

[4] *Far Eastern Economic Review,* April 16, 1976, in its account of the April 1976 elections, spoke of "a spate of shootings, bombings, and other violent incidents aimed mainly at left-wing and reformist parties." *Prachachart Weekly Digest* 20 (March 16, 1976) and 21 (March 23, 1976) listed the names of close to fifty victims of political assassination in the period 1974–76, all of them on the left.

[5] On the repression following the "rebellion" of Phraya Song Suradet in 1938, see Wilson, *Politics in Thailand*, p. 261. On March 3, 1949, four well-known members of parliament and former cabinet ministers were murdered by Phao's police while being moved from one prison to another. See Samut Surakkhaka, *26 Kanpattiwat Thai lae Ratthaprahan 2089–2507* [Twenty-six Thai Revolutions and Coups, 1546–1964] (Bangkok: Sue Kanphim, 1964), pp. 472–89. In December 1952, two prominent northeastern politicians, Thim Phuriphat and Tiang Sirikhan, disappeared. Later it was revealed that they had been strangled by Phao's police. See Charles F. Keyes, *Isan: Regionalism in Northeastern Thailand*, Data Paper No. 65 (Ithaca, NY: Cornell University Southeast Asia Program Publications, 1967), p. 34; and Thak Chaloemtiarana, "The Sarit Regime, 1957–1963: The Formative Years of Modern Thai Politics" (PhD dissertation, Cornell University, 1974), p. 118; this dissertation was later published as *Thailand: The Politics of Despotic Paternalism* (Bangkok: Social Science Association of Thailand, 1979), and in 2007 Cornell Southeast Asia Program Publications brought out a revised version.

[6] See, e.g., Thak, "The Sarit Regime," pp. 266–69, for accounts of the public executions of Suphachai Sisati on July 5, 1959; of Khrong Chandawong and Thongphan Sutthimat on May 31, 1961; and of Ruam Phromwong on April 24, 1962. Victims of the Thanom–Praphat era belonged to groups well beyond the circle of intellectuals and politicians. For example, an official inquiry in 1975 by the Ministry of the Interior, headed by the ministry's own inspector-general, confirmed student charges that in 1970–71 at least seventy people were summarily executed by the Communist Suppression Operations Command in Patthalung province. In the words of the report, "Communist suspects arrested by the soldiers were mostly executed. Previously, soldiers would have shot these suspects by the roadside [sic!]. But later they changed the style of killing and introduced the red oil drum massacre in order to eliminate all possible evidence. The sergeant would club the suspect until he fell unconscious, before dumping him in the oil drum and burning him alive." *Bangkok Post*, March 30, 1975. For a report on indiscriminate napalming of minority Meo (Hmong) villages in the north, see Thomas A. Marks, "The Meo Hill Tribe Problem in Thailand," *Asian Survey* XIII,10 (October 1973): 932; and Ralph Thaxton, "Modernization and Peasant Resistance in Thailand," in *Remaking Asia*, ed. Mark Selden (New York, NY: Pantheon, 1971), pp. 265–73, especially at p. 269.

even mob character. In August 1976, Bangkokians watched the hitherto inconceivable spectacle of the private home of Prime Minister Kukrit Pramote being sacked by a swarm of drunken policemen.[7] In February, Socialist Party secretary-general Dr. Boonsanong Punyothayan had been waylaid and assassinated outside his suburban home by professional gunmen.[8] Hired hooligans increasingly displayed a quite "untraditional" style of violence, such as indiscriminate public bombings,[9] that sharply contrasted with the discreet, precise murders of an earlier era. Ten innocent persons died when a grenade was thrown into the midst of a New Force party election rally in Chainat on March 25, 1976.[10] And the gruesome lynchings of October 6 took place in the most public place in all Siam—Sanam Luang, the great downtown square before the old royal palace.

What I propose to do in this article is to explore the reasons for this new level and style of violence, for I believe that they are symptomatic of the present social, cultural, and political crisis in Siam. My argument will be developed along two related lines, one dealing with class formation and the other with ideological upheaval.

The class structure of Thai society has changed rapidly since the late 1950s. Above all, new bourgeois strata have emerged, rather small and frail to be sure, but in significant respects outside of and partially antagonistic to the old feudal–bureaucratic upper class. These new strata—which include both a middle and a petty bourgeoisie—were spawned by the great Vietnam War boom of the 1960s when Americans and American capital poured into the country on a completely unprecedented scale (rapidly followed by the Japanese). It is these strata that provide the social base for a quasi-popular right-wing movement clearly different from the aristocratic and bureaucratic rightism of an earlier age. This is by no means to suggest that old ruling cliques of generals, bankers, bureaucrats, and royalty do not continue to hold the keys of real political power; rather, that these cliques have found themselves new, and possibly menacing, "popular" allies.[11]

---

[7] These policemen, in civilian clothes, were escorted by police cars with flashing lights and motorcycle outriders. Aside from stealing brandy and cigarettes, they did an estimated $500,000 damage to Kukrit's palatial home. *New York Times*, August 20, 1975. At precisely the same moment, Thammasat University, spiritual home of student radicalism, was assaulted and partly put to the torch by the right-wing hooligans of the Red Gaurs (on whom see below) with complete impunity.

[8] The murder took place on February 28. See *Far Eastern Economic Review*, March 12, 1976; and Carl Trocki's article, "Boonsanong Punyodyana: Thai Socialist and Scholar," in *The Bulletin of Concerned Asian Scholars* 9,3 (July–September 1977).

[9] On February 15, 1976, the moderate New Force party's Bangkok headquarters were fire-bombed by right-wing hooligans. See *Far Eastern Economic Review*, February 27, 1976. Though one of these hooligans got an arm blown off in the process, he was released by the police for "lack of evidence." On March 21, a bomb thrown into a mass of marchers in downtown Bangkok—they were demanding full removal of the American military presence—killed four people and wounded many others. See *Prachachart Weekly Digest* 22 (March 30, 1976): 1.

[10] *Far Eastern Economic Review*, April 9, 1976.

[11] This is perhaps the place to emphasize that the present article, being centrally concerned with the emergence of new social formations and new cultural tendencies, deliberately pays little attention to these old ruling groups, or to such powerful bureaucratic institutions as the military and the Ministry of the Interior. The political roles of these groups and institutions have been extensively discussed in the literature on modern Thai politics, including other contributions to this issue of *The Bulletin of Concerned Asian Scholars*.

The ideological upheaval was also in large part due to the impact of American penetration, and manifested itself primarily in an intellectual revolution that exploded during the "democratic era" of 1973–76. Reacting to the intellectual nullity and the crude manipulation of traditionalist symbols by the Sarit–Thanom–Praphat dictatorship, many young Thai came openly to question certain central elements of the old hegemonic culture. In response to this, there was an enormous increase in the self-conscious propagation and indoctrination of a militant ideology of Nation–Religion–King—as opposed to the *bien-pensant* "traditionalism" that reigned before. Rather than being seen generally as "naturally Thai," Nation–Religion–King became ever more explicitly the ideological clubs of highly specific social formations. The obvious audience for this self-conscious rightist ideologizing were the new bourgeois strata; the propagandists were both fanatical elements in these strata themselves and some shrewd manipulators in the ruling cliques.

TROUBLES OF NEW CLASSES

In the 1950s and 1960s most Western social scientists took the view that Siam was a "bureaucratic polity"—a political system completely dominated by a largely self-perpetuating "modernizing" bureaucracy.[12] Below this bureaucracy there was only a pariah Chinese commercial class and an undifferentiated peasantry, both with low political consciousness and virtually excluded from political participation. The relations between bureaucracy and peasantry were understood to be generally harmonious and unexploitative,[13] involving only the classical exchanges of taxes, labor, and deference for security, glory, and religious identity. Thanks largely to the shrewdness and foresight of the great nineteenth-century Chakkri dynasts, Siam, alone among the states of Southeast Asia, did not succumb to European or American imperialism and thereby escaped the evils of rackrenting, absentee landlordism, chronic peasant indebtedness, and rural proletarianization so typical of the colonized zones. The Siamese economy, by no means highly developed until the 1960s, was essentially in the hands of immigrant Chinese, who, by their alien and marginal status, could never play a dynamic, independent political role.[14] This picture of a peaceful, sturdy, and independent Siam was in important ways quite false. Western capital, Western "advisers," and Western cultural missionaries exercised decisive influence on Siamese history after the 1950s.[15] On the other hand, when compared to

---

[12] The phrase was, I think, coined by Riggs. See p. 11 of his *Thailand*. But the basic idea was central to Wilson's *Politics in Thailand*, the single most influential study of that era.

[13] Thadeus Flood, in his excellent article "The Thai Left Wing in Historical Context," *Bulletin of Concerned Asian Scholars* (April–June 1975), p. 55, quotes the following entertaining sentences from Wendell Blanchard et al., *Thailand* (New Haven, CT: Human Relations Area File, 1957), pp. 484–85: "It is doubtful whether [Thai peasants] could conceive of a social situation without distinction between superior and inferior position. Peasants and others of low social status have never viewed such a social system as particularly unreasonable or severe, and there is no history in Thailand of general social oppression."

[14] See G. William Skinner's *Chinese Society in Thailand: An Analytic History* (Ithaca, NY: Cornell University Press, 1957); and his *Leadership and Power in the Chinese Community in Thailand* (Ithaca, NY: Cornell University Press, 1958). Cf. Donald Hindley, "Thailand: The Politics of Passivity," *Pacific Affairs*, XLI,3 (Fall 1968): 366–67.

[15] Frank C. Darling, *Thailand and the United States* (Washington, DC: Public Affairs Press, 1965), p. 29, noted that, at the time of the 1932 coup that overthrew the absolute monarchy, 95 percent of the Thai economy was in the hands of foreigners and Chinese.

the changes brought about by the American and Japanese penetration in the Vietnam War era, the years before the 1960s appear relatively "golden." As late as 1960, Bangkok could still be described as the "Venice of the East," a somnolent old-style royal harbor-city dominated by canals, temples, and palaces. Fifteen years later, many of the canals had been filled in to form roads and many of the temples had fallen into decay. The whole center of gravity of the capital had moved eastwards, away from the royal compounds and Chinese ghettoes by the Chao Phraya river to a new cosmopolitan zone dominated visually and politically by vast office buildings, banks, hotels, and shopping plazas. The city had expanded with cancerous speed, devouring the surrounding countryside and turning rice-paddies into speculative housing developments, instant suburbs, and huge new slums.[16]

This transformation, which on a smaller scale also occurred in certain provincial capitals, was generated by forces exogenous to Siamese society. It may be helpful to describe these forces in terms of three interrelated factors. The first and most important was undoubtedly America's unceremonious post-1945 extrusion of the European colonial powers from their prewar economic, political, and military hegemony in Southeast Asia.[17] The second was Washington's decision to make Siam the pivot of its regionwide expansionism. Bangkok became the headquarters not only for SEATO [Southeast Asia Treaty Organization], but also for a vast array of overt and clandestine American operations in neighboring Laos, Cambodia, Burma, and Vietnam.[18] A third factor—important in a rather different way—was the technological revolution that made mass tourism a major industry in the Far East after World War II. (Hitherto tourism in this zone had been an upper-class luxury.) For this industry Bangkok was a natural nexus: it was not only geographically central to the region, but it was thoroughly safe under the protection of American arms and native dictatorships, and, above all, it offered an irresistible combination of modern luxury (international hotels, comfortable air-conditioned transportation, up-to-date movies, etc.) and exotic antiquities.[19] Elsewhere in Southeast Asia the colonial

---

[16] Over a quarter of a century the population of the metropolitan complex of Bangkok–Thonburi rose as follows:

1947	781,662
1960	1,800,678
1970	2,913,706
1972	3,793,763

See Ivan Mudannayake, ed., *Thailand Yearbook, 1975–76* (Bangkok: Temple Publicity Services, 1975), p. E28.

[17] Darling, *Thailand*, pp. 29, 61, 170–71. By 1949, US trade with Siam had increased by 2,000 percent over the immediate prewar level. By the late 1950s, the United States was buying 90 percent of Siam's rubber and most of its tin.

[18] This line of analysis is developed more extensively in Thaxton, "Modernization," pp. 247–51.

[19] Some indication of the scale of this tourism is suggested by the following figures:

	1965	1966	1970	1971	1972	1973	1974
Foreign Visitors (1000s)	225.0	469.0	628.7	638.7	820.8	1,037.7	1,107.4
United States	78.3	133.3	159.2	147.0	151.6	161.4	156.8
(R&R)	(15.0)	(70.7)	(44.3)	(26.6)	(7.7)	(4.4)	(3.5)
Japan	17.3	42.9	47.0	55.8	93.5	151.9	132.7

Foreign exchange earnings from tourism (in millions of *baht*):

	1965	1966	1970	1971	1972	1973	1974
	506	1,770	2,175	2,214	2,718	3,399	4,292
(R&R)	(50)	(459)	(390)	(240)	(63)	(13)	(11)

(continued on next page)

powers had typically constructed culturally mediocre, commercially oriented capital cities in coastal areas far removed from the old indigenous royal capitals. (Tourists had thus to make time-consuming pilgrimages from Djakarta to Surakarta, Rangoon to Mandalay-Ava, Saigon to Hue, and Phnom Penh to Angkor.)

If the American penetration of Siam was a general feature of the post-World War II era, there was nonetheless a marked difference in degree and pace after 1959, when the absolutist dictatorship of Sarit Thanarat was installed. His predecessor, Marshal Phibunsongkhram, was a relatively polished product of St. Cyr and the prewar European-dominated world. Sarit, on the other hand, was a provincial, the product of the Royal Military Academy, and a man who rose to power in the postwar era of American global hegemony. It was he who personally presided over the Americanization (in terms of organization, doctrines, training, weaponry, and so forth) of the Thai military, following his first visit to Washington in 1950.[20] Almost a decade of close ties with the Pentagon prior to his seizure of power meant that after 1959 he found it easy and natural to link Siam to the United States in an unprecedented intimacy.[21] In other ways, too, Sarit was a perfect dictator from Washington's point of view. He was willing and eager to make "development" part of his quest for legitimacy and to accept the advice of US-trained technocrats in drawing up and implementing developmental programs.[22] As unquestioned "strongman," he had far more power to act swiftly and decisively than his predecessor.[23] Most important of all, Sarit did everything in his power to attract foreign (and especially American) capital to Siam, believing it to be an essential means for consolidating his rule and that of his successors. Thus strikes were banned and unions forcibly dissolved. Branches of foreign corporations were not only permitted to remain largely foreign-owned, but could purchase land in Siam, were

---

Note: In gauging the significance of the figures for 1972–74, one must bear in mind the then high rate of inflation. Source: World Bank, "Thailand: Current Economic Prospects and Selected Development Issues," II (Statistical Appendix), November 14, 1975, table 8.7. Tourism was typically among the top eight foreign-exchange-earning industries during these years.

[20] The best single source on Sarit is Thak, "The Sarit Regime." For Sarit's role in the Americanization of the Thai military, see especially pp. 120–22. But Darling, *Thailand*, is very useful on the American side of the Sarit–Washington relationship.

[21] Sarit was especially supportive of US aggressiveness in Laos. Whereas Phibun had been born near Ayutthaya in Central Thailand, and was "central Thai" in his basic orientation, Sarit was a Northeasterner in many ways. His mother had come from Nongkhai on the Thai border with Laos, and he himself had spent part of his childhood there. Through her, he was closely related to Gen. Phoumi Nosavan, the Pentagon's perennial rightist–militarist candidate for strongman in Vientiane.

[22] There had never been a national plan in the Phibun era. Siam's six-year First National Development Plan was developed under Sarit and formally inaugurated in 1961. On this plan, and the degree to which it abjectly followed the recommendations of the International Bank for Reconstruction and Development, see Pierre Fistié, *L'Évolution de la Thailande Contemporaine* (Paris: Armand Colin, 1967), pp. 334–35. But cf. Thak, "The Sarit Regime," pp. 327–28, for an argument that Sarit did not allow himself to be wholly guided by international technocrats.

[23] While Phibun had been a virtual dictator in the late 1930s and early 1940s, during his second long term as Prime Minister, 1948–57, he was in a much weaker position. The coup group of 1947 had brought him back as a sort of figurehead who could serve to give some international "class" to their regime. Phibun survived mainly because of US support and his own astute balancing of the increasingly antagonistic factions of Police General Phao and General Sarit. By the coups of 1958 and 1959, Sarit destroyed the power of the police, and made the army, which he controlled, the undisputed master of Thai political life.

largely exempted from taxation, and were even allowed to bring technicians freely into the country, bypassing the existing immigration laws.[24] The *baht* was managed according to the most orthodox economic principles and remained a rock of stability until the end of the 1960s.

After five years in power, Sarit succumbed to cirrhosis of the liver. But his heirs, Thanom and Praphat, continued the basic thrust of his policies. The onset of their rule virtually coincided with [US president] Lyndon Johnson's escalation of the Vietnam War, and they were quick to seize the opportunities thereby presented. Washington was encouraged to treat Siam as a sort of gigantic immobile aircraft carrier: in the peak year 1968, there were almost 50,000 US servicemen on Thai soil, and the Americans had been allowed to build and operate at least eight major bases as well as dozens of minor installations.[25] Not only were the Thai rulers amply rewarded in terms of military aid, but this huge American presence generated a rapid economic expansion, above all in the construction and service sectors.[26] A massive war-related boom developed, which built on, but far outstripped, the "prewar" prosperity of the early Sarit years. It was the Thanom–Praphat regime that presided over the proliferation of hotels, restaurants, movie houses, supermarkets, nightclubs, and massage parlors generated by the torrential inflow of white businessmen, soldiers, and tourists.

If the boom itself was basically fueled by American (and Japanese) investment and spending, the mode of Thai participation in its benefits was influenced significantly by regime policies. Of these, one of the most decisive was Sarit's early decree eliminating the existing 50-rai (c. 20 acre) limit on permissible landholding.[27] This decree laid the legal foundations for large-scale land speculation, which continued to accelerate so long as the boom itself lasted. Nor was the speculative

---

[24] For a summary of Thai enticements to foreign investors, see Fistié, *L'Evolution*, p. 337.

[25] According to the *New York Times*, April 14, 1968, there were then 46,000 troops in Thailand, as well as 5,000 troops a month on R&R from Vietnam. *The Nation*, October 2, 1967, listed 46,000 troops, 7,000 personnel engaged in economic and propaganda activities, and eight airbases.

[26] Part of this transformation is shown by comparing employment in various sectors between 1960 and 1970:

	1960	1970	Change (%)
Agriculture	11,300,000	13,200,000	+ 17
Mining	30,000	87,000	+ 290
Manufacturing	470,000	683,000	+ 45
Construction	69,000	182,000	+ 64
Commerce	779,000	876,000	+ 13
Transport, storage, communications	166,000	268,000	+ 62
Services	654,000	1,184,000	+ 81

Rounded figures computed from Table 1.2 in World Bank, "Thailand," II (1975). In the years 1960–65, Gross National Income increased annually by 7.5 percent, Gross Domestic Investment by 14.4 percent. See Annex I of the "Report and Recommendation of the President of the International Bank for Reconstruction and Development to the Executive Directors of the World Bank on a Proposed Loan to the Industrial Finance Corporation of Thailand," September 1, 1976. Clark Neher, "Stability and Instability in Contemporary Thailand," *Asian Survey* XV,12 (December 1975): 1100–1, gives an average 8.6 percent annual increase in GNP between 1959 and 1969.

[27] See, e.g., Fistié, *L'Évolution*, p. 353; and Robert J. Muscat, *Development Strategy in Thailand: A Study of Economic Growth* (New York, NY: Praeger, 1966), p. 138.

wave confined to Bangkok. As the Americans built and paved great strategic highways to the borders of Laos and Cambodia (the "Friendship" Highway, inter alia),[28] metropolitan and provincial speculators followed in their train, buying up wayside land very cheaply from subsistence farmers who had little understanding of land-as-speculative-commodity.[29] Land speculation is an economic activity in which legal skills, "inside information," "pull," and access to cheap bank loans are peculiarly important. It is not surprising, therefore, that the main beneficiaries of the real estate boom were not merely the traditional Sino–Thai commercial class, but high and middle-level bureaucrats (military and civilian) and provincial notables with good political connections. Unsurprisingly, the zones hardest hit tended to be those closest to Bangkok, the funnel through which capital poured so fast. The situation in central Thailand is illustrative: whereas in the Phibunsongkhram era, scholars agree, tenancy was not a serious problem, by the latter 1960s, USAID reports indicated that fewer than 30 percent of the farms were still owner-operated.[30]

The general "dynamization" of the Thai economy as a result of the factors mentioned above served to create or expand at least four social formations that are significant for our purposes here—in the sense that their survival largely depended on the continuation of the boom. In those rural areas where the process of commercialization had spread most rapidly, strategically positioned notables, rice-mill owners, traders, headmen, and so forth, acquired sudden new wealth, a good deal of which was reinvested in land. As rural landlordism rose, so there was a complementary exodus of the young and the dispossessed to the booming urban centers.[31] In the towns, and perhaps especially in Bangkok, the flow of migrants generated two sorts of politically volatile social groups: first, a large mass of

---

[28] See Thak, "The Sarit Regime," Appendix IV, for details and a sketch map.

[29] Vivid evidence to this effect is provided by Howard Kaufman in his *Bangkhuad: A Community Study in Thailand* (Rutland, VT, and Tokyo: Tuttle, 1976), pp. 219–20. Revisiting Bangkhuad, which he had studied in 1954 when it was still a small rural community on the fringes of Bangkok, he found that: whereas in 1954 a *rai* (1 *rai* = c. 0.4 acres) was valued at 3,000 *baht* (approximately US$150), by 1971 it had gone up to 250,000 *baht* (approximately US$12,500). In addition, the most valuable land was no longer the most fertile, but the land closest to the developing road system. Thak, "The Sarit Regime," pp. 337–38, notes that many peasants with land along the major highways were simply extruded without compensation by powerful officials and their accomplices.

[30] See Anonymous, "The US Military and Economic Invasion of Thailand," *Pacific Research* 1,1 (August 3, 1969): 4–5, citing Department of Commerce, OBR 66–60, September 1966, p. 6. Neher, "Stability," p. 1110, speaks of tenancy and indebtedness having "jumped precipitously." Takeshi Motooka, in his *Agricultural Development in Thailand* (Kyoto: Kyoto University, Center for Southeast Asian Studies, 1971), pp. 221ff., observes that: 1. According to the Thai government's 1963 agricultural survey, over 60.8 percent of the farmed land in the Central Plain was operated by full- or part-time tenants. 2. From his own local study in a district of Pathum Thani province (very close to Bangkok), 90 percent of the operating farmers were tenants. On the other hand, the thesis that posits rapidly increasing tenancy has recently been strongly attacked by Laurence Stifel in his "Patterns of Land Ownership in Central Thailand during the Twentieth Century," *Journal of the Siam Society* 64,1 (January 1976): 237–74. For some comparative material on growing landlordism, indebtedness, and land-title manipulation in the Northern province of Chiengrai, see Michael Moerman, *Agricultural Change and Peasant Choice in a Thai Village* (Berkeley, CA: University of California Press, 1968), chapter V.

[31] This flow, however, was extensive even before the onset of the boom. Mudannayake, ed., *Thailand Yearbook, 1975–76*, p. E30, notes that in 1960 no less than one quarter of Bangkok's population had been born elsewhere.

unemployed, or underemployed, youthful drifters, with few substantial prospects either in the city or back home in their villages; second, a considerable number who were able to better themselves by finding niches in a broad array of burgeoning service-type occupations. This petty bourgeois army included barbers, pimps, manicurists, drycleaners, chauffeurs, tailors, masseuses, tour guides, motorcycle repairmen, bartenders, receptionists, tellers, small shop owners, and so forth. To a considerable degree this new petty bourgeoisie served and was dependent on the prosperity of a fourth group. This segment, mainly of previous urban origin, was a largely new middle bourgeoisie, in certain respects as closely tied to foreign capital as to the Thai state apparatus.

The two tables following may serve to suggest the nature of these changes in the Thai class structure and, in very rough terms, both the absolute sizes of the middle and petty bourgeoisies and their relative share of the population as a whole. The extraordinary increase in category B, and the sizeable increases in categories A, F, and I (largely middle/upper and petty bourgeois occupations), clearly reveal the nature of the boom's sociological impact over a decade.[32] Data drawn from the 1970 census, in which the above broad categories are broken down in great detail, allow one to make the following very rough calculations (see Table II). We may then provisionally estimate that by 1970 the middle and upper bourgeoisie formed about 3.5 percent of the working population (divided perhaps 3.0 percent and 0.5 percent), and the petty bourgeoisie about 7.5 percent.[33]

It is always useful to remember that social groupings become social classes insofar as they consolidate themselves through the *family*—a key institution for linking power, wealth, and status in one generation and transmitting them to another. One important sign of class formation in Siam during the Sarit–Thanom–Praphat era was a massive expansion of education at all levels, partly at the "modernizing" behest of American advisers and Thai technocrats, but also in bureaucratic response to the demands of the new upwardly aspirant social groups—and the families within them. In 1961, there were 15,000 students enrolled in a

---

[32] A striking example of such "nonbureaucratic" *nouveaux riches* produced by this era was Mr. Thawit ("Dewitt") Klinprathum, head of the large Social Justice party in 1974–76. The son of a poor government official, with not much more than a secondary school education, he started work at ten US dollars a month as a bookkeeper. He later did stints as a pedicab driver, shipping clerk, bus operator, and so forth. As his official biography records, "While working on subcontracts from the Express and Transportation Organization [ETO—a state-owned corporation intimately tied to JUSMAG, Joint US Military Advisory Group] unloading and transporting equipment, he realized the need for trailers. With the money he had saved and credit from the bank, he purchased two trailers to deliver heavy machinery and equipment … He started carrying equipment for JUSMAG and Accelerated Rural Development (ARD). Mr. Dewitt chose the right time to buy his trailers because mechanization was becoming necessary for economic development. With no other local companies possessing trailers and cranes, his company, Trailer Transport Company, secured a contract for transporting military equipment … His godown expanded and his trailers and trucks numbered in the hundreds *as the transportation network in the country expanded.*" *Bangkok Post*, December 24, 1974 (special advertisement paid for by the Social Justice party). Italics added. By 1974, "Dewitt" was a multimillionaire with an eight-story office building to himself.

[33] The figures in the two right-hand columns of Tables I and II (following) are likely to be too low. Category E, in particular, must include numbers of rural merchants and businessmen, though there is no way of telling even roughly how many.

Table I
Economically Active Population Aged 11 and Over Classified by Occupation

Occupational Group	Nos. in 1960	Nos. in 1970	% Increase
A. Professional, technical, & related workers	173,960	284,104	63.3
B. Administrative, executive, & managerial workers	26,191	246,591	941.5
C. Clerical workers	154,303	190,238	23.3
D. Sales workers	735,457	833,607	13.3
E. Farmers, fishermen, hunters, loggers, & related workers	11,332,489	13,217,416	16.6
F. Miners, quarrymen, & related workers	26,255	42,605	62.2
G. Workers in transport & communications occupations	144,610	225,204	55.7
H. Craftsmen, product-process workers, & laborers not elsewhere classified	806,205	1,109,943	37.7
I. Service, sport, & recreation workers	273,375	471,999	72.7
J. Unclassifiable	99,259	30,560	-59.2
K. New entrants to the work force	64,880	197,869	305.0
Total	13,836,984	16,850,136	21.7

Source: Adapted from National Economic and Development Board, National Statistical Office and Institute of Population Studies, Chulalongkorn University, "The Population of Thailand" [1974], in Mudannayake, ed., *Thailand Yearbook,* 1975–76, p. E 41.

Table II
Economically Active Population Aged 11 and Over
Classified by Occupation and Class (1970)

Occupational Group	Total Nos.	Nos. State Employed	% State Employed	Est. Middle & Upper Bourgeoisie	Est. Petty Bourgeoisie
A.	284,104	198,792	70.4	250,000	35,000
B.	246,591	212,752	86.3	230,000	15,000
C.	190,238	108,632	57.1	negl.	190,000
D.	833,607	1,492	.2	negl.	600,000
E.	13,217,416	10,169	.1	negl.	?
F.	42,605	568	1.3	negl.	negl.
G.	225,204	24,759	11.0	negl.	100,000
H.	1,109,943	106,292	9.6	negl.	150,000
I.	471,999	114,528	24.3	70,000	160,000
J.	30,560	—	—	—	—
K.	197,869	—	—	?	?
Total	16,850,136	777,984	4.7	550,000	1,250,000

Source: Adapted from Department of Labour, Ministry of the Interior, *Yearbook of Labour Statistics* 1972–1973 [using 1970 census figures], cited in Mudannayake, ed., *Thailand Yearbook,* 1975–76, pp. E 41–68.

total of five universities; by 1972, there were 100,000 enrolled in seventeen.[34] From 1964 to 1969, the numbers enrolled in government secondary schools rose from 159,136 to 216,621; in private secondary schools, from 151,728 to 228,495; and in government vocational schools, from 44,642 to 81,665.[35] "Traditionally" (for our purposes here from the 1880s until World War II), education had been sharply bifurcated. A tiny upper class received a gentlemanly Western-style education, while the bulk of the population either went uneducated, attended government primary schools, or received instruction in Buddhist temples.[36] Neither level of education generated nationally significant social mobility; rather, each helped to conserve its constituents in their existing social and economic positions. Western-style higher education gave polish to those already born to rule. State primary education was so elementary that it seems to have had few vectoral consequences: its existence was more a gesture by Thai governments concerned to show a modern face to the outside world than a response to peasant demand. Buddhist education was essentially ethically and cosmologically oriented, rather than geared to providing career-related skills (though for a small group of commoners success in the Sangha's tiered examination system could lead to very steep social mobility).[37]

---

[34] Neher, "Stability," p. 1101; Frank C. Darling, "Student Protest and Political Change in Thailand," *Pacific Affairs* 47,1 (Spring 1974): 6. To understand class formation in a capitalist society like Thailand's, it is important to study the "nonproductive" elements (schoolchildren, students, etc.). To build and to perpetuate their positions/wealth, the new bourgeois and petty bourgeois groups steer their children into the educational institutions. You only know when a class has really come to exist (rather than a suddenly rising elite) when you see "privileged kids"—and two generations of power. Aristocracies can consolidate themselves by intermarriage; bourgeoisies cannot, at least not to the same degree. Education tends to replace marriage.

[35] See Darling, "Student Protest," p. 6. These figures should be understood in the context of the budgetary statistics cited by Thak, "The Sarit Regime," pp. 437–38, which show the expenditures on the ministries of Education, Defense, and the Interior as percentages of the total budget over the years 1953–73. For brevity's sake I will give only his computations for the years 1958–73.

	1958	1959	1960	1961	1962	1963	1964	1965
Education	4.6	18.4	17.3	15.4	14.9	15.6	15.4	15.3
Defense	10.2	19.6	17.8	16.6	16.9	15.6	15.4	15.5
Interior	7.0	16.3	15.1	15.0	13.9	14.3	15.5	16.9

	1966	1967	1968	1969	1970	1971	1972	1973
Education	14.3	13.2	5.8	5.5	5.9	6.2	6.0	6.7
Defense	15.0	13.6	15.3	15.7	17.0	17.9	18.2	18.2
Interior	17.1	15.6	20.7	21.3	20.7	21.5	22.1	23.5

When one remembers that the costs of primary education came out of the Interior Ministry's budgets, the scale of expenditures on secondary and tertiary education (represented by the Education Ministry's budgets) is rather startling.

[36] Kaufman, *Bangkhuad*, p. 220, notes that in this community, very close to Bangkok, only 6 percent of the teenage cohort was attending any form of secondary school in 1954.

[37] See, e.g., David K. Wyatt, *The Politics of Reform in Thailand: Education in the Reign of King Chulalongkorn* (New Haven, CT: Yale University Press, 1969), chapter 1; and his earlier "The Buddhist Monkhood as an Avenue of Social Mobility in Traditional Thai Society," *Sinlapakorn* 10 (1966): 41–52.

Accordingly, the real significance of the education expansion of the 1960s was that it took place mainly at the secondary and tertiary levels.[38] For the first time, sizeable numbers of Thai began to desire and to have some access to career-oriented educations for their children, educations which, past history suggested, were the badges of or the avenues to elevated social status—above all, entry into the secure upper reaches of the state bureaucracy.[39] It is in this light that one must understand the political meaning of the proliferation of universities under Sarit and his heirs: as a kind of symbolic confirmation that the boom was not fortune but progress, and that its blessings would be transmitted to the next generation within the family. It was possible to *imagine* within the confines of a single household a successful dry-cleaner father and an embryonic cabinet-secretary son.[40] So the university boom served to consolidate the economic boom sociologically and to confirm it culturally.[41]

Yet, in spite of the rapid expansion in numbers, size, and enrollments of Thai universities, many aspiring families could not get their children into them: hence, in part, the no less rapid expansion of technical, vocational, commercial, and other colleges as second-bests. And in the context of all this stratificatory turmoil, one must understand, I think, a significant shift in the semantics of the word "student" itself. In an earlier time, "student" had been almost synonymous with "member of the national elite"—a being on an almost stratospheric plane above the mass of his

---

[38] Cf. above, p. 16. Kaufman, *Bangkhuad*, p. 220, comments that, by 1971, 60 percent of the community's teenage cohort was enrolled in secondary schools.

[39] Kaufman, *Bangkhuad*, pp. 229–31, has some excellent material on this topic. Hans Dieter-Evers, "The Formation of a Social Class Structure: Urbanization, Bureaucratization, and Social Mobility in Thailand," in Clark D. Neher, *Modern Thai Politics* (Cambridge, MA: Schenkman, 1976), pp. 201–5, indicates that this tendency had been in the making from the period of the 1932 coup on. From the sample of higher civil servants he studied, 26 percent of those who entered government service before 1933 had foreign university degrees, while the figure was 93 percent for those entering after World War II.

[40] The degree of mobility imagined possible is what needs underlining here, i.e., the change in public consciousness. Real mobility was, unsurprisingly, less spectacular, as Kraft's sample survey indicates:

Occupations of Parents of University Students (c. 1968)

Parents' Occupation	No. Enrolled	% Enrolled
Proprietors & Self-Employed	4,508	53.72
Government Officials	2,020	25.12
Employees	657	8.19
Agriculturalists	580	7.31
Others	437	5.31
Unknown	29	.35
Total Population of Study	8,231	100

Source: Richard Kraft, *Education in Thailand: Student Background and University Admission* (Bangkok: Educational Planning Office, Ministry of Education, 1968), cited in Mudannayke, ed., *Thailand Yearbook, 1975–76*, p. 117. Kraft estimated that the children of government officials had a 268 times better chance of being admitted to a university (and those of manufacturers and industrialists a 36 times better chance) than did children of farm families.

[41] True to the general shift in world power from Europe to the United States after World War II, the acme of the Thai educational pyramid came to be university schooling in California, Indiana, and New York, rather than London or Paris. Harvey H. Smith et al., *Area Handbook for Thailand* (Washington, DC: Government Printing Office, 1968), p. 175, for example, state that in 1966, of 4,000 Thai youngsters studying abroad, 1,700 were doing so in the United States. (There is good reason to believe that both figures are unrealistically low.) As late as 1955, the total number of Thai studying abroad had been only 1,969. See Evers, "Formation," p. 202.

countrymen. But by the late 1960s and early 1970s, social mobility had created conditions where "student" might still have elevated connotations, but could also signify something like "the neighbor's kid who got into Thammasat when mine didn't." It became possible to envy and resent students in a way that would have seemed incongruous a generation earlier.

But even for parents who were successful in getting their children into a university, the idea of the "student" came to have ambiguous resonances. The paradox of mobility is that movement upwards is also movement away. Rather poorly educated fathers, regarding university education in essentially instrumental terms, often found themselves appalled by quite unpredicted changes in the manners, goals, and morals of their student offspring, as these came to be influenced, in universities and teacher training colleges, by the iconoclastic ideas seeping in from the United States and China.[42] One must imagine the concern and anger of middle bourgeois or petty bourgeois parents when their sons began coming home with "messy" long hair, impertinent talk, casual morals, and subversive ideas: how would they ever make successful officials?

About 1971 or 1972, the feeling began to spread that the golden days were fading. The Americans were withdrawing their troops from Indochina, and the long-standing spectre of communist consolidations on Siam's border began to assume a threatening reality. The bureaucracy, ultimate target of many social hopes, had expanded to saturation point, and increasingly university degrees no longer guaranteed what they had been assumed to guarantee—secure and high-status employment.[43] After a long period of price stability, double-digit inflation suddenly struck the Thai economy.[44] A certain uneasiness and dissatisfaction developed among the beneficiaries of the great boom as it drew to its close. Exclusion from political participation had been tolerable so long as the dictatorship "produced" in the economic, security, and educational sectors, but became much less so as problems accumulated. In addition, neither Thanom nor Praphat had the frightening personal presence of Sarit.[45]

In this context the snowballing mass demonstrations that brought down Thanom and Praphat in October 1973—the month the world oil crisis began—are of

---

[42] See, e.g., Thanet Aphornsuwan, "Khwam khluanwai khong nak suksa thai nai yukh raek" [The Thai Student Movement in the Early Period], in *Khabuankan nak suksa Thai jak adit thung patchuban* [The Thai Student Movement from the Past to the Present], ed. Witthayakorn Chiengkun et al. (Bangkok: Samnakphim Prachan Siao, 1974), p. 28; and Sawai Thongplai, "Some Adults' Ideas about Some Youngsters," *Prachachart Weekly Digest* 22 (March 30, 1976): 15–18.

[43] Neher, "Stability," p. 1101; Darling, "Student Protest," pp. 8–9.

[44] Compare the following figures on the Bangkok consumer price index (1962 = 100): 1964, 102.9; 1965, 103.8; 1966, 107.7; 1967, 112.0; 1968, 114.4; 1969, 116.8; 1970, 117.7; 1971, 120.1; 1972, 124.9; 1973, 139.5; 1974, 172.0; Jan–Aug 1975, 176.4. Figures adapted from World Bank, "Thailand" (1975), II, table 9.1. Neher, "Stability," p. 1100, gives an inflation rate of 15 percent for 1972 and 24 percent for 1974.

[45] It is significant that, when the twin dictators finally held national elections in 1969, the civilian opposition Democrat party, in some ways a mirror of the new bourgeois strata, swept every seat in Bangkok. This sweep should be seen as a portent for middle-class participation in the events of October 14, 1973. On the Democrat sweep, see J. L. S. Girling, "Thailand's New Course," *Pacific Affairs* XLII,3 (Fall 1969), especially at p. 357.

extraordinary interest.[46] There is no doubt that the new bourgeois strata contributed decisively to the huge crowds that came out in support of students' and intellectuals' demands for a constitution and respect for civil liberties. Indeed, it can be argued that these strata ensured the success of the demonstrations—had the crowds been composed of slum-dwellers rather than generally well-dressed urbanites, the dictators might have won fuller support for repression.

At the same time, the participation of these bourgeois strata must be understood more as a product of their immediate history than as a portent of their future political role. It is clear, in fact, that they almost completely lacked political experience and so had no real idea of what the consequences of ending the dictatorship would be. The regime was simultaneously blamed both for failing to exact fuller American commitments to Siam and for excessive subservience to Washington. (The obverse side was an irritable, mystified, anti-American nationalism expressed in the combination of such sentiments as "Why have you let us down in Indochina?" and "Look how you've corrupted our girls!") The open corruption of Praphat, the dynastic marriage of Narong, Thanom's son, to Praphat's daughter, and his nepotistic, meteoric rise to power, all offended bourgeois sensibilities. It was also important that, for their own reasons, the monarch and certain senior generals supported the demonstrators, if only indirectly. Finally, one must remember that the student demands were essentially legalistic (constitutional) and symbolic. No one imagined that something dangerous or undesirable could come out of them. True enough, the students had destroyed a number of police stations in the last days of the demonstrations, but had they not kept traffic flowing smoothly and cleaned up the mess in the streets in a thoroughly responsible manner thereafter? With the corrupt and incompetent dictators gone, prosperity, peace, and progress would be restored under the benevolent supervision of the king with his enlightened entourage of senior justices, respected professors, and capable bankers.

As we know, none of these expectations came close to realization. The global oil crisis had broken out almost simultaneously with the October 1973 demonstrations. The disorder that resulted in the world capitalist economy began to make itself felt in Siam by early 1974. In the spring of 1975, the American position in Indochina collapsed with stunning speed. Siam was now no longer the safe pivot of America's Southeast Asian empire, but close to its fragile outer perimeter. It seemed conceivable that henceforth Singapore would play Bangkok's role, while the Thai capital itself would take Vientiane's. As a direct consequence of these events beyond its borders, Siam found its economy lagging badly.[47] The injury seemed compounded

---

[46] The important thing to note here is the size of the final demonstrations against the Thanom–Praphat regime. Neher, "Stability," p. 1103, gives a figure of 500,000—a mass demonstration without parallel in earlier Thai history.

[47] Gross Domestic Investment, which had grown at an annual rate of 14.4 percent in 1960–65, and 13.5 percent in 1965–70, dropped to 5.1 percent in 1970–75. The balance of payments situation deteriorated rapidly from 1973 on.

Year	Net Balance of Payments in US$millions
1973	-50
1974	-90
1975	-618
1976 (est.)	-745

Source: Annex I of "Report and Recommendation of the President of the International Bank for Reconstruction and Development," September 1, 1976.

by the post-October 1973 liberal governments' public commitment to civil rights and liberties, above all the rights of farmers and workers to organize, demonstrate, and strike. The Sanya Thammasakdi (October 1973–February 1975) government made real, if timid, efforts to respond directly to worker demands.[48] It is true that to some extent especially insecure new enterprises were vulnerable to the squeeze between declining profits and rising wage claims.[49] Under the dictatorship, workers had had to accept miserable pay while the middle classes prospered; now their turn had come. Yet the growing anger of the bourgeois strata as a whole had more complex roots. In the first place, the development of unions in itself threatened to undermine the patron–client "familial" style of employer–employee relations that had largely prevailed hitherto.[50] (It would be a mistake to underestimate the psychic "profit" that socially aspiring bourgeois elements derive from the opportunity to play quasi-feudal roles vis-à-vis their subordinates.) Secondly, many of the strikes occurred in sectors such as transportation, where it was particularly easy for bourgeois groups to interpret personal inconvenience as an affront to the public interest. Thirdly, and perhaps most importantly of all, influential sections of the Thai press under the control of large business interests constantly hammered on the theme that such strikes were anti-national, in the sense that they scared away the foreign investors on whom the "national economy" so depended. It was thus only too easy to blame the general economic deterioration on worker irresponsibility.

Finally, in still another sphere the chickens of the dictatorship came home to roost during the liberal era: rapidly growing unemployment among high school, vocational school, and even university graduates.[51] In effect, the educational boom, with its promise of rising status and security, went into a slump. Under the circumstances, it is scarcely surprising that the image of the student as unemployed (unemployable?) layabout at home and restless troublemaking agitator in shop or plant became the prime focus of a whole complex of resentments and frustrations among the new bourgeois strata.[52]

---

[48] Strikes and unionizing had been virtually outlawed by Sarit, both to crush left-wing opposition and to encourage foreign investment. Neher, "Stability," p. 1100, notes that "Over 2,000 labor strikes were carried out in 1973, almost all of them *after* [my italics] the October 1973 uprising, and some 1,500 strikes were counted in the first six months of 1974. In contrast, during the three-year period between 1969 and 1972 a total of only 100 strikes occurred." The Sanya government raised the 60¢ minimum wage, first to $1.00 and later (October 1974) to $1.25 a day. *Indochina Chronicle*, May–June 1975.

[49] The profit margins of some poorly managed Thai concerns certainly depended directly on the extremely cheap labor the dictatorship guaranteed.

[50] In 1966, only 5 percent of 30,672 manufacturing enterprises registered with the government employed more than 50 persons. Smith et al., *Area Handbook*, p. 360.

[51] "Strangely enough, vocational school graduates have a difficult time finding jobs. In the rural areas, only 25 percent are able to find jobs and in the greater Bangkok area the situation is not much better, with only about 50 percent able to find employment." Mudannayake, ed., *Thailand Yearbook, 1975–76*, p. 110.

[52] Highly significant is the fact that in the 1973–76 period perhaps the most militant of all labor unions was the Hostel and Hotel Workers' Union, led by the well-known activist Therdphum Chaidee. (By 1976, there were at least fifty first-class hotels alone in Siam, employing more than 30,000 workers. *Bangkok Post*, May 22, 1975.) No one sees more bitterly than a badly paid waiter or chambermaid how luxuriously some of their fellow countrymen really live. It is revealing that the main targets of union militancy were not foreign-owned or Chinese hotels (which were usually quite willing to recognize the union and deal with it in a reasonable way), but those owned by Thai (old and new rich), who insisted on treating their employees in

We are to visualize then a very insecure, suddenly created bourgeois stratum—Bangkok's immense traffic problems are partly the result of a flood of first-generation car owners and drivers[53]—faced by straitened economic circumstances and the menace of worse troubles still to come; not merely worried by the ending of the long boom but haunted by the fear that the boom was part of a single historical parabola, that the golden days of Sarit would never return, and that their ascent from backstreet dust would end where it had begun. Furthermore, we must understand that this bourgeoisie, with little experience in politics and unsophisticated ideas about government, but precisely therefore a strong consciousness of "not being to blame for the mess," was peculiarly liable to evince paranoiac responses to their predicament. (Depending on the circumstances, one could imagine this paranoia being vented on corruption, students, communists, foreigners, Chinese, or whatever.) In the event, in 1975–76, for reasons to be discussed below, the radicalized students—bourgeois successes who seemed to spit on that success—came to be the main target of this panicked anger. Such, I think, is the explanation of why many of the same people who sincerely supported the mass demonstrations of October 1973 welcomed the return to dictatorship three years later.

Yet they were not the immediate perpetrators of the brutalities on October 6. It remains therefore to attempt to identify the culprits and to situate them within the broad sociological framework sketched out so far. Undoubtedly the most notorious men of violence, not only on October 6, 1976, but during the preceding two years, were the Krathing Daeng (Red Gaurs). These hooligans have been given (I think somewhat mistakenly) a quasi-sociological respectability by journalists and academics who have identified them simply as vocational school students. Since vocational more than university students bore the brunt of the police repression of October 1973, so the argument goes, it is plausible to interpret Red Gaur attacks on university students as expressing the honest resentment of long-suffering low-status vocational students against high-status, arrogant, and cowardly "college kids."[54] The Red Gaur-vocational student identification was probably strengthened in many people's minds by a series of spectacularly violent (but mainly apolitical) clashes between adolescents from rival vocational schools in late 1974 and 1975.[55] Since these

patronal style. The most violent strike of 1975 erupted at the downtown luxury Dusit Thani hotel, when the Thai management hired Red Gaur gunmen as strike-breakers. See the account given in the *Bangkok Post*, May 30, 1975, which also quotes Prime Minister Kukrit Pramote's strong criticism of what he called a "private army."

[53] Chaktip Nitibhon, "Urban Development and Industrial Estates in Thailand," in *Finance, Trade, and Economic Development in Thailand*, ed. Prateep Sondysuvan (Bangkok: Sompong Press, 1975), p. 249, notes that between 1967 and 1971 the number of vehicles registered in Bangkok rose by 15 percent per annum (road surfaces increased by 1 percent). In 1973, with over 320,000 vehicles registered, Siam's capital contained more than half of the national total.

[54] See, e.g., Somporn Sangchai, "Thailand: Rising of the Rightist Phoenix" [*sic*], in *Southeast Asian Affairs 1976* (Singapore: Institute of Southeast Asian Studies, 1976), pp. 361–62.

[55] "Police said about three hundred students from Uthane Thawai Construction School, armed with bombs, clubs, guns, and other weapons, marched [yesterday] to Pathumwan Engineering School in front of the National Stadium where they engaged in a point-blank-range fight with three hundred Pathumwan students." (*The Nation*, June 1975.) Some earlier and subsequent confrontations include the following: (i) On October 29, 1974, a small boy was killed and fourteen people injured by a bomb thrown during a clash between students from the Dusit Construction, Nonthaburi Engineering, and Bangsorn Engineering schools. (*Bangkok Post*, December 9, 1975.) (ii) On December 26, one student was killed and several injured in a fight conducted with bombs and rifles between boys from the Bangsorn Engineering and Northern

boys used guns and bombs against each other, and these were the favored weapons of the Red Gaurs, it was easy to jump to the conclusion that the latter politically represented the former.

A more complex picture of the Red Gaurs is suggested by the following passage from an article in the conservative *Bangkok Post*:

> Another interesting man is Doui, who is appointed as the leader of a mobile unit [of the Red Gaurs], a force which could shift rapidly from place to place. Long-haired in hippy style and with a big scar on his face, Doui said he had fifty men under his control. Most of these are mercenaries, he said, who live in Loei Province as a security unit for road construction in the area.
>
> "I was a former soldier, but later I became a mercenary. I liked the uniform, but I disliked there being too many disciplines and regulations in the army. I like the freedom to follow my own style, wearing long hair or whatever dress I wish ..."[56]

Well-informed sources in Bangkok confirm that many of the key Red Gaur cadres were ex-mercenaries and men discharged from the army for disciplinary infractions, while their followings were mainly composed of unemployed vocational school graduates, high-school dropouts, unemployed street-corner boys, slum toughs, and so forth.[57] Hired by various cliques within the ISOC (Internal Security Operations Command) and other agencies specializing in police and intelligence work,[58] the Red Gaurs were not recruited primarily on the basis of ideological

---

Bangkok Engineering schools. (*The Nation*, December 27, 1974.) (iii) Three students suffered severe knife and gunshot wounds after a brawl between gangs from the Dusit Construction and Archivasilpa schools on December 27, 1974. (*Bangkok Post*, December 28, 1974.) A further bottle-bomb, rifle, and grenade battle between Bangsorn and Northern Bangkok on January 22, 1975, led to the death of a *Bangkok Post* cameraman. (*Bangkok Post*, January 23 and 24, 1975.) (iv) On June 12, two students died in a series of bottle- and plastic-bomb melees between boys from the Rama VI Engineering, Bangsorn Engineering, Uthane Thawai Construction, Nonthaburi Engineering, Pathumwan Engineering, and other vocational schools. (*The Nation*, June 13, 1975.) (v) On June 18, after a quarrel between Archivasilpa students and bus and construction workers, the students fire-bombed some buses, causing serious injuries. (*The Nation*, June 19, 1975.) Of these schools, only Rama VI had a somewhat political (left-wing) reputation.

[56] *Bangkok Post*, June 1, 1975.

[57] Personal communications. Compare note 51 above for unemployment rates among vocational school graduates.

[58] Two of the better-known leaders of the Red Gaur clusters are directly connected to ISOC: they are Praphan Wongkham, identified as "a twenty-seven-year-old employee of the Internal Security Operations Command"; and Suebsai Hasdin, son of Special Colonel Sudsai Hatsadin, formerly in charge of ISOC's Hill Tribes Division (see *Bangkok Post*, June 1, 1975); and Norman Peagam, "Rumblings from the Right," *Far Eastern Economic Review*, July 25, 1975. It is known that other Red Gaur groups were controlled by General Withoon Yasawat, former leader of the CIA-hired Thai mercenary forces in Laos, and General Chatchai Choonhawan, brother-in-law of the late Police General Phao, top figure in the Chat Thai party, and Foreign Minister in the Kukrit Pramote government (March 1975–April 1976). It should be noted that ISOC had also heavily infiltrated the section of the Education Ministry in charge of vocational education, and was the clandestine paymaster and manipulator of the NVSCT (National Vocational Student Center of Thailand), a small, aggressively right-wing antagonist of the large NSCT (National Student Center of Thailand), vanguard of left-wing student activism during the liberal era.

commitment, but rather by promises of high pay, abundant free liquor, brothel privileges, and the lure of public notoriety. It is striking how these rewards mirror the privileges anticipated for successful students on their entry into government service (money, prestige, expenses-paid visits to nightclubs and massage parlors), anticipated at least in the aspiring petty bourgeois *milieux* from which the Red Gaurs emerged.[59] In other words, there is a sociological underpinning to the political role played by these hooligans. Children of a new and vulnerable petty bourgeoisie, caught in a time of widespread unemployment,[60] unsuccessful in obtaining jobs in government offices and scornful of jobs in factories, they were easy targets for anti-(successful) student and anti-worker propaganda.

A second group, no less involved in the right-wing violence of 1974–76[61] but with a somewhat more respectable public image, was the Village Scouts. Founded in 1971 under the joint aegis of the Border Patrol Police [BPP] and the Ministry of the Interior, it was conceived as a paramilitary, anticommunist rural security organization.[62] In the liberal period, however, it developed a significant urban component and played an important mobilizing role for various right-wing forces. If, prior to October 1973, it had been the arena for discreet competition between Praphat, military strongman and Minister of the Interior, and the royal family, very influential in the BPP, the Village Scouts became, after the fall of the dictators, ever more openly a means for building up an activist constituency for royalist politics. Even under the dictatorship, the palace had worked hard to bind to itself the beneficiaries of the boom by a variety of public relations techniques.[63] This

---

[59] While the bulk of the Red Gaurs were probably petty bourgeois in origin (working-class Thai were much less likely to get their children as far as high school or vocational school), it is possible, even likely, that some were recruited from the migrant unemployed population alluded to earlier in this article.

[60] Prime Minister Thanin Kraiwichien, in a radio broadcast on October 17, 1976, observed that: "Another group of people facing poverty are the seasonal workers, laborers, new graduates, and other unemployed people. The unemployed now number over one million." *FBIS* (Foreign Broadcast Information Service) *Daily Report*, October 18, 1976. Italics added.

[61] They played an important role in intimidating liberal and left-wing elements during the 1976 election campaign; in expelling student activists trying to organize peasant and tenants' unions in the villages; in demanding the resignation of the Seni Pramote government's three "progressive" ministers (Surin Masdit, Chuen Leekphai, and Damrong Latthaphiphat) on the eve of the October 6, 1976, coup; and in the violence of October 6 itself. See, e.g., Sarika Krirkchai, "Do Not Corrupt the Village Scouts," *Prachachart Weekly Digest* 23 (April 6, 1976): 14–15.

[62] Much of the information on the Village Scouts contained in the following sentences is drawn from the illuminating, detailed article by Natee Pisalchai, "Village Scouts," *Thai Information Resource* (Australia) No. 1 (May 1977): 34–37.

[63] Thak, "The Sarit Regime," pp. 414–25, offers instructive material on three such techniques. First, the king stepped up both the absolute number of weddings at which he officiated and the relative number involving the upper bourgeoisie, as opposed to royal, aristocratic, or military partners. Second, by the deft distribution of official decorations, the monarch was able to levy very large sums of money from the new bourgeois strata in the form of donations for charitable (and, after 1966, anticommunist) organizations and campaigns. (However, contributions were also elicited even from poor pedicab drivers, essentially for "populist" image-making purposes.) Third, the ruler increased his personal contacts with circles outside officialdom to a very pronounced degree, as shown:

experience proved very useful when the Scouts expanded after October 1973. Scout leadership was drawn heavily from the well-to-do and the middle-aged, provincial officials, rural notables, and urban *nouveaux riches*.[64] Such people were not only ideologically amenable to assuming such roles, but had the private economic resources to enable the organization to develop rapidly and, to a considerable degree, independently of the state bureaucracy.[65] "Training programs," coordinated by BPP headquarters, were essentially political in character: lectures by right-wing monks, parades, oath-swearings, salutes, beauty and dance contests, visits to military installations, royal donation ceremonies, "sing-songs," and so forth.[66] From a right-wing perspective, the beauty of the Village Scouts was that the organization worked by the following reciprocal motion: For the palace, it provided continuous public evidence of militant political support, outside the Bangkok upper class, among the "establishments" of provincial capitals, small towns, and even some villages. (The word "Village" in its title gave a reassuring, if deceptive, picture of rustic communities organizationally engaged—as it were, a concrete manifestation of the natural ties between "Nation" and "King.") For the Scouts' leaders, on the other hand, royal patronage made it easy to legitimize private, localized repression of protesting peasants and student activists as essential for the preservation of Nation–Religion–King.

Beyond the Red Gaurs and the Village Scouts, there were other agents of right-wing violence, less well organized and directed, but no less products of the great boom and its anxious aftermath. Typically, these men came from marginal and/or recently developed sectors of the security bureaucracy: upcountry policemen and counterinsurgency personnel who saw budgets, staffs, and promotion chances

	Frequency of the King's Contacts with Non-official Groups			
Year	Private Sector Function	Citizen/Group Audience	Meeting with Students	Meeting with Subjects
1956	17	1	–	–
1961	35	45	3	–
1966	71	116	9	5
1971	121	191	10	31

Table adapted from "The Sarit Regime," p. 422. As Thak rightly observed, all this activity "clearly indicates that the throne was developing links with the rising (private) middle-class sector."

[64] Natee notes that of his 496 fellow-applicants for admission to the Scouts branch in Nakhon Pathom in September 1976, 70 percent were between the ages 35–42, 2 to 5 percent were young people, and most of the rest were in their sixties and seventies. He adds that "most of the people who joined the program were reasonably well-off." See "Village Scouts," pp. 34–35. Indeed, this would have had to have been so, for the trainees were required to: buy expensive badges and color group photographs; contribute 40–50 *baht* daily for food; make religious donations; and pay for the elaborate costumes used for the beauty and dance competitions. Ibid., p. 36.

[65] While the provincial governor was usually the local chairman of the Scouts, financing was deliberately left up to prestige- and status-conscious local notables. Ibid., pp. 34–35.

[66] For a good description, see ibid., pp. 34 and 37. Natee's group was taken to visit the Naresuan paratroop training camp near the royal resort town of Hua Hin. (These paratroops worked closely with the Village Scouts in the violence of October 6.) Some idea of the style of instruction given to the trainees may be gleaned from the songs they were required to learn. These included: "Wake up, Thai!" "Ode to the Queen Mother," "Ode to the King," "They Are Like Our Father and Mother," "Punctuality," and "Any Work!" Themes of plays put on included scenes of communists being tormented in hell.

decline as a result of world depression and US strategic withdrawal; officials assigned to the dead-end career of service in the South (whether for lack of good connections or for poor performance elsewhere); superannuated guards at US bases; and so forth.[67] Such people found the experience of the liberal years frustrating and alarming on almost every front. Accustomed to exacting cowed deference, to exercising often arbitrary local authority, and above all to enjoying virtual immunity from law and criticism,[68] they were deeply enraged by the irreverent and muckraking journalism permitted after October 1973. As salaried men, they were hurt by the inflation and by a certain decline in opportunities for moonlighting and extortion. Given the chance to enter government service by the great bureaucratic expansion of the 1960s, they had to face the same prospect as nonofficial segments of the new middle and petty bourgeoisie: stagnation, if not decline. Small wonder that out of frustration and resentment came nostalgia for the heyday of the dictatorship and fury at its insolent opponents.

IDEOLOGICAL UPHEAVAL

One way of getting a sense of the dimensions of the cultural crisis that developed out of the economic and social changes sketched above is to begin with one striking contrast between Siam and its regional neighbors. Thanks in part to their colonized pasts, most Southeast Asian countries have inherited a political vocabulary and rhetoric that is essentially radical–populist, if not left-wing, in character. It is very hard to find anywhere, except perhaps in the Philippines, a calm, self-confident conservative ideology: indeed, since the nineteenth century, conservative culture has been in epistemological shock and on the political defensive, its nationalist credentials deeply suspect. In Siam, mainly because the country escaped direct colonial control, the situation has been, until recently, almost exactly the reverse.[69] The heroes in Thai children's schoolbooks have not been journalists, union leaders, teachers, and politicians who spent years in colonial jails, but above all the "great kings" of the ruling house. In fact, until 1973, it would be hard to imagine a single Thai children's hero who had ever been inside a prison. The prevailing rhetoric had typically been conservative, conformist, and royalist. It was the left that was always on the defensive, anxious to defend its nationalist credentials against charges of being "Chinese," "Vietnamese," "un-Thai," and "anti-monarchy" (this last a clear sign of a successful identification of royal and nationalist symbols). It would even be

---

[67] In June 1975, a rather spectacular strike of two thousand "security guards" at various US bases took place. The guards not only demanded government guarantees for their future livelihood, but accused the Supreme Command of embezzling over 8,000,000,000 *baht* (= US$400,000,000) of their US-supplied severance pay—charges that Supreme Command Chief of Staff General Kriangsak Chamanan hastily denied. *The Nation*, June 19 and 21, 1975. The NSCT strongly supported the guards' demands, and, curiously enough, developed close working relations with some of them.

[68] One must imagine the shock experienced in such circles when, on January 22, 1975, the official residence of the governor of Nakhon Si Thamarat, Khlai Chitphithak, was burned to the ground by an angry crowd of about three thousand people. The governor, widely suspected of corruption and incompetence in the handling of relief supplies for the victims of recent severe flooding, had to flee secretly to Bangkok. *Bangkok Post*, January 23 and 24, 1975.

[69] I say this in spite of the material assembled in Flood's fine "Thai Left Wing." Flood ably shows the real element of continuity on the Thai Left, but also, possibly inadvertently, how oppressed and marginal that left was until quite recently.

fair to say that until the repressions of October 6, the taboo on criticism of monarchy as an institution or the monarch as a person was overwhelmingly accepted even by those firmly on the left.[70]

To be sure, the capable monarchs of the nineteenth century, above all Rama IV and Rama V, did, in some sense, "save" Siam from conquest and colonization by adroit concessions to, and maneuvers between, the European imperialist powers. But one must not forget the other side of this coin: that the "saving" of Siam made these rulers simultaneously the most powerful and the most dependent sovereigns in Thai history. For if, in the course of the nineteenth century, the Europeans threatened Siam, they also completely eliminated the menace of her traditional foes—the Burmese, Khmers, Vietnamese, and Malays. Thai armies did not fight a serious engagement with anyone for almost one hundred years (roughly 1840–1940).[71] The old enemies were too weak, the new ones too strong. This externally generated and maintained security enabled the rulers to concentrate, in a quite unprecedented way, on the consolidation of their domestic power. To a very considerable degree, however, even this consolidation was only made possible by royal reliance on European advisers, technology, capital, and weaponry.[72] In a pattern prophetic of the "absolutism" of Sarit, the dynasty was able to exploit externally created security and externally generated resources to maximize internal control. The Thai "absolute monarchy" came closest to realization precisely when Siam was most completely at the mercy of the Europeans.[73]

In 1932, the immensely expanded "Western-style" civil and military bureaucracy, earlier instrument of royal aggrandizement, turned on its master. The leaders of the 1932 coup decisively put an end to the monarchy's direct, practical political power without, however, attempting any serious or permanent undermining of its cultural centrality and "nationalist" prestige. "Thailand," as Phibunsongkhram would eventually name Siam, remained defined as a

---

[70] This applies no less to the Communist Party of Thailand in the maquis than to left-wing elements attempting to participate in parliamentary-style politics. It is true that in the 1930s the monarchy went through a difficult time, to the point that Rama VII went into self-imposed exile in England. But there seems to have been no question of getting rid of the monarchy as such, merely of bringing it into conformity with internationally respectable standards of constitutionality.

[71] It was only in 1894 that a modern-style Ministry of Defense was set up.

[72] The facts of this reliance are a commonplace of modern Siamese historiography. They are traditionally interpreted, however, in good *bien-pensant* fashion, as signs of the "modernity" and "progressiveness" of the rulers. For a very instructive picture of how Siam's Northeast (Isan) was subjugated by Bangkok in the reigns of Rama V, VI, and VII, see Keyes, *Isan*, chapter III ("The Consolidation of Thai [*sic*] Control"). He stresses the importance of external peace, extension of rail, road, telegraph, and telephone systems, and "modern" state-controlled education.

[73] The effect of European imperialism on the Thai monarchy was important in two other ways. First, it changed the effective principle of succession from political capacity and seniority to quasi-primogeniture. It is unlikely that Rama VI or VII would have come to the throne under pre-imperialist conditions, as they lacked much real politico-military competence. Second, it put an end to the possibility of a new dynasty. Realization of this must have begun about the turn of the century. Able, ruthless figures like Phibun and Sarit, in many ways very similar types to Rama I, could no longer start new royal lines. In Phibun's expansionist and irredentist policies of the late 1930s and early 1940s, however, one can see clear dynastic lineaments. He was, as it were, restoring Greater Siam (bits of Burma, Cambodia, Laos, and Malaya), as Taksin and Rama I had done before him.

(constitutional) monarchy. When Rama VII, deeply involved in the political crises of the late 1920s and early 1930s, abdicated in 1935, the coup leaders immediately offered the throne to a grandson of the legendary national savior Rama V (Chulalongkorn)—then, fortunately, still a minor.[74] The fact that this lad remained at school in Switzerland throughout World War II merely preserved the monarchy from any contamination from Phibunsongkhram's collaboration with Japanese militarism.

Yet there is a sense in which the Phibunsongkhram era of the late 1930s and early 1940s did mark a real cultural–ideological change in Siam. For the dictator worked hard to legitimize his power by nationalistic propagandizing. To a considerable degree he was able to make the bureaucracy, and above all its military sector, where his effective power lay, appear the public custodian of the nation's interests. Much more clearly than hitherto, nation and monarchy became intellectually separable ideas, with the state (essentially the armed forces) as representative of the one and guardian of the other.[75] In important ways this development helped to enshrine the monarchy as a sort of precious palladium of the nation.[76]

In spite of all this, Phibunsongkhram's deep involvement in the 1932 coup and the suppression of Prince Boworadet's royalist counter-coup of 1934 earned him the lasting hostility of the royal family. During his second tenure of office (1948–57), therefore, he was unable to exploit the symbolic resources of the monarchy as he might by then have wished.[77] Perhaps *faute de mieux*, he turned to the symbols of democracy for help when, by 1956, he felt his power ebbing away.[78]

---

[74] See Wilson, *Politics in Thailand*, p. 18.

[75] There are curious parallels here—which may not entirely have escaped Phibunsongkhram's attention—to the shogun's relationship to the Emperor in Tokugawa Japan.

[76] Among the important prizes at stake in the power struggles of traditional Laos and Siam were certain highly venerated, magically charged objects (Buddha images in particular), referred to by many Western historians of Siam as palladia. After 1932, one detects a developing interest in control of the monarch-as-sacred-object. The tendency was probably facilitated by the domestic circumstances of the royal family. In the late 1930s and early 1940s, Rama VIII was a minor and mostly at school overseas. (In effect, there was then almost no bodily royal presence in Siam.) Shortly after World War II he returned home, but almost immediately died of a gunshot wound under circumstances that are still mysterious. He was succeeded by his younger brother, the present king, who was then still a minor and thus incapable of playing an independent political role.

Palladium-ization achieved a certain spectacular climax in 1971, when Marshal Thanom appeared on television after organizing a coup against his own government, and solemnly opened before the viewers a purported letter of approval from the palladium, brought in on a gold tray.

[77] He did, however, make efforts to clothe himself with Buddhist legitimacy, especially at nervous moments. In 1956, for example, when his regime was nearing its end, he had 1,239 temples restored at government expense. (In 1955 the number had been only 413, and a puny 164 in 1954.) See Thak, "The Sarit Regime," p. 128. He also spent a great deal of money on the 25th Centennial of the Buddhist Era celebrations (1957), and attempted to keep the monarchy from sharing in the resulting glory. In return, the palace pointedly disassociated itself from the proceedings. Ibid., pp. 129–30.

[78] For a description of Phibunsongkhram's "restoration of democracy," which culminated in the rigged elections of 1957, see Wilson, *Politics in Thailand*, pp. 29–31. It is one of the oddest ironies of modern Thai political history that the famous Democracy Monument in downtown Bangkok, the central visual symbol of the October 14, 1973, demonstrations and student activism thereafter, was constructed by Siam's most durable dictator.

It was Marshal Sarit who brought out the full "shogunal" potential of Phibunsongkhram's early militarism, and thereby significantly changed the whole ideological atmosphere of Thai politics. Sarit was a homegrown product of the Royal Military Academy; he was too young to have played any important role in the 1932 coup and its aftermath; and, unlike Phibun, he had never even pretended to an interest in constitutionalist or democratic conceptions. There was thus no serious obstacle to a rapid rapprochement with the palace. Shortly after seizing power, Sarit began a systematic campaign to "restore" the monarchy, and, in giving it new luster, to fortify his own position. In Phibun's time the king and queen had scarcely ventured outside the national capital. Now they were sent on long world tours to hobnob with other heads of state, especially European monarchs; reciprocal visits by assorted European royalty were encouraged—and so forth.[79] Royal ceremonies not performed since the days of the absolute monarchy were now revived.[80] The king and queen not only were brought into much more frequent contact with the Thai population, but also were sent out to help "integrate" the tribal minorities by kindly donations. One could almost say that under Sarit a strange displacement of traditional roles occurred: the field marshal playing the part of the ruler (punisher of crimes,[81] collector of taxes, deployer of armies, and political power-boss in general), and the ruler that of the Buddhist hierarchy (consecrator of authority and epitome of disinterested virtue). We need not be surprised, therefore, that in some ways the monarchy became more "sacred" as the dictatorship entrenched itself.

Not content with utilizing the monarchy, Sarit also exploited Buddhism. In 1962, he eliminated the existing decentralized, rather democratic Sangha organization and replaced it with a despotic centralized system under the control of the Supreme Patriarchate, an office he filled with pliable characters.[82] At his instigation, two popular, liberally minded senior monks were stripped of their ecclesiastical ranks and prosecuted on fabricated charges (in the one case, for communist sympathies, in

---

[79] This side of Sarit's manipulation of traditional symbols is analyzed in Thak, "The Sarit Regime," pp. 397–402. In late 1959 and early 1960, the king and queen left the country for the first time to visit Saigon, Djakarta, and Rangoon. Between June 1960 and January 1961, they visited the United States, England, West Germany, Portugal, Spain, Switzerland, Denmark, Norway, Sweden, Italy, Belgium, France, Luxembourg, and the Netherlands (note that half of these countries are monarchies of sorts). Before Sarit's death at the end of 1963, further visits had taken place to Malaysia, Pakistan, Australia, New Zealand, Japan, and the Philippines. International "recognition" of the Thai monarchy followed with visits by royalty from Malaysia and Great Britain.

[80] Ibid., pp. 410–25, for excellent details. Thak also notes the organized and direct participation of the royal family in anticommunist and counterinsurgency propaganda campaigns.

[81] Sarit's willingness to take personal responsibility for executions and other regime violence accords well with the style of pre-nineteenth-century Thai monarchs.

[82] See Mahamākuta Educational Council, ed., *Acts on the Administration of the Buddhist Order of Sangha* (Bangkok: The Buddhist University, 1963), for full texts of the 1962 regulations and the regime (dating back to 1941) they replaced. The 1941 system was tripartite, with authority divided between legislative, executive, and judicial branches. The 1962 system created a single administrative–judicial hierarchy. As Yoneo Ishii rightly says, the new rules completely eliminated "the idea of democracy which had been the spirit of the previous law." (See his "Church and State in Thailand," *Asian Survey* VIII,10 [October 1968], p. 869.) They also permitted, I believe for the first time, the arrest of monks by the lay authorities (police) without consultation with the Sangha authorities.

the other, for sodomy).[83] Finally, important segments of the Sangha were mobilized for "integrationist" (vis-à-vis non-Buddhist hill tribes) and counterinsurgency programs, particularly in the disturbed North and Northeast.[84] More than ever before, Buddhist symbols and institutions were cynically manipulated to generate regime legitimacy.[85] It was in the Sarit era that the triolet Nation–Religion–King was transformed from placid motto to fighting political slogan, and was increasingly understood as such.[86]

It would be a mistake to suppose from the above, however, that the prestige of the monarchy and the Sangha were affected by the dictatorship and the great boom in the same way. As we have seen, there is good reason to believe that the monarchy, for one, improved its position. The "royal revival" had coincided with the start of the boom, and for many newly prosperous Thai the coincidence hardly seemed fortuitous. In a reciprocal motion, development confirmed the legitimacy of the throne, and the throne gave moral luster to development. On the other hand, it seems clear that the powerful secularizing influence of capitalism was simultaneously eroding the authority of Buddhism, particularly in aristocratic and upper bourgeois circles. Boys from these strata were less and less inclined to enter the monkhood even for a nominal period, let alone commit themselves to a lifetime of religious devotion. Even more than hitherto, the committed younger monks tended to come from lower class and rural backgrounds. The consequence, predictably enough, was sharpening politico–religious conflict within the Sangha itself.[87] Growing numbers of young monks, especially those from the impoverished

---

[83] On this case, see Somporn, "Rightist Phoenix," p. 384; and S. J. Tambiah, *World Conqueror and World Renouncer* (Cambridge: Cambridge University Press, 1976), pp. 257–60. Though the two men, Phra Phimonladham and Phra Sasanasophon, were completely exonerated by the courts, the Sangha hierarchs were too timid, venal, or jealous to restore them to their former positions. After October 1973, a quiet campaign for their rehabilitation was begun, initially to little effect. Then, on January 12, 1975, in an action unprecedented in modern Thai history, a number of young monks began a hunger strike at Wat Mahathat in Bangkok, refusing to take food till the Supreme Patriarch agreed to reopen the case (*The Nation*, January 13, 1975). The strike caused a sensation, and, on January 17, the Supreme Patriarch surrendered, promising rehabilitation within the month. (*Bangkok Post*, January 18, 1975.) On January 30, a specially appointed Sangha committee finally cleared the two men. (*Bangkok Post*, February 23, 1976.)

The Supreme Patriarch who connived with Sarit in the original frameup, Somdet Phra Ariyawongsakhatayan, died a gruesome death in a traffic accident on December 18, 1971. Many Thai regarded his end as retribution for abuse of power.

[84] See Charles F. Keyes, "Buddhism and National Integration in Thailand," *Journal of Asian Studies* XXX,3 (May 1971): 551–67, especially pp. 559–65; see also Ishii, "Church and State," pp. 864–71.

[85] When the Buddhism-promoting Sarit died, it came out that he had accumulated a $140 million fortune by corrupt practices and maintained perhaps as many as eighty mistresses. See Thak, "The Sarit Regime," pp. 427–30, who also cites much of the contemporary Thai literature on the scandal.

[86] This is naively illustrated by the section "Education and Society," in Smith et al., *Area Handbook*, pp. 175–77.

[87] See Chatcharintr Chaiyawat's article, "Protests Divide the Monkhood," in the *Bangkok Post*, February 23, 1975, for some useful material on this. Cf. Kaufman, *Bangkhuad*, pp. 224–26, for comparable data in a local community setting. Sarcastic comment on misconduct by high-ranking monks began to be heard publicly around 1971. See, e.g., Phra Maha Sathienpong Punnawanno, "Phra Song Thai nai Rob 25 Pi" [The Thai Sangha Over 25 Years], in *Sangkhomsat Parithat* [Social Science Review] IX,6 (December 1971): 28. For this citation, I am indebted to an unpublished paper, "The Buddhist Monkhood in Thai Politics," by Mr.

Northeast, moved towards social activism[88] and a left-wing interpretation of religious doctrine.[89] Others, such as the notorious Kitti Wuttho, openly linked Buddhism to an ultra-rightist ideology.[90] In all these ways, then, the Sangha was brought directly into the midst of the political fray.

So far we have considered only the transformation of elements in the hegemonic cultural tradition. But, as [Thadeus] Flood has helped to show, change was also occurring among the tradition's opponents. Students and intellectuals in particular were profoundly affected by the Vietnam War. The courage and stamina with which the Vietnamese resisted the American juggernaut aroused increasing admiration. Many bright students who had gone to study in Europe and the United States in the latter 1960s were influenced by and participated in the anti-war movement. In China, the Cultural Revolution was in full spate, and internationally the prestige of Mao Zedong's anti-bureaucratic ideas was at its zenith. In Siam itself, the huge American presence was generating serious social problems—rampant prostitution, fatherless mixed-blood babies, drug addiction, pollution, and sleazy commercialization of many aspects of Thai life. By the early 1970s an increasingly strong anti-American (and anti-Japanese) nationalism was making itself felt, symbolized by the bitter title

---

Somboon Suksamran. During the series of protests and demonstrations that led to the overthrow of Thanom and Praphat, monks were increasingly in attendance as sympathetic observers.

[88] On November 29, 1974, a group of one hundred monks, with arms linked, actually formed the front line for a massive demonstration by peasants who had come to Bangkok eleven days earlier to press demands for land reform. (Somboon Suksamran, "The Buddhist Monkhood," p. 6.) Predictably, this move aroused a rabid reaction in the "moderate" and right-wing press, which straight-facedly insisted that the Sangha had always been above politics and should remain so. On December 8, the "radical" monk Phra Maha Jad Khongsuk announced the formation of a Federation of Thai Buddhists to promote democratization of the Sangha and orientation of Buddhist education towards social service. (*Prachathipatai*, December 9, 1974; see also *Bangkok Post*, December 10–12, 1974.) The hunger strike referred to in a footnote above, which occurred in January 1975, was organized by a group called Yuwasong (Young Monks), which since 1974 had learned a good deal about political organization from the NSCT.

[89] See, e.g., Phra Maha Jad Khongsuk's speech to the Seminar on "Is Thailand a Genuinely Buddhist Country?" published in *Pha Tat Phutsasana* [Operating on Buddhism] (Bangkok: Pharbsuwan Press, 1974), pp. 48–49, cited in Somboon Suksamran, "The Buddhist Monkhood," p. 22.

[90] The best account of Kitti Wuttho's career and political ideas that I have seen is in Charles F. Keyes, "Political Crisis and Militant Buddhism in Contemporary Thailand," in *Religion and Legitimation of Power in Thailand, Burma, and Laos*, ed. Bardwell L. Smith (Chambersburg, PA: Anima Books, 1978). This essay includes a fine analysis of Kitti Wuttho's famous 1976 speech, "Killing Communists Is Not Demeritorious." Keyes quotes the speech as follows: "[Killing communists is not killing persons] because whoever destroys the nation, the religion, or the monarchy, such bestial types are not complete persons. Thus, we must intend not to kill people but to kill the Devil (Mara); this is the duty of all Thai. ... It is just like when we kill a fish to make a stew to place in the alms bowl for a monk. There is certainly demerit in killing the fish, but we place it in the alms bowl of a monk and gain much greater merit." Keyes's translation is of Kitti Wuttho's *Kha Khommunit mat bap* (Bangkok: Abhidhamma Foundation of Wat Mahadhatu, 1976). In spite of the vociferous protests of the liberal press, the NSCT, and others at the "anti-Buddhist" nature of this speech and Kitti Wuttho's membership in the secretive ultra-right-wing organization Nawaphon (for which, see below at note 95), the Sangha hierarchy refused to administer even a mild reprimand, though earlier it had arranged to have Jad Khongsuk and others (temporarily) expelled from their monasteries for "political activities unbecoming a monk."

of an influential book published in 1971: *White Peril.*[91] In 1972, students successfully organized a boycott of Japanese commodities in Bangkok.[92]

Yet the censorship that the dictatorship imposed (to be sure, weaker under Thanom than under Sarit) concealed from almost everyone the real extent of the intellectual ferment going on. After October 14, 1973, censorship disappeared overnight, and, to general astonishment, a steadily swelling torrent of critical poetry, songs, plays, essays, novels, and books flooded first the capital and later the provinces. Many of these works had been written or composed under the dictatorship but had never seen the light of day.[93] Others were produced by the radicalizing effects of the October days themselves, and the rapid increase in political consciousness among students in the free atmosphere of the liberal era.

The cultural and ideological consequences of October 1973 took two diametrically opposite forms. On the left, an almost giddy sense of exhilaration, iconoclasm, and creativity was born. For a time it seemed that one could say, sing, or do almost anything. On the right, the illusion rapidly took root that the newly established liberal regime was the cause of the sudden epidemic of subversive ideas. Democracy was quickly blamed for the consequences of the dictatorship and its complicity with American and Japanese capitalism.

Predictably, the issue came to be joined on the ideological tools self-consciously forged to buttress Sarit's autocracy: Nation–Religion–King. Of these, religion was the least important and did not at first generate much heat. But on the national issue, the left quickly went onto the offensive, making its case more or less along the following lines: Just as Phibunsongkhram had collaborated with the Japanese, so Sarit and his heirs had betrayed the country to the Americans. Never before in Thai history had almost fifty thousand foreign troops been stationed on Thai soil. The economy had been allowed to fall overwhelmingly into foreign hands. For all the talk of national identity, the dictators had complacently permitted the corruption of Thai society and culture. So slavishly had the old regime aped the Americans' anticommunism and paranoia about Chinese expansionism that it was left ludicrously paralyzed by the Machiavellian Nixon–Kissinger approach to Peking. All in all, the policies of the right had proven not only venal and opportunistic, but shortsighted and ultimately bankrupt.

Of even greater significance in the long run were clear signs of a Copernican shift of perspective on the core element of conservative Thai ideology: the historical centrality and nationalist legitimacy of the monarchy. The popularity of Jit Phumisak's *Chomna Sakdina Thai Nai Patchuban* is symptomatic here because this closely argued book, dealing exclusively with pre-nineteenth century (and thus pre-European imperialist) Siam, interpreted the whole course of Thai history in terms of fundamental conflicts between oppressive rulers and struggling ruled. But Jit's book was only one element in a broad array of scholarly and journalistic writings

---

[91] See Thanet, "Khwam Khluanwai," p. 30.

[92] See Neher, "Stability," p. 1101.

[93] Of crucial importance were the varied works of the brilliant Marxist historian, poet, linguist, essayist, and social critic Jit Phumisak, killed by agents of the dictatorship at the early age of thirty-six. Most of his works had either been suppressed shortly after publication or existed only in manuscript form prior to 1974. Indeed, even the mention of Jit's name was publicly taboo under the Thanom–Praphat regime. In 1974–75, however, his *Chomna Sakdina Thai Nai Patchuban* (The Face of Thai Feudalism Today) had gone through three editions and become the bible of a whole generation of radicalized youth.

appearing after 1973 that explored the Thai past in categories that implicitly denied or marginalized the traditional royalist–nationalist mythology. It is useful to try to visualize the everyday social feedback from such cultural–ideological developments. One must imagine Thai students discussing in their parents' presence a Siamese nineteenth century not in terms of the great King Rama V, but of the commercialization of agriculture, the growth of compradore communities, foreign penetration, bureaucratic aggrandizement, and so forth. Simply to use a vocabulary of social processes and economic forces was to refuse centrality to Thai monarchs as heroes in or embodiments of national history. Indeed, in some ways this *bypassing of traditional historical categories,* doubtless often perpetrated with naive insouciance or calm contempt by the young, may have seemed more menacing than any direct denial of royal prestige and authority.[94] (One should never underestimate the power of inter-generational hostility to exacerbate ideological antagonisms.[95])

It should now be possible to understand more clearly why, not long after liberal democratic government was installed and censorship abolished, prosecutions for *lèse majesté* began to be inaugurated.[96] It was not just that the ruling cliques were angered by the hostile rhetoric of radicalized students. Rather, a whole concatenation of crises in Thai society began to crystallize around the symbol of the monarchy. The end of the long economic boom, the unexpected frustrations generated by rapid educational expansion, inter-generational estrangement,[97] and the alarm caused by the American strategic withdrawal and the discrediting of the military leadership—these linked crises were experienced most acutely of all by the insecure new bourgeois strata. One must remember that for these strata the monarchy was both a talisman and a moral

---

[94] Symptomatic are the following enraged remarks delivered by the Thanin regime's Public Relations Office on November 6, 1976: "Our culture, upheld by our ancestors and customs [sic], was neglected, considered obsolete, and regarded as a dinosaur or other extinct creature. Some had no respect for their parents, and students disregarded their teachers. They espoused a foreign ideology without realizing that such action is dangerous to our culture and did not listen to the advice of those who have much knowledge of that ideology. National security was frequently threatened over the past three years. Anyone who expressed concern for the national security was mocked and regarded as a wasted product of the bureaucratic society by those who labeled themselves as progressive-minded ..." (*FBIS Daily Report*, November 8, 1976.)

[95] It is interesting that an important component of the ultra-rightist organization Nawaphon, founded in 1974 (of which Prime Minister Thanin is reputed to be a member), was (and is) middle-aged and elderly university professors. Many of these men, with MA degrees from second-rate foreign universities and long records of toadying to the dictatorship, were outraged by the openly critical, even contemptuous way they were regarded by younger men (often with PhD degrees from good universities, and influenced by the idealism of the anti-war movement). In a number of important cases, senior university officials were deposed for corruption, scandalous laziness, and incompetence, and spying on students for the state bureaucracy. On Nawaphon, see, e.g., Keyes, "Political Crisis," pp. 8–12.

[96] The first case was that of left-wing student activist Praderm Damrongcharoen, accused of slyly attacking the king in a poem written for an obscure student magazine. Praderm was fortunate to be acquitted finally at the end of February 1975 (see *The Nation*, March 1, 1975, for details). The second was that of the journalist Seni Sungnat, charged with insulting the queen by criticizing one of her speeches in the pages of the rabidly rightist *Dao Sayam*. Seni was sentenced to two years in prison on February 4, 1976. (See *Prachachart Weekly Digest* 15 [February 10, 1976], p. 36.) The punishment of a right-wing journalist is a clear indication that the *lèse majesté* prosecutions were not simply cynical conservative maneuvers against the left, but stemmed from genuine cultural–ideological panic.

[97] Kaufman, *Bangkhuad*, pp. 229–31, is good on this conflict in a local community setting.

alibi. The historical depth and solidity of the institution appeared as a kind of charm against disorder and disintegration. And whatever the venality of their lives or their actual economic and cultural dependence on foreigners, members of these strata felt their nationalist self-esteem morally guaranteed by their loyalty to the throne, the epitome of the national heritage. Thus any assault, however indirect, on the legitimacy of the throne was necessarily sensed as a menace to that alibi.

The malaise of 1974, which generated the first of the *lèse majesté* trials, was then immeasurably deepened by events in Indochina. In the space of a few weeks in the spring of 1975, Vientiane, Phnom Penh, and Saigon all were conquered by communist forces. In the short run, the main effect was a panicked capital outflow. In the slightly longer run came a crucial change in the practical, as opposed to the symbolic, role of the throne. For there can be little doubt that the abolition of the Laotian monarchy in December (the end of the Khmer monarchy at right-wing hands five years earlier had actually been applauded)[98] raised the alarming specter that Rama IX might prove the last of his line. The king took an increasingly back-to-the-wall conservative anticommunist line in his public statements. The royal shift was noted duly by a whole gamut of right-wing groupings, who were thereby encouraged to go violently on the offensive.

Thanks to the entrenched position of right-wing elements in the mass media—especially radio and television[99]—this offensive, initiated in the fall of 1975, went into high gear in the spring of 1976, particularly during the campaign for the April parliamentary elections. The head of the Chat Thai party, General Pramarn Adireksan, for example, used his ministerial powers over state-controlled media to launch openly the slogan "Right Kill Left!"—something he would not have dared to do a year before.[100] Radio stations controlled by rightists, and especially the extremist Armored Division Radio, commissioned and played incessantly such violent songs as "Nak Phaendin" (Heavy on the Earth) and "Rok Phaendin" (Scum of Earth). Kitti Wuttho's dictum that Buddhism endorsed the killing of communists was given wide and constant publicity. Nor, of course, was the violence merely verbal. The spring and summer of 1976 witnessed a whole series of physical outrages, as sketched out at the beginning of this article.

The essential point to bear in mind is that the pivot on which this whole right-wing offensive turned was the monarchy, increasingly identified with and under the

---

[98] The Thanom–Praphat government immediately reopened diplomatic relations with Phnom Penh, and in the summer of 1970 came very close to sending Thai troops into Cambodia in support of the Lon Nol regime and the US–South Vietnamese "incursions." Even in the early 1950s, when the Khmer monarch Norodom Sihanouk had come to Bangkok in the course of his "Royal Crusade" for Cambodian independence, the Phibunsongkhram government treated him with scarcely veiled contempt. See Roger M. Smith, *Cambodia's Foreign Policy* (Ithaca, NY: Cornell University Press, 1965), p. 48. Nonetheless, political change in Cambodia was not left wholly unexploited over the border. Kitti Wuttho, for example, justified his anticommunist militancy in part on the grounds of alleged communist massacres of Khmer monks during the final stages of the Cambodian civil war.

[99] At that time, the military alone owned more than half the radio stations in the country and all but one of the TV stations in Bangkok, according to The National Anti-Fascism Front of Thailand, "Three Years of Thai Democracy," in *Thailand Information Resource*, No. 1 (May 1977), p. 3.

[100] Pramarn, a well-known partner of Japanese big business, is a brother-in-law of the late unlamented Police General Phao Siyanon, whose brutalities in the late 1940s and early 1950s were briefly detailed near the beginning of this article.

influence of the enemies of the liberal regime. It was therefore characteristic that the "flash point" for the overthrow of the regime on October 6, 1976, should have been a fabricated case of *lèse majesté*. Some days earlier, on September 24, two workers at Nakhon Pathom, putting up posters protesting former dictator Thanom's re-entry into Siam under the cloak of monkhood, were beaten to death by some local policemen and their corpses hanged.[101] Two days before the coup, a radical student troupe staged a dramatic re-enactment of the murder in the Bo-Tree courtyard of Thammasat University as part of a nationwide campaign for Thanom's expulsion.[102] The rabid right-wing newspaper *Dao Sayam* touched up photographs of the performance in such a way as to suggest that one of the actors "strangled" had been made up to look like the crown prince.[103] In a coordinated maneuver, the Armored Division Radio broadcast the slander, urged the citizenry to buy copies of *Dao Sayam*, and demanded retribution for this "cruel attack" on the royal family.[104] From this stemmed the lynch mobs that paved the way for the military takeover.

It is perhaps worth stressing that this type of frame-up and coordinated media campaign is quite new in Thai politics. When Sarit framed Phra Phimonladham and Phra Sasanasophon, or when Phao murdered opposition parliamentarians, they committed their crimes administratively, behind closed doors. The mass media of the 1960s had always warned that the government would deal severely with communists and subversives. In 1976, however, the frame-up was staged out in the open, and the public was invited to exact vengeance for subversion.

The reason for this, I hope to have shown, is that the old ruling cliques, weakened by developments at home and abroad, have been seeking new domestic allies, and have found them in the bewildered, buffeted, and angry middle and petty bourgeoisie created under the old dictatorship. The crudity with which such formulations as Nation–Religion–King are being elaborated and deployed is symptomatic both of a growing general awareness that they are no longer genuinely hegemonic, and of the real fear and hatred generated by the cultural revolution of the 1970s.[105]

---

[101] Natee, "Village Scouts," p. 35, claims that several hours before these murders took place the Village Scout training camp at Nakhon Pathom had staged a mock killing and hanging of the corpses of "bad students." He also avers that some of the real-life murderers had come from this camp.

[102] The Bo-Tree courtyard had become a national symbol of resistance to dictatorship, for it was from this courtyard that the demonstrations started which overthrew Thanom and Praphat in October 1973.

[103] It is worth noting that *Dao Sayam*, founded by a typical nouveau riche figure, ran a regular Village Scout activities column. Wealthy donors and activists could see their names given good publicity and even intermingled with those of royalty, aristocrats, and important government officials. The newspaper was thus the logical place to launch a swift, violent Village Scout mobilization campaign.

[104] The eminence grise of the Armored Division Radio, Col. Utharn Sanidwong na Ayutthaya, is a relative of the queen—and thus of the crown prince. See *Far Eastern Economic Review*, February 11, 1977. His key role in the fabrications of October 5–6 is an indication of the complicity of the palace in the overthrow of the parliamentary constitutional regime. Another effective hate-monger was Dr. Uthit Naksawat, Cornell University graduate and president of the Chomrom Witthayu Seri (Independent Radio Group of Thailand).

[105] It is a bizarre, but characteristic, sign of the almost cosmological panic involved that the Thanin regime should have banned the teaching of all (i.e., even right-wing) forms of political theory in Thai schools. See *New York Times*, October 21, 1976; and *Far Eastern Economic Review*, November 5, 1976.

The consequences of October 6 point therefore in two different but related directions. On the one hand, the coup has obviously accelerated the secular demystification of Thai politics. Direct and open attacks on the monarchy loom imminently.[106] Sizeable groups, both liberal and radical, have come to understand that they have no place in the Bangkok order, and so, in unprecedented numbers, have left for exile or the maquis. On the other hand, the political conceptions and symbols of the once hegemonic right have become self-conscious slogans with an increasingly specific social constituency. In the 1950s and 1960s, it was possible for many Thai conservatives to view the Thai left quite sincerely as a kind of alien minority ("really" Vietnamese, Chinese, or whatever), and the anticommunist struggle as a loftily national crusade. Today, such ideas have become less and less plausible even to the right. The events of October 6 have served to speed up the process whereby the right gradually concedes, almost without being aware of it, that it is engaged in civil war. In the long run, this change is likely to prove decisive, for modern history shows very clearly that no revolutionary movement succeeds unless it has won or been conceded the nationalist accolade.[107]

---

[106] This is clear from recent broadcasts over the maquis radio and from clandestine leaflets circulating in Bangkok. Interestingly enough, there are indications that certain dissatisfied right-wing groups are becoming increasingly critical, if not of the monarchy as an institution, at least of the present incumbent and his consort.

[107] I hope I have made it clear that, in the analysis presented in this article, I have deliberately focused on the new elements in the Thai political constellation. I certainly do not mean to suggest that the new bourgeois strata are more than a secondary element in the Bangkok power structure; they are probably even an unreliable secondary element from the point of view of the ruling cliques. It is instructive that, after the October 6 coup, the junta returned as far as possible to the old "administrative" style of repression. The Red Gaurs were silenced or packed off to combat zones in the North, Northeast, and South (where they reportedly suffered severe casualties). Nawaphon was encouraged to crawl back into the woodwork. Col. Utharn was removed from control of the Armored Division Radio. The generals currently on top—"moderates" all—would probably like to run the regime in the Sarit–Thanom–Praphat style. But one suspects that this may no longer prove feasible. The new bourgeois strata are there, the new provincial landlords are there—and these erstwhile allies cannot be safely ignored or discarded. Nor, probably, can the problems of these strata be solved by the generals. The boom is unlikely ever to return with its old élan: the ideological seamlessness of the past cannot be restored; unemployment swells; the bureaucracy grows ever more congested and expensive; the university paradox is seemingly insoluble. The new right-wing groups have experienced participation, and it is improbable that they can be totally excluded from it again. The genie has been let out of the bottle, and it will be very difficult for the junta or its successors to put it back again for good.

INTRODUCTION TO
IN THE MIRROR

The literature of modern Siam is still little known outside the country itself. Only a handful of foreigners have acquired sufficient knowledge of, and love for, the Thai language to read it with discriminating pleasure. Fewer still have attempted to pass on some of that pleasure by translating texts that they admire into their own languages.*

The case of English is characteristic. If we set poetry aside, and concentrate on the relatively accessible world of modern Thai prose fiction, we find the following situation: only two serious Thai novels have been translated into English by native English-speakers, both very recently. Furthermore, neither offers an English-speaking public much in the way of a broad perspective on a rapidly changing Thai society. The year 1977 saw the publication of *Letters from Thailand*, Susan Fulop Morell's deft version of *Jotmay jak muang thai*, for which the author, "Botan" (Supha Lusiri), had received the 1969 SEATO Prize for Literature. A gripping account of the lives of a young Chinese immigrant and of the family he acquires and loses in the two decades after World War II, it is claustrophobically preoccupied with the small world of Bangkok's "Chinatown" and includes only two "Thai" characters of any importance. Four years later, Gehan Wijeyewardene published *The Teachers of Mad Dog Swamp*, a thoughtful rendering of *Khru ban nok* (Rural Schoolteachers) by "Khamman Khonkhai" (Somphong Phalasun). This novel, a popular hit on its appearance in 1978, and quickly made into an even more popular film, is again very narrowly focused—this time on the tribulations of two idealistic young primary schoolteachers in a remote village close to Siam's borders with Laos and Cambodia.[1]

---

* In writing this introduction I have relied on the valuable historical material assembled in Suchart Sawatsi's prefaces to the four volumes of his pathbreaking anthology of modern Thai short stories: namely *Laeng khen* [Drought] (Bangkok: Duang Kamon, 1975), pp. 13–35; *Thanon sai thi nam pai su khwam tai* [The Road that Leads to Death] (Bangkok: Duang Kamon, 1975), pp. 19–47; *Meuan yang mai khoey* [As If It Had Never Happened] (Bangkok: Duang Kamon, 1976), pp. 1–33; and *Kham khan rap* [Response] (Bangkok: Duang Kamon, 1976), pp. 1–55.

[1] In addition, two significant novels have been translated into English by a native Thai-speaker, Janjaem Bunnag, under the pen name "Tulachandra." In 1964, she published *Prisna* (name of the heroine), a version of *Pritsana* by "W. na Pramuanmak" (the late Wiphawadi Rangsit); and, in 1981, she published the first volume of an abridged rendering of Kukrit Pramot [Kukrit Pramoj]'s *Si phaendin* [Four Reigns]—the concluding volume is due to appear in 1984. Mention should also be made of *Red Bamboo* (1961), a translation, by an unspecified person, of Kukrit's *Phai daeng*—itself a wholesale, if unacknowledged, borrowing from an English translation of Giovanni Guareschi's *Don Camillo* stories. Of this text, the critic Sulak Siwarak (Sulak Sivaraksa) pointedly observed: "... if any Thai wrote anything against the Communists, such a book would receive tremendous applause. That is why USIS saw to it that

With respect to short stories, there exist, to my knowledge, only three published collections of English-language translations. Far and away the best of these is the version of Khamsing Sinok's collection *Fa bo kan* (The Sky is No Barrier) published in 1973 under the title *The Politician and Other Stories*. Not only is Khamsing arguably Siam's best short-story writer, but the translation by Damnern Garden is unusually sensitive and subtle. Earlier, in 1961, P.E.N. Thailand had published *Thai Short Stories* (a second edition appeared in 1971), containing six tales by as many writers. Finally, in 1975, Jennifer Draskau put out *Taw and Other Stories*. This volume contained eleven stories by nine Thai authors, in addition to two by Ms. Draskau herself. So far as can be ascertained from the introductions to these later volumes, the choice of stories for inclusion was determined primarily by the personal tastes of the editors. For there are few obvious links between the stories in terms of themes, styles, perspectives, or historical period.

In contrast, in the present collection, a deliberate effort has been made to achieve some temporal coherence by offering a representative sampling of the work of a single generation of Thai writers—those born after World War II—and some orderly variety, by including stories dealing with many of contemporary Siam's problems. The moral, political, and literary concerns of this youngest generation of writers are such that the above principles of selection can be followed without any serious sacrifice of literary quality. The purpose of this collection is thus both to serve the interests of literature, and to offer readers interested in modern Siam some perspectives on Thai life and society that parallel, complement, and perhaps confront those typically to be found in academic social science studies and popular descriptions by journalists and travelers.

THE HISTORICAL CONTEXT

Thais have been writing texts that can be readily classified as "short stories" for almost a century. From their first appearance in the 1880s up till the present, these texts have been shaped by three powerful interlocking influences: the residues of traditional Thai Buddhist culture in the broadest sense (including aristocratic written literature and popular oral narratives and poetry); the rise of print-capitalism and the steady growth of a mass market of anonymous, habitual readers; and the increasing pace and intensity of economic, political, and social change.

The "interlock" is already visible in the pages of the first newspaper ever published in Siam, the English-language *Bangkok Recorder,* issued for one precarious year (1844) by Dr. Dan Beach Bradley, the American medical missionary and scholar who was then acting as tutor to the man who in 1851 would ascend the throne as King Mongkut (Rama IV).[2] For in these startlingly new pages appeared, alongside news of the outside world, versions of popular Buddhist Jataka tales, episodes from the *Thousand and One Nights,* and Aesop's fables. When Thai-language periodicals began to be printed in the 1870s, they not only included Jataka tales and the like, but invited readers to submit "solutions," in everyday prose, to hypothetical "problems"

... *Red Bamboo,* a mediocre novel, was translated into eighteen languages." See his *Siam in Crisis* (Bangkok: Kamol Keemthong Foundation, 1980), p. 321.

[2] For much of the material in the following paragraphs I am indebted to Sudarat Seriwat's fine *Wiwatthanakan khong ruang san nai meuang thai tangtae raek jon P.S. 2475* [The Evolution of Thai Short Stories from the Beginning up to 1932 CE] (Bangkok: Ministry of Education, Teacher Training Division, Thai Language Department, 1977).

drawn from contemporary life. Out of these beginnings grew the first self-conscious "imaginative fictions" of modern Siam, which appeared in the pages of the magazine *Wachirayan Wiset* (1883–1894), a journal published by and for the first generation of (upper-class) Thai to have had extensive Western education, often abroad, and thus accustomed to the format and contents of contemporary European magazines.

It is symptomatic of the era, and of the role that imaginative fiction has continued to play in Thai life until the present, that one of the very first samples of these new fictions precipitated a political storm and provoked the first modern-style imposition of censorship. In 1885, *Wachirayan Wiset* published the first part of a composition called "Sanuk nuk" (Fun Thinking) by Krom Luang Phichit Prichakon, a prominent young foreign-educated nobleman. It took the form of an imaginary conversation between four young Buddhist monks at one of Bangkok's most famous temples, Wat Bowonniwet, about their futures: some spoke of soon leaving the monkhood to resume civil service careers, while one rather matter-of-factly pointed out the practical advantages—economic security and peace of mind—offered by remaining in yellow robes. The insertion of an imaginary conversation into a well-known "real-life" setting is, of course, a commonplace, and effective, literary device of modern Western-style "realism." But to the abbot of Wat Bowonniwet and to the Supreme Patriarch, Phichit's text appeared as an irreverent, insulting rapportage of the actual state of mind of young monks at the temple. They made their anger known to King Julalongkon (Rama V), who then banned publication of any further episodes of the tale.

The spread of literacy, the growing numbers of Thai being educated abroad, the penetration of Victorian English culture, and the development of an (increasingly female) leisured, urban reading public from the 1890s on provided a strong social stimulus to the production of the new style of literature. A virtual revolution in taste followed the publication in 1901 of a translation of Marie Corelli's sentimental melodrama *Vendetta*. A well-to-do readership was growing, with a voracious appetite, no longer for classical Thai poetry and chronicles, or Chinese romances, but for "realistic" representations of its own pleasures and problems. (Translations of tales by Guy de Maupassant, O. Henry, and Arthur Conan Doyle offered formal models of how this mirroring could effectively be done.) Magazines multiplied and competed with one another for the print-market by paying for short stories and serialized novels. Thus was born a new figure in Thai society: the professional writer, usually a combination of journalist, essayist, and composer of fiction. By 1926, this fiction-creating figure had made his appearance as fictional hero—in Kulap Saipradit's story "Watsana Manut" (Man's Fate).

If the dominant genres of prose fiction in the first three decades of the twentieth century were those of the popular literature of late Victorian and Edwardian England—sentimental romances, "tales of mystery and imagination," adventure stories, and vignettes of family problems and intergenerational friction—we should not be altogether surprised. As in an earlier England, both writers and readers came out of a comfortable, secure, urban milieu sustained by a mass of badly paid domestic servants, a strong and stable currency—and a new sense of national well-being. The tide of European imperialism had engulfed the traditional external adversaries of the Thai—Burmese, Khmer, Malay, and Vietnamese—but, thanks to luck, concessions, and adroit diplomacy, Siam had escaped the same fate. By 1910, Europe's last territorial demands had been met, and the modern boundaries of the country effectively guaranteed by the new world order of which the League of Nations was to become the most pregnant symbol.

Yet forces were at work transforming the "Victorian" order, and, with it, the character of Thai fiction. The ambitious program of administrative centralization and education launched by King Julalongkon in the early 1890s unwittingly generated serious political and social conflict in the reigns of his sons, Rama VI (1910–1926) and Rama VII (1926–1935). For, on the one hand, the monarchy, traditionally absolutist in its formal claims, came closer than ever to being absolutist in practice, thanks to the absence of wars, and the massive new financial and administrative resources created by the reorganization of the state along Western lines. On the other hand, absolutist modernization meant an enormous expansion of the bureaucracy, which quadrupled in size between 1892 and 1905.[3] Such a bureaucracy could not be manned exclusively by Siam's traditional nobility, and into its lower ranks flooded ambitious young commoners, some of whom studied abroad on government scholarships and returned infected with liberal, meritocratic, and egalitarian ideas. The shock of the Great Depression exacerbated the tension between "merit" and "blood," since the strict austerity programs insisted on by the monarchy's foreign advisers were implemented to the former's disadvantage. On June 24, 1932, a coalition of civilian and military "new men" overthrew the absolutist monarchy in a bloodless coup, and three years later Rama VII abdicated the throne in voluntary exile.

As so often happens, the political storm was heralded by the rumble of distant literary thunder. All three of the founders of Siam's serious modern fiction published their first major novels on the eve of the coup: "Dok Mai Sot" (Buppha Kunchon) her *Khwam phit khrang raek* (The First Mistake) in 1930; Akat Damkoeng his *Lakhon haeng chiwit* (Life is a Play) in 1929; and Kulap Saipradit his *Songkhram chiwit* (The War of Life) early in 1932. In all three, if from very different perspectives, class consciousness and conflict added a new problematic to Thai literature and enormously widened the stretch of its concerns.[4] If Akat and "Dok Mai Sot" were sensitive aristocrats aware of the impending decline of the old order, Kulap, a commoner, wrote polemically for the "new men," attacking snobbery and class discrimination and propagating the virtues of democracy, equality, and social justice. It was with Kulap that a self-consciously "progressive tendency" made its first appearance in Thai fiction, and his influence remains strong to the present day.

After 1932, with the monarchy and aristocracy for the time being removed from political power, a growing conflict developed between the civilian and military components of the "Coup Group." The dominant civilian leader, Pridi Phanomyong, was a typical "new man," the brilliant son of a Chinese immigrant and a Thai mother, successful student at the Sorbonne Law Faculty, and chief public exponent of the Coup Group's claims to be inaugurating a new era of democratization and social reform. Around him gathered progressive-minded politicians, journalists, academics, and writers (including Kulap). Symbolic of his role was his founding in 1934 of Siam's second (and at that time "open") university, Thammasat, which ever since has been the single most important institutional center for the spreading and

---

[3] By 1910, the 15,000 officials of the Ministry of the Interior outnumbered the 12,000 bureaucrats, of whom the entire salaried state bureaucracy had been composed in 1892. See William J. Siffin, *The Thai Bureaucracy: Institutional Change and Development* (Honolulu, HI: East–West Center Press, 1966), pp. 80, 94.

[4] An excellent study (in English) of these three novelists can be found in Wibha Senanan's *The Genesis of the Novel in Thailand* (Bangkok: Thai Watana Panich, 1975).

defense of democratic and egalitarian ideas in Thai society. Meanwhile the military increasingly came under the control of Plaek Phibunsongkhram, another "new man" educated in France (but at the conservative, nationalist St. Cyr military academy), who, attracted by the examples of Italy, Japan, Kuomintang China, and Germany, became the proponent of a right-wing populist nationalism. Like Pridi, Plaek had his literary allies, notably the jingoistic playwright, poet, and novelist Wijit Wathakan. In the late 1930s, Pridi's group declined in influence, and when the Pacific War broke out, Plaek quickly brought his country in on the side of the Axis powers. By the summer of 1944, the waning of Japan's military power led to Plaek's fall, and the reemergence, by stages, of the civilian progressives. Between 1945 and 1947 Pridi dominated Thai politics and presided over Siam's first real elections. The military-imposed censorship was abolished, and there was a new flowering of socially concerned literature.

Highly dissatisfied with their now marginal position in Thai politics, the military exploited the economic difficulties of the post-war era, and the mysterious shotgun death in 1946 of the boy-monarch Rama VIII, to make a comeback. The coup of November 8, 1947, forced Pridi into exile and inaugurated a quarter of a century of almost unbroken military government. While Plaek Phibunsongkhram resumed the office of prime minister in 1948, real power more and more gravitated into the hands of his two rival subordinates, Generals Phao Siyanon and Sarit Thanarat. These were "new new-men," in the sense that they came from provincial small towns, were educated wholly in Siam, and (unlike the urbane, polished Plaek) knew no foreign languages. They were also "old men," in the sense that they made no pretence of attachment to democratic, egalitarian values, and behaved with the ruthlessness of old-style warlords. Between 1947 and 1957, Phao in particular became a dreaded figure for organizing the imprisonment, torture, and assassination of political opponents, including progressive politicians and intellectuals.

The post-war military dictatorships differed from their pre-war predecessors in one other fundamental respect: they were heavily supported by an outside power, the United States. Plaek, Phao, Sarit, and their associates discovered early on that they could get sizeable financial and military aid from Washington if they were prepared to collaborate closely with America's prosecution of the Cold War in Asia. Bangkok recognized the puppet Bao Dai regime in Saigon, sent troops to Korea, instituted stringent "anticommunist" legislation along American lines, offered accommodation to SEATO's headquarters, and in due course became an essential base for American aerial warfare and intelligence operations against Vietnam, Cambodia, and Laos.[5]

One effect of the strong American backing of the post-1947 military regimes, and of their public justification of violent domestic repression in terms of American-style anticommunism (the American Embassy in Bangkok had initially been sufficiently alarmed by the Thai government's casual attitude to the red menace to sponsor a Thai translation of the *Communist Manifesto*), was to move a significant number of Thai intellectuals and literati (among them Kulap Saipradit) to a more Marxist view of the world. Another stimulus to this shift was admiration for the triumph of Mao

---

[5] Useful accounts of the relationship between the Americans and the Thai military and police during this period can be found in Frank C. Darling, *Thailand and the United States* (Washington, DC: Public Affairs Press, 1965); and Thomas Lobe, *United States National Security Policy and Aid to the Thailand Police* (Denver, CO: University of Denver, Monograph Series of World Affairs, 1977).

Tse-tung in 1949, as well as sympathy for the newly independent states and struggling liberation movements of Southeast Asia. Between 1955 and 1957 the growing power-struggle between Phao (who controlled the police and was strongly backed by the CIA for his help in supporting clandestine Kuomintang operations inside Southwestern China) and Sarit (who controlled the army, and was backed by the Pentagon for his role in modernizing the military along American lines) afforded these writers and intellectuals a certain room for maneuver. This freedom was even enlarged in the immediate aftermath of the coup of September 16, 1957, which drove Phao and Plaek into exile. The years 1955–58 thus saw a flowering of critical, socially committed literature, perhaps best symbolized by the publication in 1958 of Khamsing Sinok's admired short-story collection *Fa bo kan.*

But on October 20, 1958, Sarit overthrew the provisional regime installed after the fall of Plaek and Phao, and established the first absolutist (i.e., constitutionless) regime in Thailand since 1932. A rigid censorship was imposed, dozens of intellectuals, writers, and progressive politicians were imprisoned, jailed, driven into exile (and in one or two cases executed). So severe was the repression in what came later to be remembered as the Yuk Thamin (Dark Age) that a kind of cultural amnesia overtook Thai intellectual life. Much of the literary heritage of the progressives disappeared for a generation (Khamsing stopped writing at all for a decade, while Kulap stayed in China until his death in 1974) and had to be laboriously "excavated" in the middle 1970s.

The years of Sarit's dictatorship (1958 till his death from cirrhosis of the liver in 1963) and that of his associates and successors, Thanom Kittikhajon and Praphat Jarusathian (1963–1973), can justifiably be called the "American Era" in modern Thai history. The American presence was enormously intensified, and as a result Thai society began changing at an unprecedentedly rapid pace. Almost all the writers represented in this volume grew to maturity during the American Era, and were profoundly influenced by the transformation it engendered. Accordingly, it is appropriate to delineate briefly the most important elements of this transformation.

Sarit came to power at the height of the Dulles era [John Foster Dulles, US secretary of state, 1953–59], and died at almost the same time as [US president] John Kennedy. It was a period of great American alarm about "Red Chinese" expansionism, the entrenchment of a communist regime in the north of Vietnam, the weaknesses of the anticommunist regime in the south, the growth of the Left in Laos, and neutralist tendencies in Cambodia. Siam was thus conceived as a bastion of the "Free World," and its strength, stability, and ideological orthodoxy regarded as of the utmost importance to the United States. Successive American administrations, drawing their conclusions from their experience in Vietnam, believed that Siam's "security" in the widest sense required an intensification of Bangkok's administrative control of the country's population, and an energetic promotion of Western-style development, not least in the rural areas. They used all their influence to push the Thai dictatorship to act accordingly, undeterred by the fact that armed communist insurgency only began well *after* these programs had been instituted, and appeared to increase in proportion to their intensification.[6] It so happened that these

---

[6] Far the best and most comprehensive account of American political, military, and economic activity in Siam in this period is Sean Randolph, "Diplomacy and National Interest: Thai–American Security Cooperation in the Vietnam Era" (PhD dissertation, Fletcher School of Law and Diplomacy, 1978).

objectives fitted well with those of Sarit and his successors. If Plaek's claims to legitimacy had derived from the 1932 Coup Group's anti-aristocratic appeals, the introduction of the principle of constitutionalism, and a certain populist nationalism (including economic nationalism), these were either unavailable to Sarit, or he had no interest in them. He therefore seized on "development," and a marked revival of the monarchy and pre-modern Thai traditions, to justify his absolutism.[7]

"Development" meant, first and foremost, unhindered access to Siam by foreign capital (in his lifetime mainly American). Accordingly, Sarit dismantled many state enterprises, smashed trade unions, enforced low wages, offered very favorable conditions for the repatriation of corporate profits, and abolished the Plaek-era 50-*rai* (roughly twenty acre) statutory limits on landownership. Partly as a result of these measures, partly as a consequence, after 1964, of huge American military expenditures in Siam as the Indochina War intensified,[8] the Thai economy went into a sustained decade-long boom, which gave birth for the first time to a real Thai middle class.[9] "Rural development," heavily financed by the United States,[10] meant a drive to tighten Bangkok's administrative grip on the country's overwhelmingly agricultural population;[11] a vast expansion of the nation's various police forces, the military, and the educational bureaucracies; the rapid commercialization of agriculture; the building of roads and highways (whose location was often determined by American strategic planners);[12] the spread of electrification and extension services to the countryside; and the harnessing of the rural Buddhist monkhood to the government's public relations and security programs.

To achieve these goals, and also to satisfy the demands of Siam's growing middle class, a major expansion of education was required. In 1961, the country had only five university-level institutions, with no more than 18,000 students all told; by 1972, she had seventeen colleges in which over 100,000 students were enrolled.[13] At the same time, thanks to changes in government policy, and the financial assistance of various public and private American institutions, more and more able young Thais were going to America for advanced study, rather than to Europe (especially

---

[7] See the lucid and penetrating discussion in Thak Chaloemtiarana, *Thailand: The Politics of Despotic Paternalism* (Bangkok: Thammasat University, Thai Khadi Institute, 1979), especially chapter III. [Revised edition published by Cornell Southeast Asia Program Publications, 2007.]

[8] More precisely: total US "regular military assistance" to the Thai armed forces between 1951 and 1971 amounted to $935,900,000, a sum equal to 59 percent of the total Thai government military budget for that period. A further $760,000,000 was spent for the acquisition of military equipment and the ($200,000,000 over four years) hiring of a Thai division to fight in Vietnam. US payments for the construction of air and naval bases amounted to a further $250,000,000. Expenditures by American servicemen in Siam for "rest and recreation" and other items added a further approximately $850,000,000. See John L. S. Girling, *Thailand: Society and Politics* (Ithaca, NY: Cornell University Press, 1981), p. 236.

[9] For further detail, see my "Withdrawal Symptoms: Social and Cultural Aspects of the October 6 Coup," *Bulletin of Concerned Asian Scholars* 9,3 (July–September 1977): 13–31, at pp. 15ff. [In this volume, see "Withdrawal Symptoms," pp. 52ff.]

[10] Between 1950 and 1975, the United States provided Siam with $650,000,000 in support of economic development programs. Most of the money was granted in the years after Sarit's ascension to power. See Girling, *Thailand,* p. 235.

[11] Lobe, *United States National Security Policy,* p. 16, indicates that nearly half of all US *economic* aid in the years 1965–69 went to the Thai police.

[12] For instructive details, see Randolph, "Diplomacy and National Interest," pp. 51–54.

[13] Girling, *Thailand,* p. 177.

England) as had been the case before.[14] Most of the young writers represented in this volume were among the beneficiaries of this educational explosion.

Aside from the burgeoning of a new middle class, one basic social consequence of this period of dynamic growth was the spread of capitalist relations to many parts of the country where till then residents had largely lived by subsistence agriculture. Rapidly rising land prices, caused in part by a fever of land speculation, produced a new stratum of provincial rich, worsened rural tenancy rates, and forced the migration of large numbers of dispossessed peasants into urban slums in search of work.[15] The urban labor force, which until World War II had consisted largely of Chinese immigrants, became more and more ethnic Thai.[16] (Emblematic of this change is the life of one of our writers, "Si Dao Ruang," born in 1943, who in the later 1950s came to Bangkok from the rural north to seek work, first as a maid, then as a factory worker.)

Scarcely less important in its impact on Thai society was the massive American military buildup of the mid-1960s, such that by 1968 there were no less than 46,000 US servicemen stationed on Thai soil.[17] Eight major military bases and many more minor installations, scattered around the country,[18] brought "Americanization" to rural Siam in a very immediate way. The construction of these installations poured money into the countryside, but also meant the penetration of the sleaziest aspects of American civilization. The results were a vast increase in prostitution,[19] births of

---

[14] In the late 1930s, no more than 500 Thais were studying abroad. By 1973, almost 6,000 were studying in the United States alone. By the late 1970s, "about 36,000 Thais go abroad to study every year (some 30,000 of them to the United States)." As of early 1974, one in every four of more than 26,000 officials in the top four grades of the civil service had had training in America. Ibid., pp. 82, 150, and 96.

[15] A study done by the National Council on Social Assistance in 1968 showed there were already two hundred slums in Bangkok. A subsequent Thammasat University survey of one of the most crime- and drug-ridden of these slums, Khlong Toey, showed that 71 percent of its 25,000 inhabitants were ex-peasants who had "fled" to the capital to find work. See Wiraprawat Wongphuaphan, "Salam" [Slum], *Sangkhomsat Parithat* 10,2 (February 1972): 43–49. The statistics are painfully illustrated by the interviews with slum-dwellers, un- or menially employed, relayed in Anonymous, "Chiwit na beua meuan reua mai mi jutmai" [Lives of Boredom Like Drifting Boats], *Sangkhomsat Parithat* 10,5 (May 1972): 45–49.

[16] The size of the core of the working class—in manufacturing—rose from less than 200,000 in 1947 to almost 700,000 in 1970, and about 1,000,000 in 1976. By then, several hundreds of thousands of others were employed in the construction, transport, and communications industries. Girling, *Thailand*, p. 178.

[17] *New York Times*, April 16, 1968.

[18] The fullest account of these bases, their history, and varied purposes, is in Randolph, "Diplomacy and National Interest," pp. 108–23.

[19] For example, see the vivid rapportage of Wiraprawat Wongphuaphan, "Takhli: khaya songkhram" [Takhli: War Garbage], *Sangkhomsat Parithat* 10,8 (August 1972): 44–55. The author describes the two huge American waves that hit the sleepy northern township, first after 1961, when it became the site of an American airbase for missions over Laos and the Ho Chi Minh Trail, and then during [US president] Richard Nixon's 1972 all-out bombing war. The author notes that, by 1972, the township had more bars and nightclubs (46) than temples (44). The number of prostitutes checking in for VD inspections rose from 91 in January 1972 to 2,954 six months later, in June. A detailed academic study of Takhli, based on a questionnaire issued to 320 Thai airbase personnel, 150 women "partners," and 420 local citizens, is Narong Sinsawat's "Rayngan kanwijay ruang phon krathop thang setthakit lae sangkhom khong kanprajamyu khong thahan amerikan" [Research Report on the Economic and Social Impact of the Presence of American Troops], December 1968.

"red-haired" (fatherless Amerasian) children,[20] narcotics addiction,[21] and the like. And along with the military came a swelling army of American businessmen, missionaries, technocrats, academics, and tourists.[22] The impact of all this was as much cultural as social: decay of traditional arts in the face of American films and their imitators; decline in the legitimacy of the monkhood as television sets and Mercedes-Benzes entered the temples,[23] while young men stayed away from them; deracination of youth and their partial absorption into the orbit of Atlantic consumer culture; and, eventually, in the 1970s, something quite new in Thai history—the permanent settlement of large numbers of Thai in a California to which they were already culturally acclimatized before their departure.

Such massive and various changes were bound to produce a complex response. If one considers the contours of that response between the installation of the Sarit dictatorship on October 20, 1958, and the collapse of the Thanom–Praphat dictatorship on October 14, 1973, in the face of the huge popular demonstrations, two features immediately strike the historian's eye. First, the critical reaction was initially cultural and limited to small groups of young metropolitan intellectuals, then gradually spread through the rapidly expanding student population and the wider society, becoming steadily more political in the process. Second, this reaction, though firmly grounded in Thai traditions and contemporary realities, was nonetheless paradoxically shaped to a significant degree by quite another sort of "Americanization" than what has been detailed so far.

---

[20] See Anan Wiriyaphinit, "Dek phom daeng: luk raboet thi amerikan thing nai thai" [Red-haired Kids: Timebombs Abandoned by the Americans in Siam], *Sangkhomsat Parithat* 10,8 (August 1972): 58–65. He sadly noted that 88 percent of the 2,000 or so children estimated to exist by the Pearl S. Buck Foundation were born between 1964 and 1970; only 11 percent got any paternal support; and 68 percent lived in conditions from poor to extremely poor. The ratio of black to white fathers was 1 to 3.5.

[21] In his "400,000 khon nai man khwan" [400,000 People in a Haze of Smoke], in *Sangkhomsat Parithat* 11,3 (February 1973): 67–82, Wiraprawat Wongphuaphan estimated that by 1973 the number of addicts in Siam (Chinese, ethnic Thai, and minorities) had risen to 400,000, compared to about 120,000 in 1956, and these addicts spent 8.6 billion baht ($430,000,000) a year on drugs. At the same time, there existed only one rehabilitation center in the entire country, which treated 3,123 patients in 1971, fewer than 400 of them successfully.

[22] Compare the following figures:

	1965	1966	1970	1971
Total Foreign Visitors	225,000	469,000	628,700	638,700
Americans	78,300	133,000	159,200	147,000
(Servicemen on R and R)	(15,000)	(70,700)	(44,300)	(26,600)

Adapted from Anderson, "Withdrawal Symptoms" [p. 51 in this volume].

[23] Late in 1971, Phra Maha Sathiaraphong Punnawanno, a brilliant young monk (only the third youth to pass the highest [ninth] level of Pali examinations while still a novice since the start of the nineteenth century), published "Phra song thai nai rop 25 pi" [The Thai Sangha over 25 Years], in *Sangkhomsat Parithat*, December 1971, pp. 20–28. It is an astonishing attack on the modern Thai monkhood: High positions in the Sangha are the object of intrigues and chicanery worse than in lay politics. The main criterion for advancement is the construction of lavish temples. Conversation between monks is not the old religious greeting, but "How's the temple doing?" "Got 3 millions, still 500,000 short ..." Monks know more about boxers, football champions, and which movie star is sleeping with whom, than laymen do. Temples have become dirty, noisy places in which quiet meditation is impossible. And so on.

The first ripples of the later tide manifested themselves in the last years of the Sarit autocracy. As was to be expected in an era of rigid political control, the reaction started in the confined sphere of the metropolitan intelligentsia. In 1963, the idiosyncratic conservative–monarchist intellectual Sulak Siwarak established, with the help of the Asia Foundation, a new journal somewhat misleadingly named *Sangkhomsat Parithat* (Social Science Review).[24] In spite of his excellent American connections, Sulak maintained a pointedly critical stance vis-à-vis the Americanophilia and "developmentalism" of the Sarit era. Although his insistence on trying to repopularize traditional upper-class Thai costume, and to revive "Siam" in place of the Plaek-period mongrelization "Thailand,"[25] earned him ridicule in some quarters, the thrust of many of his articles—a defense of Thai cultural and political autonomy from excessive American influence—won him a small, but increasingly influential, youthful intellectual following.[26] From a secure conservative political position, he was able to open the pages of *Sangkhomsat Parithat* to more radically inclined critics, such as Nithi Tawsiwong (Nidhi Aeusrivongse),[27] as well as the poet Angkhan Kanlayanaphong, who, though largely apolitical, broke radically with the formal traditions of Thai poetic language to pursue a personal vision of Buddhist humanism.

---

[24] See Sulak's own amusing account in *Siam in Crisis*, pp. 324–25. There is no reason to suppose that Sulak was aware that the Asia Foundation was indirectly receiving CIA funding, something the Foundation only conceded publicly in 1967. See *New York Times*, March 22, 1967. Sulak also served on the editorial board of Sionil José's *Solidarity*, a sort of Filipino counterpart to *Sangkhomsat Parithat*, which was supported by the Congress for Cultural Freedom, another beneficiary of CIA largesse (see *New York Times*, May 8 and 14, 1967).

[25] He was not the first to do so. When Pridi Phanomyong returned to power after World War II, he brought back the traditional name of the realm, doubtless because Plaek's innovation implied that the country belonged exclusively to the ethnic Thai, and he preferred a name giving the many ethnic minorities their share. The military reimposed "Thailand" after the coup of 1947.

[26] See, for example, his editorial "Antaray samrap pannyachon khon num" (Dangers Facing Young Intellectuals], *Sangkhomsat Parithat* 2,1 (June 1964): 3–6, warning recently returned graduates from American universities against initial arrogance and impatience and subsequent mental laziness and easy cooptation by the establishment. Sharper still was his "Itthiphon khong farang" [The Influence of the Whites] in *Sangkhomsat Parithat* 4,3 (December 1966): 3–6, a biting attack on blind imitation of the West and its consequences. He deplored the way Bangkok was being destroyed by the tearing down of temples and filling in of canals to build congested thoroughfares; satirized the absurd pride in being the first nation in Asia to have air-conditioned movie houses and television; criticized wasting money on huge hotels rather than on better education; and warned against rising greed, declining morals, and a willingness to turn even funerals into tourist shows, especially since the inflow of huge numbers of American soldiers.

[27] See, for example, Nithi's riposte to Sulak entitled "Krung Si Ayutthaya sin khon di" [Ayutthaya Has Lost Its Good Men], *Sangkhomsat Parithat* 5,8 (September 1967): 81–90, which, while praising the editor for having the courage to raise the issue of the bad influences exerted by the American bases, reminded him that the Thai have been absorbing Western influence for more than a century. He noted that for all Sulak's criticism of "Americanism," he had nonetheless unselfconsciously adopted the American demonological conception of World Communism. (He concluded with some penetrating remarks on the differences between Russian, Chinese, and Vietnamese communism.) See also Nithi's fine critique of conservative-nationalist historiography, "Somdet Krom Phraya Damrong Rachanuphap kap Arnold Toynbee" [Prince Damrong Rachanuphap and Arnold Toynbee], in *Sangkhomsat Parithat* 7,1 (June–August 1969): 17–36.

At about the same time, a young writer calling himself 'Rong Wongsawan created a sensation with a series of novels and stories about Bangkok's demimonde of prostitutes, pimps, decayed aristocrats, drunkards, school dropouts, and nihilist *jeunesse dorée*. On the surface "apolitical," these works, in their matter-of-fact, unmoralizing descriptions of a twilight world, and their satirical barbs against the metropolitan elite, had their own subversive effect. Moreover, 'Rong's imaginative literary style, casual, abrupt, close to the speech of the streets, and often defying the norms of Thai grammar, had a liberating effect.[28]

The stylistic and cultural innovations of Angkhan and 'Rong Wongsawan, important as they were in different ways for stirring up what later came to be called the "stagnant water" of Thai literature, nonetheless were isolated, idiosyncratic achievements. But in 1967 two loose associations of young intellectuals came into being that began a major shift in the character, style, and themes of Thai writing. The first, which came to be called the Phrajan Siaw (Crescent Moon) group, was composed largely of young writers associated with Thammasat University, and was under the intellectual leadership of Suchart Sawatsi. To express their sense of boredom, alienation, and political impotence, these writers borrowed consciously from abroad, introducing into Thai literature the techniques of surrealism and stream-of-consciousness narration, and producing a body of literary work characterized by enigmatic symbolism and melancholy satire. The second, a group loosely attached to Sinlapakon University, called itself Num Nao Sao Suay (Spoiled Boys and Lovely Girls). Dominated by Sujit Wongthet and Khanchai Bunpan, it took the opposite tack. Writing in a vivid, often humorous prose initially much influenced by 'Rong Wongsawan, it strongly championed an *echt* "Old Siamese" culture and literature against what it regarded as the decadence and superficial Westernization of the contemporary establishment. Though their cultural orientations were very different, and their political leanings in some ways opposed (Phrajan Siaw was vaguely liberal and Num Nao Sao Suay rather explicitly conservative), they belonged to the same generation and shared a common target. After 1969, they came to cooperate more and more closely and jointly shaped the outlook of a new generation of Thai intellectuals.

In June 1969, Suchart succeeded Sulak as editor of *Sangkhomsat Parithat* and quickly made it the single most important outlet for nonconforming opinion on almost every subject—politics, education, sexual mores, religious values, as well as literature.[29]

Paradoxically enough, some of the most important contributions to Suchart's "campaign" came from the United States. For the flow of capable Thai students to the United States, which had begun in the late 1950s, reached the proportions of a

---

[28] It was characteristic of 'Rong that when an outraged critic brought him some lines that he had written and demanded that he explain them, 'Rong roared with laughter and simply wrote them down again. See the comments of "Jinda Duangjinda" in the "Men and Books" section of *Sangkhomsat Parithat* 3,1 (June 1965). No less revealing is Jacqueline de Fels's quotation of a typical passage from 'Rong's novel *Ai malaengwan thi rak* [Dear Fly], in which the eponymous fly proposes as a New Year cocktail "some gin, plus a drop or two of a Chinaman's piss ... or, if you prefer something sweeter, a cabinet minister's—these people eat so much sugar that they all get diabetes." See her "Littérature Populaire: Les éditions bon marché en Thaïlande," in Pierre-Bernard Lafont and Denys Lombard, eds., *Littératures Contemporaines de l'Asie du Sud-est* (Paris: L'Asiathèque, 1974), pp. 57–72, at pp. 67–68.

[29] Originally published three times a year, *Sangkhomsat Parithat* became a monthly in 1971 under Suchart's energetic leadership.

small flood in the late 1960s, when many American campuses were in turmoil over the Indochina War, and when American youth, in a wider sense, were in dramatic rebellion against the conventional pieties of their country's political leadership, social mores, and cultural values. "Americanization" at this juncture of American history had a powerful double impact on many of these young Thai.

First, they obtained direct experience, either as close observers or even as occasional participants, in an extraordinary movement of popular opposition in the heartland of the capitalist, liberal-democratic West—their own country's closest political ally.[30] Between 1965 and 1973, a growing coalition of middle-class students, academics, intellectuals, journalists, clergymen, professionals, and politicians, using a wide variety of rather novel political techniques and tactics, drove two presidents from power, and forced the withdrawal of the bulk of American troops from Indochina. Nor was America alone in providing a model of populist, radical-democratic opposition to the established order. In France, too, student power had come very close to toppling De Gaulle's authoritarian Fifth Republic in the heady days of May 1968. To a lesser extent in most of the other advanced capitalist democracies—Britain, West Germany, Sweden, The Netherlands, and Japan—a similar tide was flowing. Inevitably, many young Thai living abroad came, little by little, to think of working along the same lines at home.

Second, immersion in the America of the late 1960s and early 1970s meant a two-stage intellectual transformation, which in a very short time made itself felt back home. The process began with the students' exposure to startling information about the activities, not merely of the US government, but of their own. From the hearings of the [US] Senate Foreign Relations Committee under Senator William Fulbright's chairmanship, from the pages of the *New York Times* and the *Washington Post,* no less than *Ramparts* and the *Nation,* from the nightly news broadcasts of the major television networks, from academic monographs, from American students' exposés of "war related research,"[31] from the *Pentagon Papers* and many other sources, these young Thai became aware of the realities of what the Americans were doing in and

---

[30] A good example of the articles reporting back on the anti-war movement in America is Thak Chaloemtiarana, "Sinlatham khong khon num sao lae panha songkhram wiatnam" [The Morality of Youth and the Problem of the Vietnam War], *Sangkhomsat Parithat* 8,2 (September–November 1970): 44–48.

[31]   Cf. Warin Wonghanchao, "Nak wichakan amerikan kap kanwijai kiaw kap meuang thai" [American Scholars and Research on Siam], *Sangkhomsat Parithat* 8,1 (June–August 1970): 126–27; and "Panha samkhan khong ngan wijai nai meuang thai" [A Serious Problem of Research in Siam], *Sangkhomsat Parithat* 8,3 (December 1970–February 1971): 18–28. Both articles were based on allegations aired at the Association for Asian Studies conference in San Francisco in the spring of 1970, asserting that the Academic Advisory Committee on Thailand had secretly contracted to do counterinsurgency work for the US government. The letter makes reference to two well-known muckraking articles in *Ramparts:* Warren Hinkle's "Michigan State: The University on the Make" (1966), and David Ransom's "The Berkeley Mafia and the Indonesian Massacre" (1970). Note also Charnvit Kasetsiri, "Ngan wijai khong amerikan nai thatsana thai" [American Research from a Thai Perspective]," in *Sangkhomsat Parithat* 8,3 (December 1970–February 1971): 70–71, citing Noam Chomsky's attack on the Vietnam War-era social-science technocracy in *American Power and the New Mandarins;* and especially Thirawet Pramuanratthakan's very detailed "Ngan wijai khong nakwichakan amerikan kap khwam mankhong khong prathet thai" [Research by American Scholars and the Security of Thailand]," in *Sangkhomsat Parithat* 8,3 (December 1970–February 1971): 30–40.

to their country. They learned of deployment of Thai mercenaries to fight in Laos;[32] of Washington's hiring Thai troops to fight in southern Vietnam;[33] and of the horrors of the air war over Indochina[34]—all of which had been kept from them in Siam itself by the dictatorship's rigid censorship. Living in the United States, they were, at least for the nonce, at liberty, outside the dictatorship's control, and so started to send back reports of what they had learned. These reports, often couched, deadpan, as mere transmissions from the American media and academies, began to appear in Bangkok, first in the pages of *Sangkhomsat Parithat* and later in a variety of new journals and magazines.

The second stage can be thought of as the revival of Marxism.[35] It was a romantic Marxism to begin with—a Marxism in which the Third World heroes of our time, Che Guevara, Ho Chi Minh, and Mao Tse-tung, were much more central than the European ancients, Marx, Engels, Lenin, and Stalin. And it was marked by the youth-style of the 1960s: Che Guevara T-shirts, Ho Chi Minh posters, Mao buttons, and the radical-populist folk music of Bob Dylan and Joan Baez, among many others.[36] More importantly, the Marxist texts and vocabulary came mediated, by another irony, through the high-capitalist paperback industry, not by state printing presses in Moscow or Peking. For this was an age of anthologies: Ho Chi Minh assembled by Bernard Fall, Mao Tse-tung anthologized by Stuart Schram, Kolakowski introduced by Carl Oglesby, Marx and Engels culled and displayed by respectable American scholars like Lewis Feuer and Richard Tucker.[37] The youthful imagination was better

---

[32] See Sombat Waniphok, "Thahan thai nai lao: reuang jing reu ing niyai?" [Thai Troops in Laos: Truth or Fable?], *Sangkhomsat Parithat* 9,1 (June–August 1971): 24–31. The author ridicules the government for its furious response to reports in the *New York Times* and the *Washington Post* about 4,800 Thai troops hired secretly by the CIA to fight in Laos, for the price of $10,000,000 a year. Everyone knows about these things except the Thai people! See also the editorial "Thahan rap jang: kiatiphum khong chat yu thi nai? [Mercenary Troops: Where Is Our National Honor?], *Sangkhomsat Parithat* 11,10 (October 1973): 10–12, which terms these mercenaries *sunak rap chai* (running dogs).

[33] Late in 1969, Senate Foreign Relations Committee hearings revealed that the "Queen's Cobras" and the "Black Panther" Division sent from Bangkok to South Vietnam in 1967 and 1968 were not voluntary contributions by the Thai government, but were wholly paid for by Washington under a secret agreement concluded on November 1, 1967. See *United States Security Agreements and Commitments Abroad: Kingdom of Thailand*, Hearings before the Committee on Foreign Relations of the United States Senate, Ninety-First Congress, First Session, Part 3 [November 10, 11, 12, 13, 14, and 17, 1969] (Washington, DC: US Printing Office, 1970), pp. 624–26, 657, 842–44 , 896–97.

[34] See, for example, Suchart Sawatsi's "Songkhram ngiap nai Indojin" [The Silent War in Indochina], *Sangkhomsat Parithat* 10,7 (July 1972): 72–76, which drew heavily on *The Air War in Indochina*, done at Cornell University's Center for International Studies and published early in 1972 by Beacon Press.

[35] This interest is already evidenced by two (worried) articles of late 1970: Akon Huntrakun's "'Sai mai' nai thatsana khong khon num" [The "New Left" in the Eyes of Youth], *Sangkhomsat Parithat* 8,2 (September–November 1970): 9–11; and Woraphut Chaynam, "Khon num sao kap kanpatiwat" [Youth and Revolution], ibid., pp. 16–19.

[36] A nice example of this tendency was the setting of a romantic tribute to the dead Thai Marxist intellectual Jit Phumisak (see below at n. 38) to a Thaified version of the old English folk song "John Barleycorn," which many rock- and folk-singers repopularized in the United States in the 1960s. The song became a trademark of the best-known Thai progressive folk-ensemble of the early and mid-1970s: Surachay Janthimathon's *Kharawan* [Caravan].

[37] See, for example, Suraphong Chainam, "Khrai pen sai?" [Who is Left?], *Sangkhomsat Parithat* 8,4 (March–May 1971): 104–16, who cites, inter alia, David Caute's *The Left in Europe* (1966),

caught by Eldridge Cleaver's claim to immortality "If you are not part of the solution, you are part of the problem," than by Marx and Engels's "Working Men of All Countries, Unite!" Back in Siam these currents led by 1972 to a slow "rediscovery" of the radical Thai intellectuals of the 1950s, above all the work of the brilliant polymath Jit Phumisak.[38] (By the later 1970s, these older home-grown Marxists, writing in Thai for Thai, had largely replaced the international New Left as central influences; and with them came a style of old-time Marxist thought that belonged to the age of William Z. Foster and the Mao Tse-tung of "Talks on Art and Literature.")

There was still another way in which the America of the 1960s contributed to the transformation of the intellectual climate among the educated young in Siam: by helping to bring them into direct touch with the growing social problems in the Thai countryside. Once again, the observer is struck by the irony of this assistance—in other words, that it had its effects largely by inadvertence. At one level, it meant the introduction of American-style social science—the product of the training Thai students were getting in the United States, the growing Americanization of the structures and priorities of Thai universities, and the counterinsurgency research sponsored by American military and civil institutions in Siam.[39] The pages of *Sangkhomsat Parithat* after 1970 show that for the first time the journal was beginning to live up to its name: one finds statistical studies of growing landlessness, of the social mobility implications of the educational system, of working conditions in factories, and a whole range of other social problems.[40]

George Lichtheim's Vintage paperback *The Concept of Ideology* (1966), and Carl Oglesby's *The New Left Reader* (Grove Press Paperback, 1966), containing Leszek Kolakowski's essay "The Concept of the Left."

[38] Jit had been an outstanding student at Julalongkon University's Literature Faculty in the early 1950s, but ran afoul of his teachers and was expelled. (He also worked very closely with Prof. William Gedney, the dean of American scholars specializing in Thai language and literature.) He was eventually permitted to finish his degree, and profited from the "liberalization" of 1955–58 to publish a number of pathbreaking works on Thai history and literature. He was among those arrested after Sarit's 1958 coup and remained in prison for Sarit's lifetime. On his release he went underground and eventually joined the communist maquis. He was shot dead under mysterious circumstances in 1966. His name was largely unknown to the younger generation until the publication of an article by Chukiat Uthakaphan in *Witthayasan* 23,45 (December 1, 1972). See Chaloem Yuwiangchai, "Thiphakon: sinlapa pheua chiwit, sinlapa pheua prachachon" [Thiphakon: Art for Life, Art for the People], *Sangkhomsat Parithat* 11,3 (March 1973): 77–89. This article also announced the reprinting of Jit's *Art for Life, Art for the People* (written under the pen-name "Thiphakon") by a group of Thammasat students, who said they were "starting to clear the ground for a literature with value for the life of society." They had run across Jit's text in an obscure corner of the university library and decided to reprint it on their own, since "after fifteen years" author and printer were "hard to trace."

[39] As the Thai communist party's insurgency grew, so did American-directed and -funded study of the rural bases of its success. A significant number of young Thai were involved in these projects, which took them into the hills and rice-paddies for their first close-up look at the lives of their rural compatriots. One major source of funding was ARPA (Advanced Research Projects Agency), a Pentagon-created research organization. A detailed reminiscence by one former ARPA employee is "Special Correspondent," "Buang lang kanjarakam khong saharat amerikan tor prathet thai" [Behind American Spying on Thailand], *Sangkhomsat Parithat* 12,2 (February 1974): 37–46.

[40] On agrarian problems, see the Special Issue on Peasants put out by *Sangkhomsat Parithat* in September 1970, especially the withering, radical, statistic-packed text of Mangkun Chaiphan,

At another level, it was what one can think of as the example of the Peace Corps. For whatever the actual failures or accomplishments of this organization, it provided the novel sight of well-educated, prosperous, urban youth going out to "help the villagers" in a very American spirit of utilitarian idealism. Under the sponsorship first of the Thai government itself, and after 1971 of the National Student Center of Thailand (NSCT), sizeable numbers of Siam's privileged students became involved in programs of rural development.[41] For many, it proved to be a powerful emotional experience, as they experienced rural poverty at first hand, and began to develop a sense of the political causes of the farmers' difficulties.

These tendencies were markedly reinforced after November 1971, when the aging dictators, having gingerly experimented with some steps toward restoring constitutional forms and representative institutions, made a coup d'état against their own creations, and attempted to restore a Sarit-like absolutist regime.[42] But Siam had changed, and been changed, too much by this time. Moreover, the sudden rapprochement between Peking and Washington (symbolized by Nixon's visit in February 1972), on which, naturally, the Thai dictators had not been consulted, drastically undermined the credibility of one major rationale for military domination ever since 1947: the danger from Communist China. Accordingly, in 1972 and 1973, Thanom and Praphat, for all their dictatorial powers, were unable to prevent a continuing erosion of their authority. In November 1972, students in the NSCT, led by Thirayut Bunmi,[43] organized a boycott of Japanese businesses—ostensibly a nationalist protest against foreign economic domination, but also, in view of the close ties between Japanese multinationals and segments of the Thai military elite, an indirect attack on the regime.[44] At about the same time, a group of radicalized

---

"Chaona kap botbat khong sahakon nai prathet thai" [Peasants and the Role of Cooperatives in Thailand], pp. 31–44, which is vitriolic in its attacks on *nai thun* (capitalists), land speculators, corrupt provincial officials, and TV-owning monks. Of equal interest are Mongkhon Dansiri's interviews with peasants from various parts of the country (ibid., pp. 82–93). On education, see Udom Koetphibun's English-language article, "Education and Social Stratification: A Thai Study," in *Sangkhomsat Parithat* 8,4 (March–May 1971): 78–85. On labor conditions, see Phiphat Thai-ari, "Raeng ngan khong thai nai rop 25 pi" [Thai Labor over 25 Years]," in *Sangkhomsat Parithat* 9,6 (December 1971): 40–47; Suwit Rawiwong, "Kan nat yut ngan: reuang jing reu ing niyai" [Strikes: Truth or Fable?], in *Sangkhomsat Parithat* 10,5 (May 1972): 40–43; and Jamnong Somprasong, "Prakat khana patiwat chabap thi 101 kao na khong krabuankan raeng ngan thai [Revolutionary Group Decree No. 101, a New Step for the Thai Labor Movement]," *Sangkhomsat Parithat* 10,5 (May 1972): 24–35. See also the articles cited above in notes 15, 19, 20, 21, and 23.

[41] As late as the end of the 1970s, less than 6 percent of Thai students came from Peasant backgrounds. See Girling, *Thailand*, p. 89.

[42] In 1968, a highly restrictive constitution was finally promulgated. In 1969, an elected Lower House was added to a 164-man appointed Senate (to which the armed forces and the police contributed 117 members). Praphat's Ministry of the Interior ensured that massive victories for the government party in the rural areas easily outweighed the success of the opposition Democrat Party in the capital.

[43] Thirayut became the NSCT's secretary-general in 1972 and was largely responsible for turning it from an insignificant inter-university liaison group into a powerful political organization. See Girling, *Thailand*, p. 190.

[44] The ground was prepared by a detailed article in *Sangkhomsat Parithat* listing the major Japanese businesses in Siam, their size, labor force, and purpose, and the percentage of shares held by Japanese (as opposed to Thai). Characteristically for this period, the material originated from the *Eastern Economic Statistics* published in Japan, and was translated by a Thai student at Keio University. "Arai oey ... meuang ja bot huajai hai pen phlae? kham torp:

Thammasat students produced a pamphlet called *Phay Khao* (White Peril), which was a bitter, wide-ranging attack on American imperialism and its effects on Siam and Indochina.[45] In December, student protests succeeded in blocking a regime plan to abolish the residual independence of the judiciary.[46] Finally, in the fall of 1973, a movement for the restoration of constitutionalism, started by a small group of academics, politicians, and students, snowballed into huge demonstrations, which led on October 14 to the collapse of the dictatorship and the exile of the twin dictators themselves.[47]

In the aftermath of October 14, Siam entered an extraordinary new era in its national life. Censorship was virtually abolished. Workers and peasants were permitted to organize in the defense of their interests. The military was, for a time, removed from the center of power, and the two freest elections in Thai history were held (in January 1975 and April 1976). Between 1973 and the summer of 1976, the NSCT became the driving force behind campaigns for a whole series of social reforms. In November 1974, its activists helped to set up the Farmers' Federation of Thailand, which fought for the rights of hard-pressed peasants. They cooperated with emerging trade union leaders to campaign for higher wages and better working conditions for labor. They exposed gruesome abuses of power by provincial authorities.[48] Finally, they agitated successfully for the near-total withdrawal of American military personnel from Siam and the closing of the American bases.[49] Many played key roles in setting up the Socialist Party of Thailand in late 1974.

Abolition of the censorship dramatically accelerated the radicalization of the cultural life of the younger generation of intellectuals, writers, and students.[50]

---

kanlongthun khong yipun" [What Is It that Feels Like It's Crushing One's Heart till It's a Bloody Wound? The Answer: Japanese Capital Investment]," *Sangkhomsat Parithat* 10,4 (April 1972): 30–33. For a lucid, sympathetic discussion of the reasons for the boycott and its failure, see Phansak Winyarat, "Songkhram thang kankha thai–yipun" [The Thai–Japanese Commercial War], *Sangkhomsat Parithat* 11,1 (January 1973): 12–16.

[45] This one-hundred-page booklet, edited by Phichit Jongsatitwatthana and Kamon Kamontrakun, and published by Aksonsamphan in 1971, contained sixteen essays denouncing "American neocolonialism" in every sphere of life: military, economic, intellectual, and moral. The tone throughout is strongly nationalistic.

[46] See Girling, *Thailand*, p. 190. This episode is well described in Wiraprawat Wongphuaphan, "Meua dokmai 3,000 dok ban" [When 3,000 Flowers Bloomed], *Sangkhomsat Parithat* 11,1 (January 1973): 51–57. Already the regime was being openly referred to as *rabop phadetkan bet set* (total dictatorship) and *amnat thamin* (barbarian authority).

[47] The course of events is effectively summarized in David Morell and Chai-anan Samudavanija, *Political Conflict in Thailand: Reform, Reaction, Revolution* (Cambridge, MA: Oelgeschlager, Gunn, and Hain, 1981), pp. 146–48.

[48] See, for example, Ruangyot Jansiri, "Raingan jak Phatthalung; thip long khao, phao long thang" [Report from Phatthalung: Kicked out over Mountains, Burnt in Oildrums], *Sangkhomsat Parithat* 13,1 (January 1975): 41–71, for a detailed account of such atrocities in the southern province of Phatthalung. He writes of "suspects" being pushed out of airplanes, or beaten senseless and then burned alive in used oil drums by government counterinsurgency forces.

[49] Largely achieved by June 1976.

[50] The new freedom, and the beginnings of new sources for Thai student radicalism, are exemplified by Suraphong Chainam's "Thammai Sangkhomniyom?" [Why Socialism?], published in *Sangkhomsat Parithat* 11,11 (November 1973): 37–47, which is a sophisticated discussion of Marxism and neo-Marxism, based on: Althusser's *For Marx*, Garaudy's *Marxism in the Twentieth Century*, Lukacs's *History and Class Consciousness*, Gramsci's *Prison Notebooks*,

Disinterment of the work of the radicals of earlier periods of Thai history, cautiously initiated, as we have seen, even before October 14, proceeded rapidly. In this revival the central figure was the late Jit Phumisak, whose books *Chomna sakdina thai nai pajjuban* (The Face of Thai Feudalism Today)—a biting revisionist analysis of Thai history—and *Sinlapa pheua chiwit, sinlapa pheua prachachon*—a polemic in favor of politically committed art—became very influential. In literature, one consequence was an increasingly self-conscious movement for a Thai-style "socialist realism."

Meanwhile, a backlash was not slow in coming. As early as 1975, and very obviously in 1976, student activists, as well as leaders of peasant and labor unions, were subjected to intimidation, beatings, and assassination.[51] In March 1976, the secretary-general of the Socialist Party of Thailand, Dr. Bunsanong Bunyothayan, a young American-trained sociologist, was gunned down outside his home in Bangkok. An orchestrated media campaign, above all over radio and television, propagated the slogan "Right Kill Left" and depicted student activists and their allies as "burdens on the land," and "scum of the earth."[52] (The communist triumphs in Indochina in 1975, and the abolition of the Laotian monarchy at the end of 1976, had aroused enormous alarm in conservative circles in Siam, above all among the military and in the Palace.) The backlash culminated on October 6, 1976, when Thammasat University, long regarded as the "spiritual center" of student activism, was assaulted by hired hooligans, police, and rightwing fanatics, and hundreds of students were massacred in horrifying ways.[53] That evening the military took power once more, and shortly afterwards the extremist right-wing regime of Thanin Kraiwichian was installed. In the wake of these events, hundreds of left-inclined intellectuals, writers, students, and politicians went underground, many of them seeking refuge eventually with the Communist Party of Thailand (CPT) in the jungles of the North, Northeast, and South.

There they might well have remained but for the extraordinary events of 1978–79: the first open wars between communist states in world history (the Vietnamese invasion of Cambodia and the Chinese assault on northern Vietnam). These wars, between states which had only recently cooperated to drive American imperialism from Indochina, had in themselves a shattering effect on youthful idealists committed to the idea of international left-wing solidarity. But, in addition, the CPT's rigid adhesion to the Chinese position—doubtless the consequence of its leaders' long periods of residence in China and the fact that many were of Sino–Thai origin—caused the expulsion of the party and all groups associated with it from earlier secure base areas in Laos and western Cambodia, and a complete loss of political momentum and military strength. Finally, a shrewd liberalization policy pursued by General Kriangsak Chamanan (who overthrew the Thanin regime late in 1977)—a policy which included virtual amnesty for all those willing to return from the

---

and Miliband's *The State in Capitalist Society* (all published in London in the late 1960s and early 1970s), as well as texts of Marx himself in the standard Moscow edition.

[51] Detailed statistics on the assassinations of peasant leaders is given in Table 8.3 (Assassinations of Members and Leaders of the Farmers' Federation of Thailand) of Morell and Chai-anan, *Political Conflict*, p. 227.

[52] "Nak Phaendin" and "Rok Phaendin," for example, were the titles of two propaganda songs constantly broadcast over military-controlled radio stations in 1976.

[53] The events of October 6 are minutely detailed in the anonymous 140-page underground pamphlet "Thung ... phu yang yu" [To ... Those Who Remain], which also contains twenty pages of horrifying photographs of the killings.

jungle—led to a swelling stream of defections. By 1981, it is safe to say, the overwhelming majority of those who had fled in 1976 were back where they had come from, sadder, older, and less illusioned, but by no means wholly abandoning the ideals of their generation.

• • •

IN THE MIRROR, THIRTY YEARS LATER

The purposes of this new preface are: (1) to say something brief about the circumstances in which the book appeared, and why I attempted a project of this kind; and (2) to reflect on some of the changes in Siam over the past twenty-five years in relation to artistic production.

When my colleagues in Cornell University's "Government" (i.e., Political Science) Department saw *In the Mirror*, they were more than puzzled. "After writing a high-theory book like *Imagined Communities*, why on earth are you translating Thai short stories? 'Government' surely has nothing to do with literature, in which, anyway, you have no professional training." I didn't then feel like explaining myself. The truth was that from Mor Sor 1 (first year of junior high), I had been studying English and French, as well as ancient Roman and Greek literature, not political science, and loved the former more than the latter.

Furthermore, in 1972 I had been kicked out of Indonesia by the Suharto military dictatorship, and knew that it would be many years before I could go back. So for the first time I started to study Indonesian literature, which was easily available in Cornell Library's wonderful Southeast Asia collection. Furthermore, I had now to think about studying politics somewhere else; for a short time, I seriously considered Sri Lanka. But early in 1974, I settled on Siam, for two reasons. The first was 14 Tula [October 14], when, to my great pleasure, a military dictatorship was overthrown, and the possibility of a progressive Thai democracy seemed real. The second was the wave of interesting and high-quality Thai graduate students at Cornell in the late 1960s and early 70s. Many of their names will be familiar to you. First and foremost was Charnvit Kasetsiri, who was active in the anti-Vietnam War movement both in the US and, indirectly, back home in Siam. Others included Warin Wonghanchao, Bunsanong Bunyothayan (later secretary-general of the Socialist Party of Thailand, assassinated in early 1976), Akin Rabibhadana, Pramote Nakhornthab (later a leader in the Palang Mai party), Thak Chaloemtiarana, and Chalardchai Ramitanond. Pranee was being courted by Sujit Wongthet, who stayed in Ithaca long enough to get the material for his splendid novel *Made in the USA*. Thanet Aphornsuwan, studying nearby in Rochester, NY, often came down to visit. A little later on Nidhi, planning to write what proved to be a stellar thesis on (imagine!) Indonesian literature and reading in the late Dutch colonial period—he mastered both Dutch and Indonesian—came to work in the Cornell Library and lived with me for several months. Even though I knew no Thai at that time, I learned a lot from them all, so that when I got a one-year sabbatical in 1974–75, I decided to go to Bangkok to learn the language and to think about doing political science research on Siam. But in the next year, 1976, came the horror of 6 Tula. The cabinet of Thanin Kraiwichian, backed by the military, banned political parties and did its best to suppress the Left. Many progressive youngsters fled into the jungle, along with two of the short-story writers whose work appears in *In the Mirror*, namely, Khamsing and Wat. Thanet, too, fled. What should I study?

During a visit to Bangkok, I had a very interesting talk with Suchart Sawatsi (earlier the famous editor of *Sangkhomsat Parithat*, and now, after the journal's suppression, the editor of *Lok Nangseu*) and Khun Suk, the progressive publisher of Duang Kamol, who, one could say, gave Suchart a new life. They had a plan to "go inter," publishing English translations of Thai literature to allow foreigners to get a better and more close-up view of "real Siam," and to combat superficial tourist stuff and conventional academic works. It was also a way of fighting against the Thai state's ambition to "delete" 1973–76 from the modern history of the country. Thinking this way, I offered to do some translations of short stories for them. I had greatly enjoyed, and learned from, translating works of various kinds of Indonesian literature. Hence I knew that by doing the Thai translations, I would have fun and also learn a lot, not least about Thai literary language.

I completely trusted Suchart's broadmindedness, honesty, selflessness, and good taste. I told him that since I was a beginner, it would be best if he made the selection for me. Then a nice misunderstanding arose that, ironically, made me the unconscious selector of the stories to be translated. Suchart mailed me photocopies of thirteen stories, intending them simply to be samples of different styles and themes. Literary merit was not always the criterion for inclusion. But I mistook the copies to be what he considered the best, and immediately started the translation work. As often happens in life, chance played a good role. I soon saw that the stories were perfect for my purposes. In 1977, I had published "Withdrawal Symptoms: Social and Cultural Aspects of the October 6 Coup," analyzing the background to the right-wing violence of 1975–76.[54] Now I could write a companion piece to develop a partial account of the social and cultural history of the younger generation Thai Left, and by resurrecting some of their fiction, allow them to speak uninterruptedly in their own voices.

Meantime, Suchart also graciously sent me a huge amount of biographical material on the writers, which was invaluable for trying to see some patterns in and behind the stories. The first was generational. All but three of the writers were born in the six years between 1943 and 1949. The second was that only two of the writers were born in Bangkok (Thonburi in those days was still a city on its own). The great majority came from provincial towns in Central Thailand. You could say that they were, at bottom, *dek baan nork* (provincial kids; "hicks"). The third was that, with one exception, all of them were between twenty and thirty-one years old at the time of the October 6 coup, and that eight of the stories were published between 1977 and 1979—i.e., just after the horror. So, it was easy to see that the collection had real historical, political, and cultural unity-in-diversity. With this foundation in my mind, it then made sense to look at the stories comparatively, with an eye specially on "narrative strategies," i.e., how the stories were actually told. Seen from this angle, these tales showed a lot about the writers themselves and their changing mood across the last part of the "American era" in Siam.

---

[54] *Withdrawal Symptoms* was published by the *Bulletin of Concerned Asian Scholars* 9,3 (July–September 1977), pp. 13–31. Much later, Aj. Kasian Tejapira hilariously translated the first two words as *Baan Meuang khong Rao long daeng* ("*long daeng*" means "bloody dysentery"). *Withdrawal Symptoms* is reprinted in the current volume, pp. 47–76.

I should finally comment on one other consideration. From my Thai friends and from the pages of *Sangkhomsat Parithat* I learned that the dictatorship of Sarit and his henchmen had made a real effort to efface the writings of earlier Thai radicals from public memory and from the educational system. In the early 1970s, however, youngsters were digging up writings that had been banned for almost a generation: above all, the brilliant and diverse books of Siam's first modern genius, Jit Phumisak. It seemed to me that if I was successful, some of the work of the younger generation of progressives could be preserved and distributed beyond the reach of the Thanin Cabinet and its supporters. Little did I foresee the enormous political, economic, and social changes that lay just ahead.

* * * *

On the world stage, the long era of militant socialism and communism was drawing to an end. Already in 1972, Mao received Nixon in Peking, opening the way for an early end to the Cold War in Asia. By the early eighties, communist guerrilla movements in South America, Asia, and Africa had mostly petered out. By 1991, the USSR had fallen apart, and Stalin's East European empire disintegrated, like Yugoslavia. Although the armed communist parties of Vietnam and Cambodia took full control of their countries and inflicted a huge humiliation on the United States in 1975, only three years later they were fighting nationalist wars with each other and China.

In Western Europe, almost all existing communist parties died or were in ruins. Working-class areas where they had once been dominant started to support right-wing racist groups against foreign immigration, especially from Africa. Democratic socialist parties became fossilized, bureaucratized, and fragmented, not merely because they had difficulties in dealing with new social movements represented by feminists, gay and lesbian activists, ecological vanguardists, and increasingly dissatisfied ethnic and religious minorities. One by one, the famous newspapers and magazines that depended on left-wing intellectuals started to go bankrupt, or shifted to the commercial Right. American political propaganda and neoliberal dogmas dominated the world ideologically, and even in the remaining communist-led countries, capitalism was making rapid inroads.

To be sure, "communist" regimes and political parties still exist in Asia: China, the Korean peninsula, Japan, the Philippines, Vietnam, Laos, India, and Nepal, but they speak a frozen language that has little bearing on their policies. Everywhere one sees nationalism trumping socialism.

And Siam? Perhaps because the country had not been fully colonized, did not have huge haciendas, and still lacked a large working class, Leftist movements arose comparatively late, and were never really strong. The case of the CPT (Communist Party of Thailand) illustrates this character rather well. It began a guerrilla war against the military dictatorship only in 1965, and needed a lot of help from communist forces outside Siam. When China went to war with Vietnam, the CPT knelt to Peking, and was then kicked out of havens in Vietnam and Laos. China made a deal with Bangkok to cease providing significant help to the CPT, which very soon was on its deathbed. Fortunately or not, at that moment General Kriangsak Chomanan, far the most intelligent Nayok (prime minister) of the post-war era, having overthrown the Thanin Cabinet in November 1977, declared conditional amnesties for members and student followers of the CPT, and managed the feat of opening good relations with both China and Vietnam. Alas, early in 1980 he was forced to resign by a hostile Palace and ambitious enemies in the military. He was replaced by Palace favorite General Prem Tinsulanond, who for the next eight years headed a cabinet largely composed of leaders of conservative political parties. A spectacular economic boom got underway, supported mainly by American and Japanese investors, and it lasted till the great crash of 1997. Meantime, Bangkok was collaborating with China and the United States in supporting the murderous Khmer Rouge along the Khmer–Thai border, where they had been driven by an effective Vietnamese invasion. Who could have foreseen all this in 1976?

But it was not only a transformed set of cross-national alliances that mattered. In 1975 and 1976, Siam held the only two genuinely honest elections in its history. Imagine, a poor, progressive young man, who campaigned on a bicycle, was actually elected a member of parliament to represent a constituency in Yasothon. The Socialist Party of Thailand and the liberal-left Palang Mai won respectable numbers of seats in parliament. Five years later all of this was gone. Throughout the eighties and nineties, virtually all the parliamentary parties were conservative, and all relied on money politics made possible by a vast extension of Bangkok's huge banks into the provinces. It was the summertime of organized crime's *jao phor* (godfathers), also of the institution of the monarchy, which grew more powerful every year.

One could see the effects most clearly in poverty-stricken Isan, which had a long tradition of sending progressive politicians to represent it in the national capital; and had also been a strong recruiting base for the CPT. In the 1980s and 90s, Isan was full of corrupt and dangerous *jao phor* and was notorious for its acquiescence with money politics. But what other choice did the Isan people really have?

Meantime, leading student activists of the middle 1970s, having mostly accepted the amnesty offered by Kriangsak, had to deal with the consequences of a return to ordinary urban society. Some managed to resume studies in overseas universities (including Cornell), and later returned to work as professors; some joined successful family businesses or started new ones of their own; and some became writers, journalists, and NGO organizers. A few committed suicide or succumbed to narcotic addiction. By the 1990s, a number of them entered the arena of electoral politics as members of the existing (conservative) political parties. I still remember my astonishment on learning that Sutham Saengprathum, one of the famous Bangkok 18 (imprisoned in 1976 and held without trial till freed by Kriangsak in September 1978), had in 2001 become Minister for University Affairs in Thaksin Shinawat's first government—after more than a decade in the forgettable Kao Na and Palang Thai parties. I vividly recalled the time when Thongbai Thongpao brought him to Cornell, as part of a tour, to describe first hand the violence of 6 Tula and its aftermath. Aged twenty-one in 1976, he was now a middle-aged forty-six. If he was the first October 14–October 6 activist to become a minister, he was not alone. The next year, Pinit Jarusombat became Thaksin's Minister of Science and Technology, after five years with Arthit Urairat's Seritham party, and Praphat Panyachatrak became Siam's first Minister for the Environment. Phuntham Vejjatachai became Minister of Communications and Transportation in 2005. He had spent ten years working in the world of NGOs till, in 1997, he joined one of Thaksin's businesses and subsequently became a founding member of the billionaire's Thai Rak Thai (Thais Love Thais) party.

Perhaps I would have been less surprised by all of this if early on I had thought to look at some of the male activists' choices in girlfriends and wives. A significant number chose young women belonging to families of much higher social, political, and economic status than their own: daughters to high-ranking military or police officers, senior bureaucrats, and successful magnates who also attended Bangkok's top universities where these activists had studied. In the mid-70s, such young men had generally regarded themselves as the political vanguard of a new socialist society; in the jungle, they expected key roles in the CPT and the ear of the party's leaders, who were much less educated than themselves. In both instances, their hopes were dashed. Returning to the Bangkok of the eighties and nineties, some looked once again for ways to become intellectual or political leaders—by now they were turning forty, in any case. Until the economic crisis of 1997, they did not have much luck. Till that moment, the "existing system" had brought about rapid economic "development," regular high increases in GDP, and, of course, equally rapid growth of inequality. It was the devastating consequences of the 1997 financial crisis that opened the way, a few years later, to the meteoric rise to power of Thaksin Shinawat.

For reasons of his own, the Chiang Mai billionaire recruited numbers of the ex-activists into his entourage, and they had a decisive influence on his successful "populist" electoral strategy. Now mostly in their fifties, their ambitions were finally rewarded.

It is not difficult to surmise that in this choice two residues of the past were fundamental. Both became even clearer after the 2006 military coup that overthrew Thaksin. The first, I suspect, was a kind of revenge against the institutions that had first oppressed and later marginalized these ex-activists for oh so long: the military, the police, the bureaucratic elite, and the institution of the monarchy. The Surayud government, imposed by General Sonthi and his allies, was not a replica of the savage Thanin Cabinet, but it once again marginalized many of the October 6 politicians and thwarted their rise to national power. The second was, for some at least, a chance to revive long somnolent Leftist ideas and policies. Still, there was a huge difference from the time of their youth, when they lived with, and were directly dependent on, the rural poor and the mountain minorities. Now they lived in Bangkok and were dependent, ironically enough, on the country's most successful (and ruthless) capitalist. This situation meant swallowing a lot: extrajudicial murders of hundreds of so-claimed drug dealers, a disastrous and brutal policy against the discontent in the rural Far South, plenty of corruption, and authoritarian attempts to monopolize or intimidate the mass media. Still, the color red was back again after a quarter of a century.

Meantime, a big change in the politics of Isan became visible. Thaksin was too imperious, too impatient, and too rich to bother with the laborious task of building a genuinely mass-based political organization in Isan. Characteristically, he chose the simpler path of forcibly including the *jao phor* and their entourages as obedient parts in his electoral machine, a condition they were forced to accept or face violent elimination. Old-style fragmented "money politics" could also be superseded by programmatic "populist" policies, above all in the area of cheap and universal health care. Occasional election handouts, as in the pre-1997 era, could be displaced by state policies. Isan flocked to his banner. Access to hospitals was a vast improvement over the small election-day bribery of the era of "money politics." There is no doubt that the military overthrow of Thaksin and the later creation of an incompetent government had the effect of re-radicalizing many parts of Isan. Traditional hostility to the military, the police, and the arrogant bureaucratic elite reappeared after 2006.

For the first time in a generation, "Bangkok," which had calmly sucked the poorer provinces dry, came under open popular attack.

On the other hand, Thaksin's style of rule created suspicion and hostility among other members of the 6 Tula generation of activists. Those with political ambitions veered towards Sonthi Lim and Chamlong Simuang's right-wing nationalist and monarchist PAD (People's Alliance for Democracy)—an eerie revenant of the right-wing pro-monarchy and pro-military groups (Nawaphon, Luk Seua Chao Baan, et al.) Emblematic, but not typical, was the vociferous support given to PAD by Chontira Satayawadhna, once the firebrand Maoist broadcaster, from Yunnan, of the CPT's radio station, called Voice of the People (Siang Prachachon). Others, feeling trapped by the country's bizarre polarization, kept quiet in public, or tried to delink Thaksinism from progressive politics. To their credit, writers follow their own drums, and try to avoid moral follies. Ours, too.

Still, there are plenty of people of the October 6 generation who have labored patiently to achieve genuinely progressive changes in Thai society through NGO work, journalism, labor organization, academic writing, medical and legal services, and so on—without ambitions for personal political power.

Nonetheless, for the whole generation time is running out. If you were an activist university student in 1973, you would have to have been born around 1955, and today are heading for your late fifties. What lies ahead for you? In the 1970s it was still possible to imagine oneself as part of a global Left, with enemies who were only too easily identifiable. Today, nothing is so easy. Gramsci famously said that when the new is struggling to be born, and the old refuses to die, monsters appear.

One shouldn't be surprised that in the present circumstances there has been no outpouring of committed short stories such as those translated in *In the Mirror*. This is partly the result of the computer revolution of the early 1990s. The role of blogger is open to anyone with access to an internet café. Blogs can be amusing, biting, absurd, confused, intelligent, and very relevant politically. But, written rapidly, in semi-telegraphese, for the immediate occasion, they are not meant to be permanent works of art. Seen in this light, the very form of the stories in the book may belong to another era. Walter Benjamin famously wrote about the strange beauty of things at the moment they are about to disappear forever. But this pessimism may not be warranted in our case.

In the early 1970s, activists found inspiration in the suppressed and nearly forgotten writings of the early generations of Thai Leftists, symbolized by novelist Kulap Saipradit, the poet "Nai Phi," and poet, historian, and songwriter Jit Phumisak. It would be nice to think that the "forgotten" tales in *In the Mirror* will, in the turbulent years ahead, stimulate a youthful readership.

MURDER AND PROGRESS IN MODERN SIAM[1]

In 1983, one of the biggest box-office hits in Siam was a remarkable film entitled *Mue Puen*. English-language advertisements translated this title as "The Gunman," but an alternative, probably better, translation would be "The Gunmen." For the director invited his audiences to contemplate the contrast between two hired assassins—hero and villain—one working for private enterprise, the other for the state. In an early flashback, the two men are shown as comrades in the "secret" mercenary army hired by the CIA to fight in Laos in the late 1960s; there they learn to become crack shots with high-powered automatic rifles. In one savage firefight, however, the hero is seriously wounded and then abandoned to the enemy's tender mercies by his cowardly comrade. The story proper of the film is set in contemporary Bangkok, and depicts the subsequent careers of the two protagonists. The hero, one leg badly damaged, officially supports himself by working as a barber; but we are soon shown that he is secretly a highly paid professional killer. His paymasters are wealthy businessmen—and so are his victims.

The villain, on the other hand, has become the head of a high-publicity SWAT team of the Bangkok metropolitan police. He specializes in luring criminals into traps, where he shoots them down with icy, pinpoint accuracy. He is known to the mass media as *Mue Dam* (Black Hand) because he ostentatiously puts a black glove on his gun hand when preparing to kill for his employer, the state. In another society he would be the natural boss of a death squad.

The killers are distinguished morally by what we are shown of their circumstances and motivations. The hero has been abandoned by his wife, and is left to care for his critically ill child on his own. Murder is his only means of raising the money needed for expensive surgery for the little tyke. The villain kills to compensate for the memory of his earlier cowardice, to gain media attention, and to impress an alcoholic wife, with whom his sexual relations are distinctly sadistic. He thus exploits his position as a state-licensed killer to gratify a range of unpleasant, private desires. But lest the audience think that the villain is a pathological aberration, the director makes sure to provide him with a young police henchman who takes an even grimmer pleasure in assassination-for-the-state.

It is hard to imagine a film of this sort being made, let alone screened, anywhere else in Southeast Asia. Nor, I think, would it have been possible in Siam except in the 1980s. It is particularly interesting that the Thai police insisted on only two changes in the original print before the film's public release. The hero's main paymaster could not be shown to be a moonlighting senior police officer; and the masked motorcycle gangsters gunned down by Black Hand could not be shown to be young

[1] This article originally appeared in *New Left Review* 181 (May–June 1990): 33–48. Reprinted with permission.

women. On the other hand, there is also something curious about the film's popularity with the public. One can readily understand why young audiences would enjoy the rare filmic spectacle of villainous police. But a hero (even one played by top box-office star Soraphong) who kills "innocent people" for money? The answer, I suspect, is "yes," provided the victims are clearly middle-aged, male, and very rich (in other words, big capitalists). Provided, too, that there is some resonance between what is seen on the screen and the contemporary realities of Thai society.

This reality, or rather the part of it with which I am here concerned, is that in the 1980s, political killing in Siam has assumed a completely unprecedented character, one which, oddly enough, is probably a positive omen for the future. For it seems tied to the eclipse of a long-standing tradition of military–bureaucratic dictatorship and its supersession by a stable, bourgeois parliamentary political system. To get a sharper focus on the relationship between "The Gunmen" and the rapidly changing structures of Thai politics, it may be useful to sketch out antecedent patterns of political murder in Siam.

EARLY PATTERNS

The modern era of Siam's history is conventionally said to have begun in 1855. In that year, Sir John Bowring, representative of Queen Victoria and coiner of the immortal axiom "Free Trade is Jesus Christ and Jesus Christ is Free Trade," imposed his commercial Divinity by means of a treaty that compelled the Thai state to abolish all substantial barriers to imperialist economic penetration.[2] Prior to 1855, the pattern of political killing was exactly what one would expect in a society where political participation was confined, most of the time, to a very small, largely endogamous, "feudal" upper class. The victims were typically members of this class—princes, noblemen, courtiers, and high officials—and so, on the whole, were their assassins. If commoner bodyguards or soldiers participated, it was rarely on their own behalf, rather they acted at the behest of their patrons. Political murder was an intra-family affair, pitting fathers against sons, uncles against nephews, half-brothers against half-brothers. Most killings took place in the royal capital itself, which was the only real arena of political competition. The state was still so archaic and so personalized in the ruler himself that there was no sharp conceptual line between execution and murder, between "state" and "private" killing.

Between 1855 and 1932, this pattern of intra-upper-class murder went into suspension, most likely because of fear of European intervention in the political sense, and thanks to European intervention in the economic. Political leaders in Bangkok could see that in neighboring Southeast Asian states, where ruling circles permitted themselves too much fratricidal carnage, European imperialists found easy pretexts for marching in to establish "law'n'order" or to restore a "rightful," compliant claimant to the local throne. On the other hand, the rapidly expanding free-trade economy of the last half of the nineteenth century lessened the ferocity of intra-elite competition by enlarging the available pie. (The contrast between Siam's experience and the blood-drenched final decades of the Burmese monarchy, deprived by two Anglo-Burmese wars of more than half its territorial revenue base,

---

[2] The quotation is drawn from Charles R. Boxer, *The Dutch Seaborne Empire, 1600–1800* (London: Penguin, 1965), p. 249.

is instructive.) These conditions remained sufficiently stable so that even when the old nobility faced political and economic challenges from the "new men" of the modern-style bureaucracy created by Rama V (reign: 1868–1910), the conflicts were handled without bloodshed.

Something rather like the pre-1855 pattern only began to emerge after 1932, when the would-be absolutist monarchy was overthrown in a bloodless coup plotted by military and civilian commoner civil servants.[3] During the later 1930s, serious assassination attempts were directed against the two paramount military leaders of the coup group, generals Phahon Phonphayuhasena and "Plaek" (Weird) Phibunsongkhram, by members of their own circle; and violent retribution (by "legal" execution) was exacted by a still significantly "personal" state. By then, there was no real fear that such killings would precipitate external intervention, as the imperial powers were abandoning even their longstanding extraterritorial rights. At the same time, the inauguration of a constitutional monarchy—and the twentieth-century impossibility of starting a new (say, Phibunsongkhram) dynasty—meant in principle a much wider circle of participants in the struggle for political and economic dominance. The pattern became still clearer in the late 1940s and early 1950s, when violent conflict between the residual elements of the 1932 coup group, their followers, and some potential successors erupted. We may take as characteristic of this period the assassinations, on March 3, 1949, of four former cabinet ministers, all of them civilians hailing from the impoverished northeast, by the ferocious *asawin* ("knights") of Police General Phao Sriyanon.[4] The four victims moved in the same social milieu as Phao; they were killed in the capital, and for nothing to do with class, or even regional, conflict in the wider sense. As in the pre-1855 era, it is almost beside the point to ask whether the murders were committed by the state or by private individuals. Certainly no form of legal process was involved; but even if it had been, we know from the executions of perfectly innocent people in the so-called regicide trials of the period that legal mechanisms were easily used for private murders.[5] Yet it is also true that the clumsy moves made by Phao and Phibunsongkhram to cover up these murders indicate their awareness of a widened political public in the post-World War II world.

---

[3] The fullest English-language account is in Thawatt Mokarapong, *History of the Thai Revolution: A Study in Political Behavior* (Bangkok: Chalermnit, 1972).

[4] For details, see Thak Chaloemtiarana, *Thailand: The Politics of Despotic Paternalism* (Bangkok: Social Science Association of Thailand, Thai Khadi Institute, and Thammasat University, 1979), p. 48. [Revised edition published by Cornell Southeast Asia Program Publications, 2007.]

[5] On June 9, 1946, twenty-one-year-old King Rama VIII was found shot dead on his bed. The circumstances of his death have never been cleared up. But the Thai military, temporarily sidelined after 1945 because of Allied anger at Phibunsongkhram's wartime alliance with Tokyo, seized on the affair to accuse the civilian government of complicity in the king's alleged murder, and eventually, in late 1947, to overthrow it. The staging of the show trials was managed by General Phao. The fullest account of the king's death (with a substantial exploration of alternative explanations) and the trials is in Rayne Kruger, *The Devil's Discus* (London: Cassell, 1964). This book remains banned in Siam.

STATE KILLINGS

As with so much else in modern Thai history, political killing assumed a new character under the despotic regime of Field Marshal Sarit Thanarat, installed by coup d'état in October 1958.[6] During his time, the range of victims of political murder expanded outwards and downwards, while the killers became, more unambiguously than before, the state-qua-state and its employees. Illustrations of the change are afforded by the executions in 1958 of five "notorious" arsonists, in 1961 of two left-wing ex-members of parliament, and in 1962 of an alleged leading Communist.[7] The victims were completely outside Sarit's elite circle (he had probably never met any of them); all were accused of endangering *state* security; and the executions were performed in public by acknowledged agents of the state.[8] The real reason for these murders was simply the desire to build up Sarit's image as absolute strongman for a now national audience of newspaper readers and radio listeners, and, potentially, voters.[9] In other words, these killings were done in a spirit of public relations, mass-media-style.

The appearance of a mass-media audience for which political murders needed to be staged also meant that certain other political killings had to be kept secret from that audience. A good example of this paradox is the case of the Red Drum (*Tang Daeng*) slayings in Patthalung province in 1971–72.[10] These murders, designed to terrorize a *local* peasant population suspected of Communist sympathies, were not acceptable to a *national* audience that even the military regime of Sarit's successors felt somewhat constrained to respect. Similarly, in the immediate aftermath of the fall of the military regime in October 1973 (see below), student activists were able to expose the locally public, nationally secret Ban Na Sai affair to undermine severely the state security apparatus's legitimacy.[11] A conspicuous gap was opening up between the state as law and the state as apparatus.

---

[6] The fullest account of the Sarit regime is in Thak Chaloemtiarana's *Thailand*. "Bronze-throat" Sarit died of cirrhosis of the liver in 1963, but his regime survived until October 1973 under the control of his two chief lieutenants, Field Marshal Thanom Kittikajorn and General Praphat Jarusathien.

[7] Ibid., pp. 193–95, 203–204.

[8] The executions of the "arsonists" were carried out on Bangkok's vast downtown Pramane Square, in front of the Grand Palace, with the victims lined up against the wall of the imposing Mahathat Buddhist temple.

[9] On coming to power, Sarit abolished the existing constitution; closed down parliament; liquidated political parties and trade unions; arrested hundreds of intellectuals, politicians, and journalists; and established severe censorship. After his death, the iron grip was somewhat relaxed, a provisional constitution created, and (heavily manipulated) elections held.

[10] The victims, some dead, most still alive, were incinerated by the security forces in gasoline-filled, used oil drums. See Norman Peagam, "Probing the 'Red Drum' Atrocities," *Far Eastern Economic Review* 87,11 (March 14, 1975).

[11] The village of Ban Na Sai, suspected of Communist sympathies, was burned to the ground, and many of the villagers summarily executed. See Marian Mallet, "Causes and Consequences of the October '76 Coup," in *Thailand: Roots of Conflict*, ed. Andrew Turton, Jonathan Fast, and Malcolm Caldwell (Nottingham: Spokesman Books, 1976), pp. 80–103, esp. p. 82; and David Morell and Chai-anan Samudavanija, *Political Conflict in Thailand* (Cambridge, MA: Oelgeschlager, Gunn, and Hain, 1981), pp. 169–72.

Armed Struggle

The other big change in the era of Sarit, Thanom, and Praphat was the emergence of two very important new types of participant in Thai politics. The first of these was the Communist Party of Thailand (CPT), which, after 1965, waged an increasingly successful armed struggle in the state's territorial peripheries.[12] The CPT leaders did not belong to the old capital-city political elite, nor did they attempt to participate directly in capital-city politics. They took very good care to remain out of the reach of the state's executioners. And they carried on their struggle in remote rural areas that traditionally had had next to no political importance, but which now, in an age of territorially defined nation-states, had become accepted by the state as a significant political arena. Because the CPT was successful in many rural communities in mobilizing lowland peasants and upland minorities—in effect, getting them to participate in a national struggle for power—these people began to join the ranks of potential victims of political murder. In the early years of the state's counterinsurgency campaigns, violence (including murder) against the rural population remained largely the prerogative of the central state apparatus itself. But as the conflicts deepened and widened, with arms of the CPT attacking not merely official emissaries of the state but also its local private supporters, a significant "private enterprise" sector emerged alongside the "state sector" in the murder field. In the northeast, the north, and the south, vigilante groups, village toughs, moonlighting security personnel, and so on started to step up their activities. The unprecedented availability of firearms—thanks to American aid to the Thai military and police, as well as to the American "secret war" in Laos—substantially intensified the level of violence in rural politics.[13] Of particular interest were the sizeable numbers of rural and small-town Thai who were enrolled in paramilitary security units while the American money lasted, but demobilized when this money ran out.[14] Demobilization meant that they were no longer in the employ of the state; but they took back to private life militarized attitudes and terroristic skills that, as we shall see, began to acquire real commercial value in the 1970s. The final point to note in this context is that the CIA's secret army was a *mercenary* army, fully understood as such by its recruits. In this way, one could say that the profession of hired gunman—a profession rather new to Siam—derived directly from America's prosecution of its Indochina War, and was thus political from the start.

The New Bourgeoisie

The second new participant in Thai politics can be broadly described as an extra-bureaucratic bourgeoisie. Its origins lay in the Sino-Thai merchant and trading communities of Bangkok, Chonburi, Paknam, and a few towns of the prosperous

---

[12] See Morell and Chai-anan, *Political Conflict*, pp. 80–81; and Patrice de Beer, "History and Policy of the Communist Party of Thailand," in *Thailand*, ed. Turton, Fast, and Caldwell, pp. 143–94.

[13] See Andrew Turton, "Limits of Ideological Domination and the Formation of Social Consciousness," in *History and Peasant Consciousness in Southeast Asia*, ed. Andrew Turton and Shigeharu Tanabe (Osaka: National Museum of Ethnology, Senri Ethnological Studies No. 13, 1984), pp. 19–73.

[14] See my "Withdrawal Symptoms: Social and Cultural Aspects of the October 6 Coup," in this volume, pp. 47–76, esp. pp. 64–65. The essay was originally published in *Bulletin of Concerned Asian Scholars* 9,3 (July–September 1977): 13–30.

south.[15] In the 1940s and 1950s their numbers were still fairly small, their wealth limited, and their political influence negligible (not least because in many cases the process of assimilation was not yet complete). But by the early 1960s, a generation of fully assimilated Sino-Thai was reaching high-school and college age, just at the point when the great Vietnam War boom got under way. They arrived in time to take advantage of the huge growth of tertiary education in the 1960s, and of the massive expansion and diversification of employment that the boom engendered.[16]

Never in its history had Siam been so deluged with external economic resources—the result not merely of American capital investment in military bases and strategic infrastructural development, but also of direct American aid to the Thai regime, and substantial Japanese and American private investment in a low-wage, union-free society. There were three especially notable consequences of the deluge. First, it was by no means wholly concentrated in the metropolitan region, but had a major impact, direct and indirect, on many parts of the northeast, north, and south. Second, it encouraged a stratum of businessmen to emerge who were far less sharply counterposed to the modern bureaucrat than had been the case with the older Sino-Thai merchants. Among its leaders were the proprietors and managers of good hotels, shopping plazas, automobile franchises, insurance companies, and, of course, banks.[17] These were people who dressed like bureaucrats, lived in the new suburban housing complexes alongside bureaucrats, and dined, partied, shopped, and traveled in the same places as bureaucrats. Increasingly, from the 1960s on, they came out of a single common institution—the university. Third, it meshed nicely with the meteoric rise of the Sino-Thai banking system, and, indeed, was probably the major factor in its rise. These Sino-Thai banks were not elbowed aside by Japanese and American giants. Surely advantaged by the difficulties foreigners faced in mastering the Thai and Chinese languages, to say nothing of their formidable orthographies, the banks moved briskly to develop the domestic capital market. They quickly discovered that, in the age of the boom, there were substantial profits to be made by elaborating their provincial operations. In the early 1960s, by far the most imposing edifice in most provincial capitals was the governor's office, symbol of the old bureaucratic domination of Thai social and political life. A decade later, many of these Thai–Edwardian buildings had been completely overshadowed by spectacular glass-concrete-marble structures housing local branches of the great Bangkok banks.

EMERGENT PARLIAMENTARY DEMOCRACY

One needs therefore to look at the rise of the extra-bureaucratic bourgeoisie from two angles. The first, and most familiar, highlights the emergence of a very large number of educated youths (a portion of whom made the National Student Center of Thailand [NSCT] the briefly formidable political force it was in the early 1970s).

---

[15] The standard works are two books by G. William Skinner: *Chinese Society in Thailand: An Analytical History* (Ithaca, NY: Cornell University Press, 1957) and *Leadership and Power in the Chinese Community of Thailand* (Ithaca, NY: Cornell University Press, 1958).

[16] See my "Withdrawal Symptoms," section "Troubles of New Classes," pp. 50–66, this volume.

[17] Suthy Prasartset, *Thai Business Leaders: Men and Careers in a Developing Economy* (Tokyo: Institute of Developing Economies, 1982).

Already in the late 1960s they could no longer be absorbed into the bureaucracy as earlier university cohorts had been. But they were aware that they were in institutions that had traditionally prepared the new generation of the ruling class for its tasks: thus, they felt that they had a natural right to participate politically. Insofar as many of them were now coming from the provinces, they expected to exercise that right not merely in Bangkok but wherever in their careers they later ended up. Hence, for the first time in Thai history, arose the real possibility of significant non-bureaucratic mini-intelligentsias in the regions. A second, less familiar, angle focuses on the strengthening (on the basis of bank credit and the general, rapid commercialization of provincial life) of small-town entrepreneurs—some independent, some operating as agents of metropolitan giants. In most provincial towns people of this type quickly developed incomes, then lifestyles and status-pretensions, that were competitive with those of locally stationed state officials. Furthermore, since they were not subject to the officials' routine transfer to other locales, they put down strong local roots, social as well as commercial. For these roots to engender local power, it was necessary only that the unity and authority of the central state apparatus, standing behind local officialdom, be substantially compromised.

The historic "break" came with the popular movement of 1973, which culminated, on October 14, with the collapse of the Thanom–Praphat regime.[18] It is true that the duumvirate would not have fallen without high-level factional interventions by the King and by Army Commander General Krit Sivara. But the fact that Krit removed his seniors, not by a coup d'état, but by abetting the activism of students and intellectuals, joined by the popular masses in Bangkok (including segments of the middle and lower-middle classes), signaled his own recognition that the traditional form of "legitimate politics" was no longer viable. The country had changed too much. Events between 1973 and 1977 showed that, even though reactionary groups remained powerful, this recognition was becoming widespread even within the state apparatus, which was thus incapable of acting with its earlier unity of purpose.

What was emerging was that characteristic bourgeois political system we know as parliamentary democracy—the style of regime with which all ambitious, prosperous, and self-confident bourgeoisies feel most comfortable, precisely because it maximizes their power and minimizes that of their competitors. If one thinks of 1973 as Siam's 1789, then one can view the entire subsequent period (up to the present) within a single optic—that of the struggle of the bourgeoisie to develop and sustain its new political power (institutionalized in parliamentary forms) against threats from both left and right, the popular sector and the state apparatus. The patterns of political killing over these sixteen years provide good evidence that this optic is a useful one.

PERIOD OF CONSOLIDATION

The period might plausibly be divided into two: 1973–78 and 1978–89. In the first period, one of great instability and uncertainty, the bourgeoisie, feeling its way, was in an openly contradictory position. On the one hand, it needed the support of the popular sector, ideally channeled mainly through electoral mechanisms, to

---

[18] For a good, brief account, see Morell and Chai-anan, *Political Conflict*, pp. 146–50.

strengthen its legitimacy and power against military and civilian officialdom: in this struggle, "democracy" was a domestically powerful and internationally respectable weapon. On the other hand, it also felt the need for the support of the repressive arm of the state apparatus to contain "popular excesses" in the urban areas, to fight the rising CPT in the countryside, and, given the rapid decline of the American position in Indochina, to defend the nation-state from its new Communist-ruled neighbors to the east.[19] In the second period, the main problem for the bourgeoisie has been fending off the efforts by opportunist and ultra-rightist elements in the security bureaucracy who have sought to regain their old dominance by exploiting the "external threat" and resorting to sham-populist, "anti-capitalist" public rhetoric.

In the bourgeoisie's successful struggle, the importance of the press should not be underestimated; above all, that of the popular newspaper *Thai Rath,* which, with its huge nationwide readership, represents another kind of imagined national community, alongside those conjured up by parliamentary institutions or the Nation-Buddhism-Monarchy shibboleth of the old regime. Most of this press has been, if not explicitly antagonistic to military–bureaucratic pretensions (let alone coups), at least skeptical and suspicious. After all, successful newspapers are large business enterprises, which succeed because they voice, at least to some extent, their readers' aspirations. Correspondingly, the role of the press in this period can be viewed as that of an ally of the new bourgeois political ascendancy. However, of still greater interest is that in this second period the bourgeoisie has become so confident of its power, and so certain of the value of the parliamentary system for the protection of its own interests, that it has proved willing to permit violent internal competition among its own ranks. In the 1980s, we have had the extraordinary spectacle of members of parliament being assassinated, not by Communists or military dictators, but by other MPs or would-be MPs.

Before turning to look more closely at the contrasting patterns of political killing in the two periods, we may remind ourselves again of the reasons why the parliamentary system is so attractive to new middle classes of the current Thai type. In the first place, in the face of domineering civilian and military bureaucracies, it opens up channels to political power in both vertical and horizontal dimensions. To be elected to parliament one does not need to have a university degree, or to have entered in early youth the low rungs of an institutional hierarchy. Femaleness is no longer a fatal political disadvantage. Hence, there has been a huge, at least theoretical, increase in vertical social and political mobility for the less educated and non-male. At the same time, in a territorially based electoral system, provinciality is no special handicap, and may even be an advantage. One can be based in Nakhon Sawan and still be a cabinet minister; indeed, it may be that *only* by being solidly based in Nakhon Sawan can one obtain a cabinet seat. Parliament thus gives provincial elites the opportunity to short-circuit the Ministry of the Interior's powerful, territorially based hierarchy, and to make themselves felt, on their own terms, in the metropolitan home base of the bureaucracy itself—Krung Thep Maha Nakhon. Put in more general terms, electorally based parliamentary systems, more than any other type of regime, serve to reduce the power-gap between the provinces and the metropolis: this, of course, is why they are so attractive to provincial

---

[19] Given Siam's massive complicity in the American war effort, the Thai bourgeoisie had good grounds for fearing revenge.

notables.[20] Second, reduction in the power of the bureaucracy tends to weaken the regime of bureaucracy-controlled and protected monopolies, which always works to subordinate the bourgeoisie to the state apparatus. While such monopolies, of course, benefit particular businessmen or business cliques, they are against the general interest of the class. Third, electoral politics favor bourgeois interests in more narrow, technical ways. Money is crucial for sustained electoral success, and money is precisely the resource with which the bourgeoisie is most amply endowed.[21] On the other hand, the prestige of electoral politics, if it can be solidly entrenched, serves to delegitimize extra-parliamentary political activity—especially strikes, demonstrations, and popular movements, which the bourgeoisie is less likely to be able to control and may, on occasion, profoundly fear. Finally, it is evident that in countries like Siam, where "feudal" residues remain strong, especially in rural areas, the position of MP may offer possibilities of becoming far more powerful at the local level than is usually the case in industrial societies. It is thus no accident that the consolidation of the parliamentary system in Siam has coincided with the visible rise of so-called *jao phor*—or mafioso-like politician capitalists—who, by the use of violence, political connections, and control of local markets and rackets, become feared provincial bosses.

LOCAL AND NATIONAL KILLINGS

We may now return to political killings. In the period from late 1974 to the coup of October 6, 1976, the typical victims were middle-class student activists associated with the NSCT, leaders of peasant organizations, trade unionists, and left-wing, muckraking journalists.[22] The murders seem to fall into two broad groups. (1) Local killings—typically of peasant leaders, trade unionists, and journalists who were felt to threaten the power or profits of provincial notables, including landowners, businessmen, and corrupt village headmen. Most of these killings were private-enterprise murders, with the gunmen (*mue puen*) hired by local notables from the Vietnam-era pool of professional assassins, former security guards, moonlighting policemen, and petty gangsters.[23] (2) National killings. A conspicuous example is the ambush assassination, in Bangkok, of Socialist Party leader Dr. Boonsanong

---

[20] See the exceptionally detailed, well-informed article by Anek Laothamatas, "Business and Politics in Thailand: New Patterns of Influence," in *Asian Survey* 28,4 (April 1988): 451–70. Anek notes that in 1979 only four provinces had local chambers of commerce, but by 1987 all seventy-two provinces had established them. Furthermore, interprovincial alliances of these chambers of commerce have fought with increasing success to expand their influence vis-à-vis the metropolis (both the metropolitan bureaucracy and the capital city big bourgeoisie) using parliamentary channels.

[21] Anek has some striking figures to illustrate this point. In the three cabinets of the 1963–73 period, under military dictators Sarit, Thanom, and Praphat, there were precisely two businessmen—less than 4 percent of the total. In the election-based cabinets of 1975–76, there were thirty-five—roughly 40 percent. In the aftermath of the October 1976 coup (1976–early 1980), the proportion dropped to 13 percent. Under the restored election-based parliamentary system of the 1980s (1980–86), it shot up again to almost 44 percent. Ibid., p. 455.

[22] For a solid discussion, with detailed statistics, of these killings, see Morell and Chai-anan, *Political Conflict*, pp. 225–53.

[23] Most of the killings were carried out in small towns and villages. The highly uneven geographical distribution (most were in the north) underscores the absence of the central state-qua-state in the violence.

Punyothayan on February 28, 1976. But the periodic assassinations of prominent student leaders, and, above all, the massacre that took place at Thammasat University in Bangkok on October 6, 1976, itself, form the general category. These victims threatened no particular private interests. Rather, they were regarded as enemies of the *state,* or were cynically depicted as such for Machiavellian reasons (e.g., to create the atmosphere in which the state apparatus could plausibly reverse the parliamentary tide). Hence the killers were more or less direct agents of this apparatus.[24] The massacre of students at Thammasat University on October 6 is especially useful for showing the difference between category (1) and category (2) murders. For the victims were, many of them, the privileged children of the bourgeoisie itself (one has only to look at the Sino-Thai faces of the students inside Thammasat's gates, any day of the working week, and the Thai-Thai faces of the vendors outside, to sense this). There is very little reason to think that the Thai bourgeoisie wished for these killings—which were replicated nowhere outside the capital city.

The "national" killings," performed by agents of the state, were thus anti-middle class, and intended to return the political order to what it had been before October 14, 1973. The "local" killings, performed by private mercenaries, were pro-middle class, and intended to intimidate members of the subaltern classes and their self-appointed tribunes.

THE COLLAPSE OF RURAL INSURGENCY

It has been plausibly argued that Siam, Thai parliamentary democracy, and/or the Thai middle class benefited from an extraordinary stroke of luck in the collapse of the CPT's rural insurgency as a result of the triangular Cambodia-Vietnam-China war that opened in December 1978. It is true that the party was gravely damaged by its leadership's decision to remain wholly loyal to Peking's positions. It thereby lost its secure retreats in Laos and Cambodia, its opportunities for training cadres in Vietnam, and even its powerful radio transmitter in Yunnan. (Prime Minister [General] Kriangsak Chomanan was shrewd enough to see the advantages of cementing close ties with "Little Bottle" and his henchmen.[25]) But it can also be argued that the damage was especially severe because the party was already struggling with the problem of what to do with the hundreds of middle-class, youthful activists who fled to its jungle protection in the wake of the bloody October

---

[24] Most notoriously, the so-called Red Gaurs, many of them ex-mercenaries from the CIA's "secret army" in Laos, who operated at the behest of the dominant clique in the ISOC (Internal Security Operations Command) of the armed forces; but also the Village Scouts, right-wing vigilante groups under the aegis of the palace. See my "Withdrawal Symptoms," pp. 62–65, in this volume, and the sources there cited; and Morell and Chai-anan, *Political Conflict,* pp. 241–46.

[25] In the immediate aftermath of the October 6, 1976, coup, an awkward compromise between the palace and the coup leaders produced an ultra-rightist, but civilian, government headed by Supreme Court Justice Thanin Kraiwichian. Almost exactly one year later, this government was bloodlessly overthrown by General Kriangsak, an unusually skillful military politician. It was Kriangsak's policy to persuade Peking to stop supporting the CPT in exchange for Siam's cooperation in supporting the Khmer Rouge against the invading Vietnamese forces. The deal was publicly sealed when "Little Bottle" popped up in Bangkok as a distinguished guest at the ordination ceremonies of the Crown Prince. (In Siam, it is customary for most young males to enter the Buddhist monkhood for a short period.)

6, 1976, coup. From a much younger generation, from comfortable homes, well-read and articulate, and with some real experience in national-level legal politics, these activists found it hard to accept many CPT positions automatically; the party's obtuse response to the crisis of 1978–79 made it almost impossible. Prime Minister Kriangsak was shrewd enough to offer a general amnesty, enabling the activists to come safely home. It is significant that the CPT made little effort to stop them, even though the spectacle of "massive defections" compounded the severe political damage it had already suffered. All in all, there can be no doubt that the CPT's decline, caused not by the Thai military's battlefield successes, but by international political developments and its own internal hemorrhage, redounded principally to the benefit of the new Thai bourgeoisie. After 1978–79, it faced no serious threats from the left, or from below. By then it was also no longer much alarmed by the presence of Vietnamese troops on the country's eastern border, though the military tried hard to make it so. The bourgeoisie recognized the real limits of Vietnam's power, and Siam's advantages in having the US-China-Japan axis ranged firmly behind it.

But the Cambodia-Vietnam-China fighting erupted well *after* the fall of the post-October 6 right-wing regime of Justice Thanin Kraiwichian, and it is his rise and fall that are really instructive for understanding the changing dynamic of Thai politics in the bourgeois era.

THE THANIN REGIME

Thanin himself, a Sino-Thai jurist of eccentric and extremist views,[26] had no political base of his own, and represented no substantial group or institution. His appointment as prime minister reflected the conflict between the palace and the generals. The royal family, panicked by the recent abolition of the Laotian monarchy to which it was related, wanted a strong anti-Communist, but also a civilian (since it never fully trusted the military). The generals, even more interested in power than in anti-communism, wanted the installation of one of their own. The palace initially prevailed, but not for very long. Ridiculous in its rhetoric, so that it soon became popularly referred to as the Clam Cabinet,[27] the Thanin government quickly alienated almost everyone by its incompetence and ideological extremism. But its leaders took their historic mission—anti-communism but *also* civilian supremacy and the rule of (right-wing) law—sufficiently seriously that they did something absolutely unprecedented in modern Thai politics: have a top-ranking general sentenced to death and actually executed. To be sure, General Chalard Hiransiri, leader of an attempted coup in March 1977, had managed to kill a Palace favorite, General Arun Dewathasin, in the course of his brief bid for power, but it is most unlikely that he would have been executed if a true military junta had been in control.[28] Chalard's fate was certainly one factor that helps to explain why General

---

[26] Thanin had published some dotty books on rape, brainwashing, and the Communist menace.

[27] In an early speech, Thanin foolishly compared his government to a tender mollusk needing the protection of the hard, thick shell provided by the military, the palace, and the proliferating right-wing vigilante groups.

[28] This does not exclude the possibility that some generals were content to see the choleric Chalard sped to join his Maker.

Kriangsak's successful, bloodless coup the following October was advertised from the start as a blow for "moderation" and as foreshadowing the restoration of at least quasi-parliamentary government. The audience for the advertisement was not merely the United States and Western Europe ("international public opinion"), but also, above all, the Thai bourgeoisie.[29] Kriangsak himself was the first Thai coup leader who took pains to act as a kindly, home-loving bourgeois in public. For example, in a splendid *coup de théâtre,* he had himself photographed by the press cooking curry at his home for the Bangkok 18 (eighteen students imprisoned since October 6, 1976, on the grave charge of *lèse majesté*). The point in all this is that, even before the Indochina imbroglio and the collapse of the CPT, the rise and fall of the Thanin regime attests to the continuing consolidation of bourgeois power in Thai politics.

MPs AND THE GUNMEN

Finally, we may turn to the very recent past and to the subject matter of "The Gunmen." Any reader of the Thai press after 1978 will have been struck by the sudden conspicuousness of stories about *jao phor* ("Godfathers") and *phu mi itthiphon* ("men of influence"), and also by the new dangerousness of provincial political life. While there have been few cases as spectacular as the assassination of "Sia" Jaew,[30] the celebrated *jao phor* of Chonburi, who was ambushed military-style by men driving armored cars and firing submachine guns, the killing of MPs by "unknown gunmen" has become commonplace. Next to MPs, nouveau-riche tycoons, big speculators, and/or smugglers, judges and so on (local bosses or potential bosses) have been frequent victims. These people appear to have taken the place of peasant leaders and student activists—who are now almost never the objects of attack. There is, however, good reason to think that the killers are more or less the same people, at least the same kind of people, as the murderers of 1974–76: *mue puen,* or guns for hire. Their paymasters seem almost invariably to be the victims' fellow-bourgeois political and business rivals. (The highly uneven territorial distribution of the deaths indicates little or no involvement by the state-qua-state.)

What all these killings suggest is that in the 1980s the institution of MP has achieved solid market value. In other words, not only does being an MP offer substantial opportunities for gaining wealth and power, *but it promises comfortably to do so for the duration.* It may thus be worth one's while to murder one's parliamentary competition—something inconceivable in the 1950s and 1960s, when parliament's power and longevity were very cheaply regarded.

What we are now seeing in Siam is a consolidation of the economic and political circuits created during its "American period." An almost uninterrupted thirty-year boom has given the country the most advanced, productive capitalist economy in Southeast Asia (outside the micro-principality of Singapore). The great Bangkok banks have been funneling once undreamed-of credit to the provinces, funds that are as available for politics and gangsterism as for productive entrepreneurial

---

[29] The military was becoming increasingly aware that in a vastly changed Thai society, dreams of a new Sarit-style army despotism were obsolete.

[30] "Sia" is a Thaified version of the Teochiu Chinese word for "tycoon." Earlier used only for Sino-Thai (with an ambiguous mixture of contempt and awe), in the last two years it has been increasingly applied, with less contempt and more awe, to rising Thai-Thai tycoons.

activities. Competition between the banks, at all levels, means that each has a strong interest in developing political agents and allies. As the financial backers of many MPs, the banks can exert direct, independent political influence in a way that would be very difficult under a centralized, authoritarian military regime. Furthermore, as the representatives of a national electorate, the parliamentarians as a group veil bank power (and the power of big industrial and commercial conglomerates) with a new aura of legitimacy. This is a real and valuable asset. It can thus provisionally be concluded that most of the echelons of the bourgeoisie—from the multimillionaire bankers of Bangkok to the ambitious small entrepreneurs of the provincial towns— have decided that the parliamentary system is the system that suits them best; and that they now have the confidence to believe that they can maintain this system against all enemies. These enemies still exist—in the military and in the civilian bureaucracy in particular. But they seem in secular decline. For all officialdom's grumblings about "dark influence"—self-serving propaganda meant to suggest that "benign influence" is a monopoly of the bureaucracy—it has been gradually accommodating itself to the new system.[31]

It is in this context that the assassinations of MPs by professional gunmen can be read as a historic portent. Parliamentary democracy has little trouble gaining the support of liberal intelligentsias. But they are not sufficient to sustain it. Substantial numbers of ruthless, rich, energetic, and competitive people from all over the country must also be willing to invest in the system. That in Siam such people are prepared to kill one another to become MPs indicates that something really new is now in place.

The film *Mue Puen* reflects this situation. It refuses to side with state murder over private-enterprise murder—and the state is not in a position forcibly to change its mind. It reassures its audiences that the new bourgeois world is profoundly stable. After all, if capitalists are being murdered, their killers are neither communists, student radicals, nor agents of a police state: merely employees of fellow capitalists. And there is surely this wholly intended subtext for the defeated left among the viewing masses: at least *some* capitalists are being killed, and by a maimed victim of American imperialism and the unjust social system to boot. A sort of dream revenge for October 6, 1976.

POSTSCRIPT

In the course of finishing this article, I received from a Thai student of mine, recently returned to America, a description of a recent assassination so exemplary and so rich in detail, that I can not resist including it here in somewhat edited form.

At the beginning of April last year [1990], Mr. Phiphat Rotwanitchakorn (known as Sia Huad), a prominent *jao phor* in Chonburi district, southeast of Bangkok, was spectacularly ambushed and slain, along with his driver and his bodyguard (a captain in the local police). He had known for some time that he was targeted for

---

[31] This is true even of the military. Both coup attempts since Kriangsak's *coup de main* in October 1977 have been fiascos. Their leaders, a group of ambitious colonels loosely referred to as the Young Turks, have never managed to unite the military behind their schemes. It is symptomatic, however, that the "platform" of the Young Turks claims a mission to save the country not so much from communism as from greedy mega-capitalists. The gap between these idealists' salaries and the sums required to purchase their palatial suburban homes suggests another reason for their lack of political plausibility.

assassination, and almost never left his big, heavily guarded mansion. But on "Cheng Meng" Day, when Sino-Thai families pay homage to their ancestors, he had been summoned by a close friend and prominent Bangkok banker of the multimillionaire Tejaphaiboon family to attend the rites at the Tejaphaiboons' private cemetery in Chonburi.[32] He felt he had to go because this friend had earlier given him a billion-*baht* (US$40,000,000) line of credit, enabling him to outbid a rival *jao phor,* Kamnan (Commune Head) Poh, for control of a gigantic trade-center building project in downtown Chonburi. Afraid for his life, Sia Huad called in his brother and several professional gunmen to follow him in another car. He even switched cars on returning from the cemetery, in the hope of eluding his enemies. But the assassins, in three cars, first smashed into and thus blocked his brother's car. Then they pursued him in a wild shooting spree for about five minutes, by which time his car had halted and all three men inside were dead. To make sure of this, however, a limping gunman (not Soraphong) climbed out of his vehicle, pulling on a mask, and took a close look at the corpses, surrounded by a growing crowd of curious spectators.

Sia Huad had begun his career as a small-time enforcer for a local *jao phor.* When his boss was murdered, he set up his own gang and found a new patron in a local political leader. His youngest sister subsequently married the son of a well-known Chonburi MP, who became a cabinet minister, and Sia Huad himself worked for this man as a "vote collector" at election time. As his wealth and power grew, so did the number of his enemies. He specialized in land speculation, ordering his gang to use the most ruthless methods to force small peasants owning land in areas scheduled for commercial and industrial development to sell to him dirt-cheap. He was also involved in a successful plot to overthrow a local mayor (also a political boss) and install his own henchmen in the municipal government. The arrogant way in which he and his gang treated the local police earned him many enemies in uniform. So when the powerful Kamnan Poh, angered over being outbid on the trade-center building project, gave the green light, a lot of people who wanted Sia Huad dead pooled a million *baht* (US$40,000) and plenty of guns in a united front against him.

About a month after the slayings, the police made several arrests in the case, including some of the dead man's *jao phor* rivals, some politicians and gunmen, and, most important, four members of the Special Operations Police—allegedly the actual triggermen.[33]

Though no newspaper or magazine dares to say so, it is widely rumored that the mastermind of the assassination was Kamnan Poh. But who dares touch him now? Just one week after the killings, Kamnan Poh celebrated his victory in the first mayoral election of the newly established Saensuk district (close to the tourist resort of Phattaya) by throwing a party for ten thousand people, including several cabinet ministers from the Social Action Party, other prominent MPs, popular singers, and movie stars. This was a much bigger and splashier affair than the party given by

[32] The Sino-Thai Tejaphaiboons own the giant Bangkok Metropolitan Bank. Two of the younger-generation Tejaphaiboons, including one who was former chairman of the board of the Mekhong distillery conglomerate, ran successfully for parliament in 1986—the first time that the family had thought it worth putting its sons into electoral politics. Phiphat's friend is known as the "eighth Sia"—meaning that all his seven elder brothers are also big tycoons.

[33] This organization is not under the control of the national police department, but is a special paramilitary unit under the supervision of the armed forces. It was originally created as part of the anti-CPT counterinsurgency campaign.

incoming prime minister Chatchai Choonhawan at about the same time. In response to reporters' questions about the death of Sia Huad, Kamnan Poh replied: "In Chonburi, bad guys must die." But probably not as spectacularly as Sia Huad. These days, being killed by gunmen is becoming a class privilege of the bourgeoisie. After all, who will pay gunmen a million *baht* to slay a poor man?

RADICALISM AFTER COMMUNISM IN THAILAND AND INDONESIA[1]

One might think that "after Communism" is an uncomplicated idea, experience, or socio-political condition, but in the two countries of Southeast Asia that I intend to discuss—namely, colonized Muslim Indonesia, and uncolonized Buddhist Thailand—"after Communism" has markedly different meanings, which therefore in turn affect the imaginary of contemporary radicalism. To set the stage, therefore, it is necessary to say something about the trajectory of Communism in each of the two countries.

The Netherlands East Indies was the first Asian "country" outside the Soviet Union to have a Communist Party at all. The PKI (Partai Komunis Indonesia, Communist Party of Indonesia) was founded on May 23, 1920. In the relatively "liberal" climate of the immediate post-World War I era, it developed rapidly, especially among estate laborers, dockers, and railway personnel. As there were then no universities in the colony, and very few natives had gone to Holland for tertiary education, its leaders were a mix of Indonesian autodidacts and junior high-school graduates, along with a sprinkling of Dutch radicals, whom, however, the colonial regime quickly jailed or extruded. Although the young Party leaders frequently quarreled with various Muslim political notables, the Party had no difficulty in cultivating a following among the Muslim masses, and it was in two of the most Muslim provinces of the colony that the Party's millenarian call for an uprising in 1926–27 was most courageously, if disastrously, answered. The Dutch crushed the insurrection without much difficulty, executing some leaders, and banishing or imprisoning many others. For the remainder of the colonial period the Party did not seriously exist. It did not start to rebuild itself until after the outbreak of what Indonesians remember as their "Revolution of 1945," when, between the collapse of the Japanese occupation regime and the delayed return of the Dutch, an infant Republic of Indonesia was born. During the bitter struggle that ensued till late 1949, when The Hague finally conceded the transfer of sovereignty, freed, returning, and newborn Communists played a significant but never a dominating political role.

Already, however, a difference in generations was visible. Many of the older generation were quite fluent in Dutch—some had even served in the anti-Nazi underground in Holland itself; they had traveled abroad, or been exiled there, and self-consciously saw themselves as part of a world revolutionary movement; many had European friends and sometimes wives and lovers; they worked closely with progressive local Chinese; and they were by experience "activists," above and below ground, trade-unionists, propagandists, strike organizers, and occasionally "terrorists." They had no experience of parliamentary, legal politics. The second

[1] This essay originally appeared in the *New Left Review* 202 (November–December 1993): 3–14. Reprinted with permission.

generation came to adulthood during the bloody Japanese occupation; their Dutch was usually minimal, they had never been abroad, and they had no foreign friends; they were not fond of Chinese (so that when they took control of the Party in 1951 they excluded Chinese from open Party membership); they were ardent nationalists, and also Party men and women first and foremost, because they entered politics under the infant Republic, which governed itself as best it could by a regime of parliamentary institutions and political parties with their various affiliates.

About halfway through the Revolution, the Cold War set in with a vengeance, and increasingly polarized the internal politics of the Republic. The outcome was a brief but very bloody civil war on Java in the autumn of 1948 in which the Left, branded by a Muslim-dominated government as the traitorous agent of Moscow, was ruthlessly crushed. Many older leaders were executed or murdered, and more would have been so had not the Dutch in December made a last, large military effort to suppress the Republic. A good number of second-generation Communists escaped from jail and joined the short guerrilla struggle if only in a marginal capacity. When the fighting ended and a liberal-democratic Republic covering all of Indonesia was formed in the last days of 1949, this generation emerged to take over and rebuild the Party's membership and reputation.

In this endeavor they were astonishingly successful, for reasons that are too complex to go into here. Suffice it to say that already in the 1955 general elections, the only free elections Indonesia has ever had, the Party emerged as one of the Big Four, with millions of voters behind it and a large parliamentary fraction to represent it at the center of governance. One of the key conditions of the Party's electoral success was its extreme caution on domestic issues, and its strong nationalist stance externally, which enabled it to work out effective alliances with other political parties, and to begin to live down the "treason" of 1948. While in practice the Party's electoral successes committed it to peaceful, legal parliamentary politics, more or less like those of Togliatti's PCI (Partito Comunista Italiano, Italian Communist Party), it could not bring itself publicly to say so; hence, when in 1959 the Left-leaning President Sukarno and the generally Right-wing army leaders cooperated to replace constitutional democracy with the authoritarian, populist-nationalist system of Guided Democracy, in which no elections would ever be held, the Party leaders felt they had no alternative but to go along.

Under Guided Democracy, which lasted from 1959 to 1965, the Party's mass affiliates—of youth, women, peasants, estate workers, and so on—continued to grow rapidly, because these were better adapted than the parliamentary Party itself to conditions of non-electoral competitive politics. By 1965, the PKI's leaders claimed a "family" of twenty million partisans, and the dubious honor of being the largest such Communist family in the world outside the Socialist bloc. But this success was matched by the development of comparable Muslim and so-called secular-nationalist (bourgeois) families, leading to increasing polarization, especially as hyperinflation set in and the economy spun downward. The Party clung to its legality, and in any case had no guns.

It could do little in the more advanced sectors of the nationalized economy since these were controlled by the deeply hostile military. The Party leaders tried to compensate for this weakness with vociferous support for Sukarno's anti-Western foreign policy and a narrowly chauvinist Kulturkampf against "liberal" intellectuals, which was never forgiven them.

The end started on October 1, 1965, when a small group of military officers nominally headed by an obscure lieutenant-colonel in the Presidential Guard assassinated six top generals, and seized parts of the capital city for a few hours. The "coup," if it was such, was quickly suppressed by the commander of the Army's Strategic Reserve, General Suharto, who proceeded to manipulate the horror aroused by the midnight murders to launch an extermination campaign against the Party, which he accused of masterminding the coup attempt. Between mid-October 1965 and late January 1966, the PKI was physically destroyed. At least half a million people, perhaps as many as a million, were killed either by the Army itself, or by the Muslim and secular-nationalist vigilante groups it armed and protected. Hundreds of thousands of other people thought to be associated with the Party were imprisoned and tortured. Virtually the entire Party leadership was executed, mostly without even the flimsiest legal formalities.

In March 1966, as Suharto effectively supplanted Sukarno as head of state, the Party was declared illegal, along with anything that even smelled of Marxism. It has never been reborn, not merely because of the brutal efficiency of the dictatorship's intelligence apparatus, but also because the Party leaders were profoundly discredited in the eyes of their followers. How could the leaders have permitted the catastrophe to happen, leaving twenty million supporters defenseless against their enemies? Worse still, a large number of militants, hoping to save their own lives, turned, in Suharto's gulag, into informers on their own people, and sometimes even became torturers and executioners.

Notice the timing: 1966, just as Mao's Cultural Revolution was in full swing, Lyndon Johnson's United States was becoming engulfed in the Vietnam War, and the new Brezhnev leadership in Moscow was showing every sign of confidence and vigor. Perhaps the apogee of "World Communist" success.

A CONTRASTING HISTORY

The story of Communism in Thailand is shorter, and also very different. The social and economic system of uncolonized Thailand was much more slowly assaulted by capitalism than was the case with the Netherlands Indies, and this capitalism was not dominated by giant plantation agribusiness. It was the policy of the long-reigning, highly intelligent Rama V (Chulalongkorn, r. 1868–1910) to leave indigenous Thai society as undisturbed as convenient; the brunt of capitalist modernization was therefore borne largely by young male immigrants "imported" from the coastal parts of southeastern China. Most of those who did not manage to return home to China married Thai women, producing towards the end of his reign the first substantial generation of what the Thai call *luk jin*, or Sino-Thai. A minority of these Sino-Thai moved up socioeconomically to become the core of the country's nascent bourgeoisie, concentrated heavily in the royal capital of Bangkok, and in the smaller towns that grew up along the railway lines which the king started to build for strategic-political purposes. The rest formed the country's real working class, and continued to do so until after World War II.

It was among such immigrants and their children, as well as among Vietnamese fleeing French colonialism in Indochina, that Communism in Thailand got its start— well after the absolute monarchy had been overthrown in the bloodless coup of 1932, and just before the Pacific War broke out. Thus the Communist Party of Thailand (CPT) was only formed in 1941, a generation later than in the Netherlands Indies;

was based on still largely alien minorities rather than on "natives," was urban rather than semi-urban/semi-rural, and was oriented north towards China rather than west towards Europe and the USSR. In the brief period of liberal civilian rule after World War II, its influence began to spread among the small Thai intelligentsia, and it even managed to elect one solitary MP to the Thai parliament before the Thai military seized full powers in 1947. At the strong urging of the United States, which was inclined to regard Thailand as a fortress in its struggle against Asian Communism, the CPT was declared illegal, and remained so ever afterward. No contrast could be more striking with the contemporary PKI. At the same time, the Party was small enough, and the military-dominated Thai establishment secure enough, that arrested Communists were usually well-treated in prison, and torture and execution a distinct rarity.

This situation changed quite rapidly in the 1960s as the Vietnam War deepened and the American presence in Thailand massively expanded. The Asian Communist states, especially China and Vietnam, saw every reason to support the CPT, and their influence was decisive in persuading the underground Party to move into the rural peripheries of the country and commence a guerrilla struggle. In 1966, just as the PKI was being destroyed in Indonesia. As the Vietnam War dragged on, the CPT steadily expanded its bases, while depending substantially on Beijing and Hanoi for funds, weapons, training, and ideological guidance. The fact that the Party's leadership was overwhelmingly Sino-Thai or even "Chinese" made these links especially strong. On the other hand, the American presence—there were 48,000 US military personnel in Thailand in 1968, to say nothing of huge American expenditures on infrastructure, and on the Thai military and police—initiated changes in Thai society far more rapid than it had ever previously experienced. A huge economic boom got under way, which rapidly expanded the middle class in which, however, Sino-Thai remained predominant. Concomitantly, public education, especially at the university level, expanded spectacularly, perhaps by 500 percent in less than a decade.

In October 1973, small university-based protests against the dictatorship suddenly and rapidly swelled into huge popular demonstrations in the capital, and, thanks to internal divisions in the military itself, as well as the intervention of the young monarch Rama IX, the dictatorship abruptly collapsed. Between October 1973 and October 1976, Thailand had the most open, democratic political system it has experienced, before and since. Pent-up dissatisfactions—with oppressive land laws, with corruption, with bans on strikes, with American domination—burst into the open, and a quite rapid political polarization commenced, pushing especially student activists to the Left, and many others, fearful of the way the Vietnam War was going, to the Right. It was in this period that the CPT speedily re-expanded its underground influence into the urban areas and into the intelligentsia in a way that had been impossible for a generation. In 1975, a wave of assassinations of leaders of student, worker, and farmer organizations prepared the way for the extremely brutal reimposition of military dictatorship on October 6, 1976. The repression was especially severe at the traditionally "progressive" Thammasat University in downtown Bangkok, where students were publicly shot, hanged, and beaten to death. The immediate result was a massive flight of liberal and leftist youngsters into the maquis, where the CPT initially welcomed and protected them.

With the fall/liberation of Indochina in the spring of 1975, the abolition of the Laotian monarchy (which panicked the conservative Thai royal family), and a vast increase in the CPT's potential leadership cadres, the CIA station chief in Bangkok was gloomily predicting in early 1977 that Thailand would be the next domino to fall to Communism. He could not have been more spectacularly mistaken. Instead, within three years, the CPT had lost virtually everything, and ceased to play any significant role in Thai politics—fifteen years after that fate had overtaken the PKI. Why?

The crucial factor was the outbreak of the three-cornered war between China, Vietnam, and Cambodia that opened at the end of 1978. The aging Sino-Thai leadership of the CPT decided to throw in its lot with Deng Xiaoping, whereupon the Vietnamese, highly influential in Laos and now masters of Cambodia, ceased cooperation and blocked off all border sanctuaries. The Macchiavelli of Beijing then proceeded to Bangkok, and arranged an alliance with the Thai military leaders against Vietnam in exchange for the cessation of virtually all help to the CPT, including the powerful and effective Voice of the People of Thailand radio station in Yunnan. These proved devastating blows to the Party. Massive internal dissension broke out in its ranks, typically ranging the young, university-educated refugees of 1976 against their elders. In the meantime, a new intelligent military leadership had decided to offer a complete amnesty to all those in the maquis who surrendered— and it kept its promises. By the end of 1979 a massive hemorrhage had begun, which, in tandem with its international isolation, destroyed the Party's prestige and political possibilities. 1980, shall we say? just as Ronald Reagan was successfully campaigning for the US presidency, in part on the basis of his program for countering a never-more-powerful "Evil Empire" centered in Moscow.

There are two points to underscore in all of this. First, that "after Communism" in both Indonesia and Thailand began long before the implosion of Stalin's empire, indeed, long before anyone could imagine this implosion happening. Second, that the "residues" of Communism in the two countries were utterly different.

People who had been with the Left in Indonesia before October 1, 1965, were rarely university-educated, and the Marxism they knew theoretically was 1950s Marxism-Leninism in its simpler Stalinist and early Maoist forms. They were overwhelmingly "indigenous" Indonesians rather than members of the Sino-Indonesian minority. Their political experience had been in parliamentary and para-parliamentary legal politics. They were nationalists determined to live down their enemies' accusations of "treason" in 1948. And their lives "after Communism," if they had lives at all, had meant torture, lengthy imprisonment without trial under often barbarous conditions, destruction of marriages and families, as well as continuous social ostracism, intensive military surveillance, and unemployment on their release.

In Thailand, a substantial number of the most capable recruits to Communism, especially after 1975–76, were students at the best of Thailand's universities. While some of their Marxism came from Cultural Revolution China and Vietnam, they were also, as children of the 1960s, exposed to the New Left Marxism of Northern Europe and the United States, as well as Gramsci, Althusser, and the Frankfurt school. They were often devoted to Joan Baez and Bob Dylan who, however, came too late on the international scene for any legal PKI cadres to think of enjoying them. A substantial number of them were second- or third-generation Sino-Thai, products of an assimilated middle class that had grown so vastly from the late 1950s. As so often happens with the children and grandchildren of immigrants, they were determined to demonstrate their patriotic Thai-ness—a major reason for their revolt against the CPT leadership's subservience to Peking—but this was somewhat self-conscious. They had only the briefest and most tangential experience of parliamentary politics and had been formed by extra-parliamentary activism and by life in the maquis. But their lives "after Communism" were in most cases gently normal (though there were significant numbers who took to drugs or committed suicide). They returned home to join the family business, or went back to their universities, or studied abroad, mostly in Europe, America, and Australia, or decided to participate in parliamentary politics that began to take real roots in Thailand in the 1980s once the CPT was destroyed. Nothing was seriously held against them, not least because they were the children of a well-educated, now very successful bourgeoisie.

FOOTPRINTS IN THE MIRE

If one looks at "radicalism" after Communism in the two countries, these contrasts have to be borne centrally in mind. Yet, in a strange way, there are also partly hidden connective threads linking them together, and these are nationalism, history, and print.

Indonesia first. The best known and probably the most important radical in Indonesia today is the brilliant autodidact-writer Pramoedya Ananta Toer (or "Pram" as he is generally known), whose novels and stories have been translated into dozens of languages, and who is Southeast Asia's likeliest candidate for a Nobel prize when the region's turn of the Oslovian wheel comes round. Pram's political record is unique. Born in 1926, he was first imprisoned by the Dutch in 1948–49 as a nationalist revolutionary, then by the Sukarno regime in 1959–60 for publicly defending the Chinese minority, and finally by the Suharto dictatorship in 1966–78 for his vocal leadership of the Left intelligentsia from the late 1950s until 1965. Today, nearly thirty years after the Indonesian holocaust, his works are all prohibited, and students who circulate them clandestinely have incurred long prison sentences. By far the most influential of his writings is the tetralogy, which he initiated in the mid-1970s in the remote penal colony of Buru, by oral recitation to his fellow prisoners. The tetralogy is loosely based on the life of a hitherto little known pioneer nationalist called Tirtoadisuryo, a young man of aristocratic Javanese birth, who founded the first nationalist newspaper in the first decade of this century, helped promote the first radical movement of opposition to Dutch colonial rule, and ended his days in imprisonment and obscurity.

The titles of the novels already reveal something of their character: *Earth of Mankind, Child of All Nations, Footprints in the Mire, The Glass House.*[2] The first two announce something without precedent in Indonesian literature (and on which the PKI of the pre-1965 era would have certainly frowned): that "this earth" of Indonesia is for all those who love it, not merely its passport-carrying citizens, and that the heroic originator of Indonesian nationalism was the heir of emancipatory nationalists in every country. The third title summons up the image of all those who have left nothing behind them in their struggles—1910s, 1940s, 1960s, 1990s—except "footprints in the mire"; while the fourth allegorizes, after the manner of Foucault's

---

[2] The original novels, all published by Hasta Mitra, in Jakarta, were: *Bumi Manusia* (1979), *Anak Semua Bangsa* (1980), *Jejak Lang* (1985), and *Rumah Kaca* (1988). The current English versions are those published by William Morrow, in New York, NY, under the titles: *This Earth of Mankind* (1991), *Child of All Nations* (1993), *Footsteps* (1994), and *House of Glass* (1996).

Benthamite Panopticon, the contemporary police state in the Dutch colonial regime's ambition to put everything in the colony under surveillance.

The young radical hero of the novels is not only shown to us learning about the world from the French, Dutch, Japanese, and other Java-dwelling foreigners he encounters, and from the novel newspapers that, at the turn of the century, were bringing the whole planet into the cities of the colony, but he is destined to be married successively to the most outsider of outsider women: a pitiful Eurasian beauty, a Chinese immigrant fleeing the brutality of a dying Ch'ing dynasty, and a fierce Muslim from the most remote (from Java) eastern fringes of the sprawling archipelagic colony. Still more striking is the fact that the figure who dominates all four novels is not the young hero, but his first mother-in-law, sold off, after her first menstruation, by her corrupt, servile Javanese parents to a drunken, licentious Dutch plantation-owner, but who fully masters her later destiny, against all odds, taking on the colonial secret police itself. (In a brilliant, unexpected move, Pram has the narrator of the fourth novel be the senior Indonesian intelligence-officer assigned by the Dutch to watch the hero and hound him to his end.)

Set in the period 1896–1916, i.e., "before Communism," the novels nonetheless are radically oriented to Indonesia "after Communism." The traces of an older Marxism are perfectly clear in the many episodes of oppression by plantation-owners, vice-lords, colonial officials, native aristocrats, and secret police; and resistance by peasants, small traders, journalists, women, and minorities. But the we (radical Indonesians) versus them (white colonialists and their Chinese pariah-entrepreneur collaborators) axis, which had been more or less *de rigueur* from the 1940s on, on the Indonesian Right as well as Left, is gone. The more sinister figures are most often future-Indonesians, and the heroes and heroines are not only a mixed-nationality batch, but of many types of culture and political persuasion. Perhaps we should not be too surprised at all of this. At the end of the 1970s, when the manuscripts were finished, Pram was fully aware of the roles played by US Congressman Donald Fraser of Minneapolis, Minnesota, and of Amnesty International, in securing his release after twelve terrible years in prison, and of the contrasting indifference of the "actually existing" Communist regimes to his condition. Prison had shown how wide could be the gap between Communist credentials and moral courage. At the same time, he was writing between the lines against a brutal dictatorship that claims legitimacy among its own citizens on the grounds of the total unsuitability of "Western democracy" as well as "Marxism in all its forms" for an Indonesian nation whose origins are said to lie solely and exclusively in a pristine, thousand-year-old, 200-percent native past.

A second style of Indonesian radicalism can be presented more briefly. Pipit Rochijat Kartawidjaja, now in his early forties, is more than a generation younger than Pram. He lives a precarious existence in Berlin, since his passport has long been taken away from him on the grounds of his seditious and insolent writings, but he refuses to renounce his citizenship and seek asylum. He survives partly because he has built up close personal ties with activists among the German Greens and Social-Democrats. In 1965, his father was the pious Muslim manager of a nationalized sugar plantation, who came under strong attack by the Communist plantation-worker union. As a kid in junior high school, he was naturally drawn by family loyalty into the ranks of a local anti-Communist youth group, which, when the time came, joined in the *matanza*. Among the butchers were some of Pipit's classmate friends. The memories of what he had witnessed haunted him, but he found no way to think or act coherently about them till he went to Germany to study electrical engineering. There he married the daughter of a second-rank PKI intellectual who happened to be out of Indonesia when the massacres were under way—but his relations with his father-in-law are fairly chilly. Since the early 1980s he has become famous among Indonesian would-be radicals for three things: a flow of brilliantly satirical articles directed against the dictatorship in Jakarta, of which the most striking feature is their surreal jumbling of regime officialese, street slang, ironical Marxist vocabulary, scatology, and touches of pure poetry. The aim is always to demystify both the regime and its developmental autocratic language. Second, a series of reworkings of, or new imaginations of, those ancient Hindu-Javanese legends that underpin both Javanese tradition and Javanese Tradition. Here again Krishna and Arjuna may equally talk as public information officers, transvestite prostitutes, university professors, or religious charlatans. His rule is "Anything may be said." Third is a justly famous and unique account of his high-school brush with mass murder—on the side of the murderers. He is determined both that the massacres never be forgotten, and that they never become the basis for further massacres one day. He broods on the mindless identifications that brought him and his comrades to the abattoir. This means shattering any easy walls between "us" and "them."

I can only try to give the flavor of this extraordinary text, entitled "Am I PKI or Non-PKI?"[3] by quoting two short passages. First, of the perhaps Communist corpses floating down the Brantas river through his home town: "Usually the corpses were no longer recognizable as human. Headless. Stomachs torn open. The smell was unimaginable. To make sure they didn't sink, the carcasses were deliberately tied to, or impaled upon, bamboo stakes. And the departure of the corpses from the Kediri region down the Brantas achieved its golden age when bodies were stacked together on rafts over which the PKI banner grandly flew." Second, of unemployment at the local whorehouses: "Once the purge of Communist elements got under way, clients stopped coming for sexual satisfaction. The reason: most clients—and prostitutes— were too frightened, for, hanging up in front of the whorehouses, there were a lot of male Communist genitals—like bananas hung out for sale." This is a language utterly repellent both to the old Communists who survived the horror, and to the regime and political groups that carried it out, because it makes unanswerable the question: Am I executioner or not-executioner? But Pipit is not speaking to them, but to a young Indonesia that, if it begins to think radically as surely it will some day, will also have to confront the meaning of "Communism" and "Not-Communism" in the world epoch, not the Indonesian time, of "after Communism."

A NEW SUBJECTIVITY

In contemporary Thailand it is not a question of exorcising ghosts, but rather, perhaps, of summoning them. The end of the CPT came with, as it were, a gentle whimper rather than a terrifying bang. While its fall preceded the collapse of the USSR, the dates were close enough that those reflecting seriously on the one very soon had to reflect upon the other. Radically minded thinkers in Thailand were, in the 1980s and early 1990s, living freely and usually comfortably in a buoyant, crassly rich, thoroughly corrupt, bourgeois semi-democracy, unlike their Indonesian comrades terrorized by a merciless military regime. Most of them ended up with

---

[3] It was first translated into English and published in *Indonesia* 40 (October 1985), pp. 37–56.

respectable positions in the universities, in the mass media, and in the Thai parliament. For them the questions were, characteristically, such as these: Had the CPT gone up in smoke because, as its conservative enemies had claimed all along, it had never been authentically Thai? Had their own attachments to it been the product of naive youthful illusions? Had they completely misunderstood their country's culture and history? Was there nothing left to do but anticipate Fukuyama's dicta, and tag along in the interminable train of Adam Smith and Thomas Jefferson?

One should not be surprised that the most significant radical thinkers were academics, rather than exiled or forbidden imaginers of alternative histories; and that they spent a lot of energy thinking about why they had been politically defeated, and where lay the strength of their successful adversaries. This thinking, nonetheless, was almost always historically focused, if in significantly different ways. Let me briefly discuss just three important texts written recently by Marxist activists of the 1970s, two of them Sino-Thai.

First is that of Seksan Prasertkul, preeminent student activist in the heady days of October 1973, further radicalized in 1973–75, trained briefly in Vietnam and Laos, and a vigorous participant in the armed guerrilla struggle after 1976. Like many of his generation, Seksan had concluded by the 1980s that not only had the CPT leadership been crippled by a "Chineseness" that led it to an absurd and catastrophic identification with "Little Bottle" and his Peking associates; much more importantly, it had, almost without thinking, conceded Thai nationalism to a reactionary Buddhist monkhood, rightwing military leaders, and, above all, the monarchy with its powerful hold on Tradition and the popular imagination. Most fundamental in his view was a construction of Siam's history according to which the nation had been saved from imperialism, and set on the road to modernity, by a selfless and farsighted sequence of monarchs, beginning with the Rama IV we know from Yul Brynner's fanciful impersonations. On the basis of careful and extensive archival research, he produced a "Marxist" thesis that nonetheless turned both traditional left- and rightwing historiographies upside down.[4] He was, for example, able to show that it was precisely the typically despised and marginalized "Chinese" and "Sino-Thai" bourgeoisie of the late-nineteenth and early twentieth centuries that, far from being a gaggle of compradores, had most vigorously defended the autonomy of the Thai economy from British imperialism, whereas the monarchy and aristocracy had caved in to, and then closely collaborated with, that imperialism. He also convincingly argued that the prime impetus towards liberalization and modernization was, in fact, British Free Trade imperialism that had unilaterally, and insouciantly, destroyed the complex of mercantilist monopolies on which the old royal order had been based; at the same time, however, it had thereby taken away from the local bourgeoisie the ground for undertaking its historic political task of destroying the ancien régime. Hence the survival of much of the old social order into contemporary Thailand, and a profoundly false, mystified account of Thai history. Among the CPT's greatest failings, he argued, had been its contempt for serious historical study, its lazy adoption of Stalinist and Maoist vulgar-Marxism, and, hence, its long-run inability to create a hegemonic presence.

Second is Thongchai Winichakul, nationally famous as one of the "Bangkok 18" activists tried and convicted after the bloody coup of 1976 on charges of *lèse majesté*.

---

[4] See Seksan Prasertkul, "The Transformation of the Thai State and Economic Change" (PhD dissertation, Cornell University, 1989).

Thongchai, a Sino-Thai, was sufficiently younger than Seksan that he came intellectually to maturity in what we may look back on as the age of Foucault. His radical assault on the contemporary "ancien régime" therefore came from another direction. By a brilliant micro-study of the maps produced in Bangkok during the nineteenth century, and the institutions and discourses that enveloped them, he was able to show conclusively that the eternal "Thailand" or "Siam" of the hegemonic conservative culture was an invention of the 1870s.[5] Prior to that moment of Foucauldian "break," created by the European imperialists' introduction of Mercatorian mapping, the institution of mathematically based surveying, and the imagining of continuous, invisible borders, dynastic realms had been defined by their centers, and rulers thought of their subjects as infinitely variable, and variously exploitable, assemblies of corvée laborers, foot soldiers, and taxpayers of which the last question asked was their "nationality." This was among the reasons that the armed forces of "Thai" rulers had been so full of Chinese seamen, Malay navigators, Vietnamese archers, and so forth. Thongchai went further to show how, after the 1870s, the new royal mapping service began, in the European manner, to create wholly imaginary historical maps that pushed what he sarcastically called the "Geobody of Thailand" back into the mists of the legendary past. Needless to say, the implications of an argument that, far from continuously, bravely, and patriotically defending Thailand from ancient times, the ruling class had actually invented it a little more than a century ago (and invented it in a style that powerfully supported its hegemony) were decidedly subversive. But Thongchai also saw his aim as the opening of a huge space for many kinds of alternative historical narratives, decentered, localized, egalitarian, and popular. In this way, the road would be cleared for future counter-hegemonic left-wing appropriations of historical subjectivity.

Last is Kasian Tejapira, Sino-Thai, youngest of the three, too young to participate in the *émeute* of October 1973, but a committed underground Marxist in the later 1970s. Unlike the other two, he began his studies more or less as "World Communism" was self-destructing. Perhaps this is the reason why his research, influenced substantially by Walter Benjamin, aimed at a half-ironical recuperation of Thai Marxism in its 1940s and 1950s youthful exuberance. He is the first Thai intellectual to think carefully about the historical relation of the adjective (Thai) to the noun (Marxism), and to recognize that it had always been an illusion to imagine that Marxism moved frictionlessly from culture to culture and language to language. He was also the first to think of Marxism as a certain type of cultural commodity in a capitalist society for which in different eras there was a traceably various "demand" and "supply."[6] His work is of enormous sophistication and impossible here to summarize, but you will get some idea of its thrust from the following quotation from its opening page:

> To English-reading audiences in the present post-Communist world of the final decade of the twentieth century ... [a text] on the now defunct doctrine of Marxism-Communism in its reincarnation in a remote and reposeful Third

---

[5] See his *Siam Mapped: A History of the Geo-body of a Nation* (Honolulu, HI: University of Hawaii Press, 1994).

[6] See Kasian Tejapira, "Commodifying Marxism: The Formation of Modern Thai Radical Culture, 1927–1958" (PhD dissertation, Cornell University, 1992).

World capitalist country almost half a century ago must seem superfluous; even the [text's] "right to exist" appears dubious. After all, during the past decade, the theory, practice, and organization of Marxism-Communism had already proven bankrupt and utterly collapsed in Thailand, like most of its counterparts in other countries round the world. So why bother to read, let alone write, such a lengthy and tedious obituary for this political corpse? My answer is that, though dead, the Spectre of Communism is still haunting us; that having had such a long and stormy engagement with the living, the dead did not depart without leaving deep imprints on the cultural soul of its intimate interlocutors; and that, as such, only through the writing, reading, and understanding of a communist ghost story can the living become fully aware of their own subconscious cultural selves.

He concludes his text like this:

There still exist in Thailand the residual nuts and bolts of cultural resistance that had been tempered and moulded by the long-endeavoured frictional combination of communism and Thai culture. And so long as the modern ravages of dictatorship and capitalism are still visited upon the Thais, there will be enough new radicals to reassemble them into powerful cultural weapons in the fight for their own and humanity's survival and dignity.

It is perhaps here that our three Thai radical academics run into Pram and Pipit. In different ways, they write and write and write, by no means entirely for their fellow countrymen, to retrieve treasurable parts of the debris at the Angel's retreating feet. The modern past, including the Communism that was such a central part of it, must be profoundly reexamined, interrogated, and, where possible, recuperated, as we listen, to borrow from Satyajit Ray, for the roll of distant thunder up ahead.

TWO UNSENDABLE LETTERS[1]

1. REMORSE

In 1957, Siam's prime minister, Field Marshal Plaek Phibunsongkhram, hosted an elaborate "world" celebration of the 2,500th anniversary of the Buddha's Enlightenment. Among the foreign guests was Burma's prime minister. World-famous U Nu went out of his way to visit Ayutthaya, pray at the ruins, and publicly ask forgiveness from the ancestral spirits for the Burmese sacking of the Old Capital. Thais seem to have appreciated this graceful and gentlemanly gesture of remorse, but up to this time the Thais themselves have not managed to be either graceful or gentlemanly. How good it would be if a Thai prime minister could be persuaded to go to Cambodia to ask for forgiveness for the fifteenth-century Thai sacking of Angkor; for Rama III's early nineteenth-century seizure of western Cambodia; for Field Marshal Plaek's annexation of the same region in World War II (in collusion with Japanese militarist imperialism); for plotting the overthrow of Prince Sihanouk and the Khmer monarchy in 1970, in collusion with the Americans; and for protecting, supplying, and heavily arming Pol Pot's murderous Khmer Rouge forces driven out of Phnom Penh by Vietnamese armies in 1979—in collusion with the United States and China. There is plenty of choice! Such a gesture would cost neither a baht nor a drop of blood. Siam would then be genuinely Amazing and up to U Nu's moral example. A further nice gesture of penitence would be to ask forgiveness from Laos for the looting of the Emerald Buddha.

2. MAGNANIMITY

It has to be admitted that, although the Thai people are very gifted in many ways, there are some important areas where they do not shine. This is quite normal. The UK is very proud of its literature, but isn't a chip on the Germans when it comes to music. France is good at architecture but not at sculpture, where the Italians excel. For the Thai, the deficit is in monumental architecture and sculpture. Indonesia has its Borobudur, Cambodia its Angkor, and Burma its Pagan—all "five-star" one could say—but the Thai have never built anything of comparable size, grandeur, and beauty. In itself, this isn't anything to worry about. But when UNESCO (United Nations Educational, Scientific, and Cultural Organization) set up its program for identifying World Heritage Sites and conserving them, trouble started. To date, Siam has only three of these Sakon sites: Ayutthaya Historical Park, Sukhothai Historical Park, and Ban Chiang Archaeological Site, in Udon Thani Province. Two more sites are under review: one is Phuphrabat Park in Udon, the other the "complex" of

---

[1] "Two Unsendable Letters" was originally published, in Thai, by the *Aan Journal*. See Benedict Anderson, "Jotmai thi song mai dai song chabab," *Aan Journal* 3,3 (April–September 2011). Reprinted with permission.

Pimai-Phanomrung-Meuang Tam in Khorat-Buriram, both in "uncivilized" Isan. Neither is really "satisfactory" for Thai nationalist pride, since the Park is notable mainly for its prehistorical cave paintings, and there is no way to demonstrate who the painters were; the Complex was plainly built at the behest of Khmer kings: Pimai, by Jayavarman V and Suryavarman I in the tenth to eleventh centuries; Phanomrung, by Suryavarman II in the twelfth century; and Meuang Tam mainly by Jayavarman V in the tenth century. All of them are Hindu–Mahayana Buddhist, none Theravada Buddhist. Meanwhile, unbearable UNESCO has passed over Bangkok. From this angle it is easy to see why Thai leaders wish to establish claims to Phreah Vihara, which is grander than anything in the Complex, and might be four-star. But the difficulty is that this monumental construction was completed in the early twelfth century by Suryavarman II (builder of Angkor Wat) when the Khmer Empire was at its height. There are a few strange people who argue that Phreah Vihara was "really built by Thai slaves," but there is no evidence for this, so that the Thai state's real claim is based on conquest, not creativity. Hence, the passions over this issue are compelled to rest on modern maps and four square kilometers of once-conquered territory. Bullying Bangkokians need to get over what more and more looks like an inferiority complex. The English are proud of Benjamin Britten and Henry Purcell, but they don't delude themselves that these composers are in the same class as Bach, Beethoven, Brahms, Schumann, Schubert, Verdi, Wagner, and Debussy. British and French imperialists looted a huge number of ancient Greek, Roman, Egyptian, and Assyrian statues, bas-reliefs, and so on, but they do not pretend that these objects are "genuinely British or French." In any case, the day of vast conquests is over. It is time to be magnanimous, and forge ahead. Genuine creativity, open to the world, is what is needed, not delusional jealousy and local-annexationist humbug. Why not sincerely respect the unparalleled monumental achievements of the ancient Khmer, Javanese, and Burmese?

THE STRANGE STORY OF A STRANGE BEAST: RECEPTIONS IN THAILAND OF APICHATPONG WEERASETHAKUL'S *SAT PRALAAT*[1]

In 2005, at the end of a talk for perhaps one hundred professors and students at Thammasat University in Bangkok, I took the opportunity to ask those in the audience who had heard of Apichatpong Weerasethakul and his astonishing film *Sat pralaat*[2] (2004) to raise their hands. I was quite surprised when only about fifteen hands went up. When I made the same request for those who had actually seen the film, only about eight or nine people identified themselves. How was this possible? After all, Apichatpong had won the Special Jury Prize at the 2004 Cannes International Film Festival, which is generally regarded as the single most important international film festival in the world. Nor was this triumph a one-time fluke. Two years earlier, he had won another important prize at Cannes for his *Sut Saneha* (2002).[3] One would have thought that a Bangkok public eager to claim Tiger Woods as a "world-class Thai," even though he speaks no Thai, would have been enormously proud of, and excited by, Apichatpong's impressive success. But no. The question is: why not?

If one watches the very intelligent, biting, and funny mockumentary of "Alongkot," entitled *Room kat sat pralaat* (Ganging Up on *Sat pralaat*, 2004), the beginnings of an explanation emerge.[4] The mockumentary repeatedly (and wrongly)

---

[1] *From the author*: A shorter version of this essay first appeared, in Thai, in *Sinlapawatthanatham* magazine, July 2006, pp. 140–53. I wrote the expanded version specifically for the volume *Glimpses of Freedom: Independent Cinema in Southeast Asia* (Ithaca, NY: Cornell Southeast Asia Program Publications, 2012), pp. 149–63, under the editorial guidance of May Ingawanij. At Apichatpong's request, and in a gesture of friendship to him, May and I granted permission for "The Strange Story of a Strange Beast" to be published also in the Austrian Film Museum's book about him: James Quandt, ed., *Apichatpong Weerasethakul* (Vienna: Austrian Film Museum, 2009).

[2] The English language version of the title is the rather exotic *Tropical Malady*. The Thai title, which means literally "Strange Beast," refers to the shape-shifting were-tiger of folklore and legend. Curiously enough, in the first gay magazines of the early 1980s, one can find the term occasionally used as gayspeak for a penis, or for a male homosexual. When I asked Apichatpong whether he knew of this usage, he said he'd never heard of it, and it must have died out when he was still very young.

[3] *Sut saneha* means something like "total happiness." But the English title given it was *Blissfully Yours*.

[4] "Alongkot" is actually Alongkot Maiduang, who writes film criticism under the penname "Kanlaphraphruek." He has published an excellent, searching survey of Apichatpong's films in his collection of film criticism, *Asia 4: si yod phu kamkap haeng asia tawan ok* [Four Top East

tells watchers that *Sat pralaat* played in only three Thai cinemas (all in Bangkok), and for only one week in each.[5] Why so? A series of short interviews follows with various types of Bangkokian minor celebrities and "talking heads," who say that the film is "great," "extremely interesting," and reaches a "global level above that of other Thai films." (They are responding to the Cannes prize rather than to the film itself.) But their descriptions of it as "surreal," and "*abstrak maak*" (extremely abstract) indicate both that they do not understand the film at all, and also that they are sure that it would be pointless to circulate the film in provincial cinemas. It would be way over the *cheuy* (hick, unsophisticated) heads of the *khon baan nork* (up-country people).

The mockumentary then proceeds to wonderful extended interviews with four genuine *chao baan* (villagers, rubes), three boys, one girl, after they have been brought to Bangkok to see *Sat pralaat* at a special screening put on by the Alliance Française. After the show, the unseen interviewer tells the four that many Bangkok intellectuals find the film "*yaak*" (difficult) and "*lyk lap*" (mysterious), and asks them whether they share that reaction. The *chao baan* all say that the film is great, that there is nothing especially *yaak* or *lyk lap* about it, and that they would like to see it shown at cinemas back home. They say they understand it perfectly. We shall discuss some details of their reactions later on.

Before turning to the question of why both Cannes and the *chao baan* really liked the film, while many Bangkokians did not, it is worth reporting on a brief, amateurish research trip that I recently took with Mukhom Wongthes and May Ingawanij. We decided to spend two days interviewing personnel working at video stores in Chonburi, Samut Sakhon, Samut Songkhram, Ratburi, Suphanburi, and Ayutthaya, in a rough half circle around Bangkok, all about an hour's drive away. These businesses come in two types: stores that are in the rental outlets, mostly in downtown areas, and stores, always located in malls, that sell legal and pirated DVDs at quite low prices. What did we discover? First, that all the people interviewed, except in one small store in Suphanburi, knew about *Sat pralaat*, and a good number had the DVD of this film on their shelves. How did they know about it? Not from newspapers or magazines, but from references on TV and, most interestingly, from customers' requests. When we asked what kind of customers were interested in *Sat pralaat*, the most common answer was "oh, all kinds, mostly families." Others said, "young people who already have jobs"—i.e., in their twenties and early thirties, as opposed to teenagers. But still others said they also had requests from teens. How did the film do with the public? "Not bad," "average," "in steady demand" ... in other words, not outstandingly successful, but not a flop, either. One store clerk told us the customers were mainly male, but others denied there was any difference between the sexes. One should note that these customers were not *chao baan*, but people living in small provincial towns.

At this point we can profitably turn to the film itself, in order to deepen our inquiry. Except for an enigmatic opening scene—in which a group of young soldiers out in the countryside come across a corpse, while the viewers see in the distance the obscure figure of a naked man moving through the high grass on the edge of a jungle—the first half of *Sat pralaat* shows us how a handsome young soldier (Keng)

Asian Directors] (Bangkok: Openbooks, 2005). He has also made a number of short films, which were shown at the Fourth Bangkok Experimental Film Festival in 2005.

[5] Apichatpong has written to me that it was actually shown in only one cinema, the Lido, but for three weeks.

woos an odd-looking youngster (Tong) who works in a local ice-business. The two men never take off any clothes, never kiss each other, let alone have sex, but the film shows us the progress of this *chao baan* courtship in a wide variety of village and small town settings.

Keng and Tong together in *Sat pralaat*[6]

In *Room kat sat pralaat*, the interviewer, pretending to be a middle-class Bangkokian, on several occasions asks the four *chao baan* about this courtship: "Up-country, are there really men who are in love with other men?" The villagers matter-of-factly answer, "Oh yes, it's quite ordinary." All agree that Tong and Keng really love each other, and the shyest of the boys goes so far as to say that the courtship is very "romantic."[7] The girl comments, with a broad smile, that the scene where Keng lies with his head in Tong's lap gave her goose pimples (*khon luk*). The interviewer pretends to be surprised by all this, and asks the girl whether she thinks Keng is maybe a *kratheuy* soldier.[8] She giggles and replies: "Yes, the soldier mostly likely is a *kratheuy*." And Tong? "Well ... he's a bit coy ... um ... mostly likely he is the same." It is plain that the mockumentary is trying to show how ordinary a romance between two young men is up-country, while for some Bangkok people it might seem "trendy, aping the West," "shameful," or even "un-Thai." (But it is the interviewer who introduces the word *kratheuy*, and before he does so the *chao baan* just use *chai* [man] or *khon* [person]; the boys never describe Keng and Tong as *kratheuy*.)

---

[6] Images included in this chapter are reproduced from the Mangpong DVD of *Sat pralaat*.

[7] He actually uses a Thai-ified form of the word "romantic."

[8] *Kratheuy* is an old Khmer word adopted into the Thai language. It means an effeminate man who likes to dress in women's clothes. It should be noted that the *kratheuy* are a recognized group in traditional Thai society, even if usually stigmatized. The word and the concept of "gay" only entered Thai in the late 1970s. Note that the interviewer deliberately poses his question as an oxymoron—could a macho soldier really be an effeminate?—to see how the villagers will react.

"What do you think of the two men courting?" The interviewees in
Room kat sat pralaat

The attentive viewer, however, will quickly notice one very striking feature of the first half of *Sat pralaat*—the soundtrack. For the most part, there is no background music at all: instead, we hear the sounds of everyday country life, motorbikes, dogs barking, small machines working, and so on. The mostly banal conversations are also essentially "background," and one does not need to pay careful attention to their content. Foregrounded are faces, expressions, body language, and silent communication with eyes and smiling lips. The elderly woman whom Tong calls *mae* (mum) shows by her expression that she understands the courtship going on, but she says nothing about it, nor does anyone else in the village. A Bangkok viewer who does not pay attention to the strangeness of the soundtrack could easily dismiss the first half as something very *cheuy*, even wondering when the two men will finally undress and fall into each other's arms.

The real problem for such viewers, however, arises in the astonishing second half of the film, in which almost no human word is spoken. It shows us Keng setting off alone into the jungle to track down a *Sat pralaat*, which has apparently been killing the villagers' cattle. In this half, the soundtrack moves into the foreground, and what we hear, most of the time, are the sounds of the jungle and the sounds that Keng makes as he moves deeper and deeper inside it. Much of this half takes place at night. As Keng tracks the puzzling foot or paw prints before him, human and animal, it seems to dawn on him that they belong to one creature, and this creature is a *seua saming,* or were-tiger, but also, perhaps, Tong. Eventually, he is attacked by a "beast" in whom viewers will recognize the strange naked figure from the opening scene. It is Tong, and completely human in shape, except that he has tigerish stripes self-painted on his face, and he growls and snarls without saying a human word. In the hand-to-hand fight that ensues, Tong is the winner. He drags Keng's stunned body to the edge of a steep hill, and shoves it down. No attempt is made to kill (let alone eat) Keng, who is not seriously hurt at all, and the last we see of Tong is the silhouette of him standing at the top of the hill as if to reassure himself that Keng is really all right. In the remaining part of the film, the viewer follows Keng as he resumes his search, experiencing various "magical" events (a dead, half-eaten cow getting up in perfect condition and disappearing into the jungle, a wise monkey giving him advice, and so on). The film ends with Keng on his knees in the mud looking up at a motionless tiger crouched on the high branch of a tree in front of him. We hear his inner voice saying: "Strange beast, take them, my soul, my blood, my flesh, my memory ... In every drop of my blood there is our song, a song of happiness ... there it is ... do you hear it?"

Keng recovers from the beast's attack, in *Sat pralaat*

What to make of this second part? When I showed the film to some highly educated, bourgeois Filipino gays in Manila, they quickly decided that it was "another type of the now very popular genre of Asian Horror Film," pioneered in Japan, which has spread to Korea, China, Indonesia, the Philippines, and so forth. This is not the reaction of the young up-country people interviewed by Alongkot. Two of the boys have had personal experience of the jungle, and say it is like that: *sayong* (scary) and *tyn-ten* (tense, exciting), sometimes even "hair-raising." They have never seen a *seua saming*, but are sure that "they existed in the old days." The only thing that puzzles them is the very last scene, which they felt was cut short, unfinished.

An even more interesting reaction was that of my bosom friend Ben Abel, an Indonesian Dayak who was raised by his animist grandfather on the fringes of what was then, forty years ago, the immense, largely untouched jungle of Borneo. When I asked whether he found the second half "difficult," he said "Not at all. I understand it perfectly." He had often gone hunting in the jungle, also at night, with his grandfather, his friends, and even alone, and could immediately identify all the animal and bird sounds on the film's soundtrack. "The jungle is where you really have to listen all the time, and keep as quiet as possible yourself. Yes, it can be frightening, but it is like a strange and wonderful world all of its own. You keep wanting to go back. You know you are testing yourself, and learning about yourself, too."

The tiger looks at the hunter, in *Sat pralaat*

When I asked him about were-tigers, he confirmed what Professor Nidhi Iowsriwongse told me from his childhood days.[9]

> The true *seua saming* are always human males. Only men have the spiritual power to change their shapes as they wish. They can appear as tigers, but inside the tiger is a human intelligence and soul. Usually they change shape to escape some danger, mostly from other human beings. There is another kind of *seua saming* which is female, but it is a spirit, not a human being. It can appear as a tiger or as a beautiful woman, but it is always a malevolent spirit.

A very short scene in the second half of *Sat pralaat*—which at first seems inexplicable—shows one of Keng's experienced, older military comrades on night-guard at the fringe of the jungle. Suddenly a beautiful woman appears and asks him to go with her to help her sick mother. But the soldier refuses to leave his post and tells her to go home at once, as the jungle at night is too dangerous for women. As she turns away, the man notices a long tiger tail protruding from under her skirt. She is there, one could say, to show exactly what Tong is not: she is a malevolent spirit, but Tong is human.

---

[9] Nidhi is, by general agreement, Siam's greatest historian, as well as a brilliant essayist, columnist, satirist, and principled social activist.

Drawn image of the were-tiger in *Sat pralaat*. The lines say,
"Once upon a time, there was a Khmer shaman whose magical power
enabled him to change his body into various beasts."

In any event, Ben Abel went on, more or less in the following vein:

You know, if you grow up in or near the jungle, as I did, the distance city people feel between human beings and the animal world is hardly there. You begin to understand the meaning of the different sounds the birds and beasts make hunting, mating, escaping, warning, and so on. Also, people can pass from one world to the other—an uncle who died recently can be recognized in an owl hooting at night. When they sleep, people's spirits leave the body, and bring back messages, sometimes in dreams.

He added that he thought that in the second half of the film, Keng is looking for something, answers to what he doesn't understand about himself, Tong, and many other things. "What is so wonderful about the ending is that Keng's love is so deep that he is willing to give up 'his soul, his body, even his memory,' in other words, a certain idea of human beings as gods, apart from the rest of the natural world. His spirit is in the process of finding Tong's." His final comment to me was: "This is the most wonderful movie I have seen. I can't believe that anyone making a film today could get inside the world in which I grew up, and present it with such perfection. I've never seen anything like it."

In the summer of 2005, I was invited to a scholarly convention in Fortaleza, a remote town on the north coast of Brazil, just in front of the vast, empty, wild interior prairie called the Sertão, which is the source of many Brazilian legends and also films. In the municipal museum, I found something remarkable, an exhibition of tiny hand-sewn booklets of about twenty pages, with rough etchings on the covers. These booklets are sold mainly at bus stops, and to very poor people. They are written in poetry, often beautiful, and usually without a named author. The subjects are typically famous rebellions, massacres, and miracles in the past. But the collection included a section devoted to deeply felt romances between unhappy girls and their goats, and between cowboys and their horses and donkeys. When I asked my educated friends about them, their answer was rather Bangkokian. "Well, you know, on the ranches out there deep in the Sertão, there are no women, so the men either have sex with other men or with their animals. What can you expect?" I replied that this seemed difficult to believe. "What about the poor girl who flees her cruel master in the company of her beloved goat? What about the wife who cuts the throat of her husband's horse out of jealousy? So far as I can tell, the cowboy and his horse are in love, but they don't have sex." "Hmmmm! Hmmmm! I see what you mean." But what did I mean?

If, as it seems to me likely, Apichatpong was trying to make a film, not "about" the world of the *chao baan* of Siam, but rather "from inside" that world, from inside its culture and its consciousness of itself, then one can easily see why Alongkot's four young interviewees found the film both clear and gripping. At the same time, one can see why many of the city people of today's air-conditioned Bangkok find it "difficult," and "mysterious." They are accustomed to films about themselves and their social superiors, with *chao baan* included only for local color or comical side effects. They do not find it at all odd that the poor Isan[10] lad who plays the main role in Prince Chatrichalerm Yukol's otherwise excellent film *Thongpoon khokpo ratsadorn tem khan* (The Citizen, 1977) should be played by a fair-skinned, utterly Bangkokian pretty-boy. They enjoy Tony Jaa's stunning martial arts skill in *Ong Bak* (Prachya Pinkaew, 2003), only adding, as I heard some well-dressed girls say to each other as they came out of the multiplex of the Central Mall in Taling Chan: "What a pity, the hero isn't handsome."[11] They like, up to a point, films using Thai legends, but to be agreeable, these films have to be versions of well-known "legends" and the viewers have to be able to take a certain anthropological distance from them. A good example is the very popular recent version of *Nang naak* (Snake Girl, Nonzee Nimibutr, 1999). It recreates an originally eerie folktale, which everyone knows at least in rough outline, in the Bangkok TV bourgeois manner.[12] The folktale is about a young woman who dies in childbirth while her husband is off at war, and returns as a vengeful widow ghost; the film, however, has the woman so deeply in love with her husband that she returns as a spirit who magically reappears to him as if she were still alive. When the villagers try to get the entranced husband to see the truth, she retaliates violently. So: "It's a love story!" The Snake Girl is not a Strange Beast at all, but a nice

---

[10] Isan is the usual name for northeastern Siam, the poorest region of the country. The people's main language is a dialect that is closer to Lao than Central Thai. The area is especially famous for its popular folk-derived music. Isan people are usually looked down on by Bangkokians as dark-skinned, rough, and unsophisticated.

[11] Tony Jaa's debut was a huge commercial success in Siam, and the film went on to become a hit in the international market as well. Tony comes from Isan and is rather dark-skinned. In fact, he is quite good-looking, but the girls' idea of masculine beauty was centered on skin color. Perhaps I should add that Taling Chan is a part of Thonburi on the western ("wrong-side of the tracks") bank of the Chao Phraya River, facing Bangkok proper. Charmingly still full of gardens, orchards, and canals, it retains a somewhat rural atmosphere, and very few foreigners live there. But it is being gentrified, and the Central Mall is a magnet for west bank, upwardly mobile, middle-class people. Not far away is the "hick" Pata Plaza (alas, it closed in 2010), frequented by the lower classes. If one watches a film there, one hears the audience loudly commenting and cheering on the hero—in the Isan dialect.

[12] The translation is not really satisfactory. *Naak* is not an ordinary snake, but a Naga, a fabulous kind of serpent.

woman who can't bear to leave her husband even after death. Here we can detect Apichatpong's cunning. *Sat pralaat* is, in some respects, legendary in character, yet it is not based on any legend with which people are generally familiar. But he makes sure that the film cannot be Bangkokized and banalized by strategically introducing the theme of *chai rak chai* (men love men).[13] Just imagine if *Nang naak* were turned into *Num naak* (Snake Boy)?

But I suspect there is even more to the resolution of the puzzle with which this essay is concerned. This is the difficult problem of "Thainess" (*khwampenthai*). Some years ago, the famous novelist, poet, and critic Sujit Wongthes's pioneering and iconoclastic book *Jek pon lao* (Jek Mixed with Lao) caused a stir by its argument that "Thainess" was not something truly ancient, but was the relatively recent product of the osmosis between longstanding "Jek" and "Lao" cultures.[14] As I have heard it, Sujit was quite surprised by some of the grateful letters he received from readers. They were touched and stirred by his positive invocation of *khwampenjek* ("*jek*-ness"). (This emotional response reminds one of the reaction of gay men and women to the first serious novels with attractive gay and/or lesbian leading characters. "Finally, we are represented respectfully and honestly.") In the 1990s in Thailand, many books followed in the spirit of "coming out of the *jek* closet." There really was a lot to be proud of in the history and culture of Chinese immigrants to Thailand and their descendants. What is less clear is whether these books were carefully read by many who were not in this closet. We have yet to see "*jek*-ness" celebrated in the textbooks of Thailand's primary and secondary schools.

In the nineteenth century, Bangkok was still overwhelmingly a Chinese city, and, even on the eve of World War II, a majority of the capital city's working class consisted of poor Chinese and Vietnamese immigrants—before the huge waves of migrations from Isan got under way. Today, Bangkok's successful middle classes are heavily *luk jin* (children of Chinese, Sino-Thai, a polite substitute for *jek*).[15]

In many countries the successful urban bourgeoisie is culturally removed from the countryside, yet not ethnically so; but in Siam, this removal is twofold, because of the ethnic origins of the bourgeoisie outside the country.

One might think about it this way: the *luk jin* middle classes are, as elsewhere in the world, energetic, ambitious, and social climbing. Hence, they are inclined to assimilate upwards (at least to a certain point) to the culture of the upper classes and the state. London's House of Lords today is full of successful middle-class people who adore getting titles as Baroness This or Baron That. Bangkok has plenty of female *luk jin* who would love to become *khunying* (a lady, noblewoman).[16] It follows—always up to a point only—that such people are attracted to Thailand's

---

[13] Not to be confused with Thai Rak Thai (Thai Love Thai), the name of ex-Prime Minister Thaksin Shinawatra's huge political party.

[14] The title was deliberately provocative. We have seen earlier how the Lao-speaking people of Isan are often looked down on by Bangkokians, who also regard Laos as a "little brother" of Siam. *Jek* is a derogatory word for Chinese, analogous to "chink."

[15] The upper class, including the royal family, is also of partly Chinese origins, but this is not widely recognized in the public sphere.

[16] After the coup of 1932, which overthrew the absolutist monarchy, all the titles traditionally granted by the king to favored male officials were abolished in the spirit of egalitarian democracy. Oddly enough, titles for females were preserved; it is said that this anomaly was the result of pressure by the wives of a few of the top coup leaders.

"official nationalism"[17]—especially as performed in TV "historical" dramas and ritual celebrations, and through the "River of Kings" advertising machine.[18] They can find themselves reflected in talk shows and television soap operas, but only in their roles as "Thai bourgeois," not *luk jin*. This can't be wholly satisfactory. They are not at all comfortable with popular films like *Tom yam kung* (the name of a popular spicy Thai soup) (Prachya Pinkaew, 2005), a follow-up to *Ong Bak*, which, like *Citizen* before it, features cruel and greedy villains who are patently "*jek*."

Apichatpong's film is, I think, especially "difficult" for today's *luk jin* middle classes not only because they are invisible within it, but also because it presents a form of "Thai culture" with ancient roots that is "below them," as well as alien to their experience. To be able to dismiss it as "meant for Westerners" is to show one's own patriotic Thai credentials against the implicit threat that the film poses. Self-deception is necessarily involved, since the biggest addicts of Western consumerist culture are precisely the Bangkok bourgeois. This suggestion might bring us back to Thammasat University, which is sometimes, half-jokingly, half-proudly, self-described as the Biggest Teochiu University in the world.[19] If my argument in this article is even partly correct, it might help to explain the surprising student–faculty ignorance of, and indifference to, *Sat pralaat*'s amazing achievement.

Readers will have noticed that at several places above I have emphasized the word "today's." I do so because I suspect that the deep alienation of middle-class Bangkok from "up-country culture" is something relatively new. During the opening credits to *Sat pralaat*, Apichatpong mentions his debt to, and affection for, the popular "jungle novels," collectively called *Long phrai*, written in creative imitation of, *inter alia*, Conan Doyle's *The Lost World*, by "Noi Inthanon" during the early 1950s—before the massive elimination of most of Thailand's ancient forests by legal and illegal loggers.[20] In these novels, *set in the present*, were-tigers are often featured as real, if "strange," beasts, though the hunter-hero Khun Sak is quite rationalist and scientific in his outlook. Noi's readers were mostly young, perhaps also mostly male, townspeople of varied ethnic and class origins, who listened to the radio rather than watching TV, went to noisy, crowded cinemas rather than losing themselves in cyberspace, lived contentedly without air-conditioning like everyone else, and were not locked into a mediocre "globalized" consumer culture.[21] This older kind of urban society (middle class and lower class) still exists, up to a point, in places like Samut Sakhon and Ratburi, but it has largely vanished from the City of Angels.

---

[17] "Official nationalism" emanates from the state rather than from popular movements, and was created in Europe in the second half of the nineteenth century by worried dynastic rulers fearful of just such movements. For a detailed discussion, see my *Imagined Communities: Reflections on the Origin and Spread of Nationalism* (London: Verso, 1991), chap. 6.

[18] This machine, celebrating the palaces, temples, and monuments of the rulers of Bangkok, through which the Chao Phraya River flows, was originally aimed at boosting the tourist industry's *son et lumière* shows, luxury river cruises, and so on. But more recently it has evinced as much a political as a commercial character.

[19] The great majority of immigrants from coastal Southeast China have been Teochiu-speakers. In fact the sociological profile of Thammasat is not markedly different from that of other prestigious universities in Bangkok, but Thammasat's cheerful self-mockery is unique.

[20] Noi Inthanon is the pen name of the prolific writer and journalist Malai Chuphinit (1906–63). These novels have a real-life element, as Malai himself was an experienced hunter, and, like the hero of his book, who shares a close bond with his trusted Karen guide, counted among his closest friends the Karens who led him into the heart of the Kanchanaburi jungles.

[21] In fact, these jungle novels were serially broadcast, with great success, in the pre-TV age.

It remains only to consider the Bangkok "talking heads" who claim to like *Sat pralaat* very much, but who can make neither head nor tail of it. On this question, I owe a great debt to conversations with May Ingawanij, who has been engaged in a big research project on Thai heritage films.[22] I mentioned earlier the importance these "talking heads" attach to the high-prestige awards that the film has reaped. As they are inclined to see the matter, these awards mean that "our country" is producing films at the *sakon* (international, global) level; hence, their approval of the film means that they, too, are *sakon*. The difficulty is that this word has different and sometimes antagonistic connotations. Sometimes it means that nowadays Westerners appreciate some Thai films. But which? The unsettling examples are, for example, *Satri Lek* (Iron Ladies, Yongyoot Thongkongtoon, 2000), *Beautiful Boxer* (Ekachai Uekrongtham, 2003), *Ong Bak,* and a cluster of horror films, since their success overseas seems to mean that foreigners think of "our country" as mainly populated by kickboxers, effeminates, transsexuals, and evil spirits. Sometimes it means that foreigners have helped in the making and distribution of "good Thai films." A case in point is the role of Hollywood's Francis Ford Coppola in the final editing, as well as the promotion, of his friend Prince Chatrichalerm's huge, nationalist "heritage" film *Suriyothai* (The Legend of Suriyothai, version 2003). Alas, the film was a flop overseas, and even in "our country" it made a lower net profit than the populist, nationalist, and gory *Baang rajan* (Baang Rajan: The Legend of the Village Warriors, Thanit Jitnukul, 2000), which focused not on royalty but on patriotic *chao baan*.

Sat pralaat might seem a good way out of the difficulties, since it is admired by foreign talking heads, film critics, and well-educated aficionados of "world cinema." "Our kind of people," one could say. Unfortunately, of course, they are not really "our kind of people" because they are situated differently. Sophisticated filmgoers in New York and Tokyo, Paris and Berlin, London and Toronto are accustomed by a long, intellectual tradition not to expect to "understand" a film in any fixed, unambiguous way—hence a culture of what is technically called "multiple readings." They can watch Robert Bresson's astonishing, austere *Pickpocket* (1959) as a film about the alienation of modern urban life, or a Catholic meditation on original sin, or a study of repressed homosexuality, or an allegory of French politics in the 1940s, or ... without excluding the alternatives. Typically, the intellectual commitment is in the aesthetics of the film, a personal and collective investment that French intellectuals share with their Japanese and Canadian comrades.

This kind of investment is much more difficult for Thai intellectuals, who naturally want a Thai *sakon* film to be both "world-class/global" and also Thai. This means that the investment is primarily nationalist, which by definition is not *sakon*. Since the deeper concern is political, there is bound to be some hostility, open or concealed, towards the opening up of anything "truly Thai" to the fluid operations of "multiple readings." Foreigners, like Cannes juror Quentin Tarantino, can admire *Sat pralaat*'s ambiguities and highly sophisticated narrative technique, and yet still happily say "It is wonderful, and I don't understand it." But this position is not easily available for some Bangkok intellectuals, who find it difficult to say both "It is a great Thai film" and "I don't really understand it." After all, they *ought* to understand it in a straightforward, unambiguous way, just because they are "good Thai." Apichatpong has made their position all the more difficult in that, at least in

---

[22] May Adadol Ingawanij, "Hyperbolic Heritage: Bourgeois Spectatorship and Contemporary Thai Cinema" (PhD dissertation, London Consortium, University of London, 2007).

Siam itself, he has insisted in his interviews that his film is completely Thai and rooted in Thai traditions, *including Thai popular film traditions.*[23] The "talking heads" in Bangkok, even if they are not completely committed to River of Kings official nationalism, still find it hard to see why a very expensive product of that nationalism, such as *Suriyothai,* arouses, at the *sakon* level, no interest. It is merely boring "provincial cinema" for anthropological specialists. It says nothing to anyone who is not Thai. Needless to say, these people do not relish the idea that official patriotism at home is regarded as provinciality on the world stage.

Why should this be so? One plausible line of argument is that there is some failure to distinguish between the tourist industry and world cinema. The Thai industry has been spectacularly successful in getting short-term holidaymakers to rush-enjoy the Grand Palace, the spectacular Phra Kaew temple, the ancient ruins of Sukhotai, Phanom Rung, and Ayutthaya, the beach resorts of Patthaya, Phuket, and Samui Island, as well as Thai food, Thai friendliness, and the polymorphous Thai sex industry. But this enjoyment is superficial, as befits holidaymakers, who, while they are in Siam, form a captive market. On the other hand, this local enjoyment by backpackers, retired people, vacationing Japanese businessmen, and others has nothing whatever to do with the satisfactions of global cinephilia. This discrepancy puzzles some educated Bangkokians, who find it difficult to understand why the droves of tourists who are happy to buy tickets—in Bangkok—to see the Grand Palace have no wish at all to see *Suriyothai* in Berlin or Rotterdam, where these same viewers do not regard themselves as tourists.

Probably this is why Bangkok "talking heads," in their double position as spokespeople for "Thainess" and as members of *sakon* culture, tend to find themselves trapped. Since *sakon* culture admires Apichatpong, they wish to admire him too. But they cannot take any pleasure in the idea that they "do not understand him." The way out of the dilemma is to insist that *Sat pralaat* is "difficult," and "mysterious." We can thus see why it is highly "abstract" and/or "surreal," and therefore completely unsuitable for circulation in the rural and small-town interior of the country.

One can hardly doubt that Apichatpong enjoys all this. This is why his title is so perfectly multivalent. Who, in today's Siam, are the "strange beasts?" Awkward question, no doubt about it.

POSTSCRIPT: RECEPTIONS ELSEWHERE

Events in Siam since the coup d'état of September 2006 have made it plain that discussing the reception of *Sat pralaat* among different strata and regions of Thai society is no longer sufficient, if, indeed, it ever was. Political conflicts have to be taken into account. Early in 2007, Apichatpong's latest big film, *Saeng sattawat* (Light of a/the Century, but given the English title *Syndromes and a Century*), which had been shown very successfully at various *sakon* film festivals, came up for review by the state board of censors (a mix of police, bureaucrats, and intellectuals-of-a-sort), which decided that it could only be released in Siam if four brief scenes were eliminated. In two of these scenes, Buddhist monks are depicted in ways that the

---

[23] Until quite recently, educated Thai rarely watched commercial Thai films, which they regarded as low-class, unsophisticated, and meant for the "up-country" market. Their tastes ran rather to the products of Hollywood and Hong Kong.

censor-viewers could not tolerate—in the first, one sees a young monk strumming on a guitar, while in the second two monks of different ages are pictured in a public park playing with a battery-powered toy UFO. The other two scenes take place in a hospital.[24] First one sees a tired, middle-aged lady doctor at the end of a grueling day pulling a bottle of liquor from its hiding place in a prosthetic leg and sharing a drink with a couple of younger colleagues. Later, one sees a young doctor passionately kissing his girlfriend, while the camera drifts briefly down to the man's middle, where one hand is clutching an erection concealed inside his trousers.

The censors are film-viewers of a special type. They are not interested in either quality or commercial success. While they usually share the Bangkok middle class's disdain for "up-country people," they also, as an arm of the state, share the bureaucracy's traditional paternalism. Thus, they feel entitled to decide what is good for the "infantile" masses of the people to see on the screen—above all, when the films are Thai rather than foreign. (For them there can be nothing less agreeable than Apichatpong's films, which are deeply sympathetic to "up-country people" and keep the state almost invisible.) They are not required to justify their decisions publicly. It is enough to say that scenes to be deleted are "offensive" to their nannyish notions of "Thai" propriety. In fact, Thai newspapers are full of scandals about monks' sexual misdeeds, financial manipulations, drug-abuse, and so on. But normally the names of these monks are mentioned, i.e., as individuals, and their activities are accessible only through print. What Apichatpong had done, however, was to show in visual motion some unnamed (so to speak, "any") monks enjoying themselves in a way that would interest no scandal-hungry newspaper. Even if in real life one can easily observe monks having fun, the official nationalist–Buddhist position is that monks must be dedicated, wise, austere, and always serious people. So Apichatpong's gentle satire could be regarded as lèse-Buddhism. The Thai are a liquor-loving people, and it would be very surprising if some doctors, at the end of the working day, do not have a drink or two in their hospitals, and take a little time out to kiss their girl- or boyfriends in a private nook. But the state tries to sustain the prestige of Thai hospitals and the public's trust in Thai doctors by cultivating a public image of authority, austerity, wisdom, and seriousness.[25] So to speak, secular monks.

This was not the first time that Apichatpong had run into censorship, as we shall see, but it was the first occasion where this censorship came from the state. Doubtless to the board's surprise, Apichatpong refused to cut anything, and withdrew his request for permission to circulate the film in his own country.[26] This was also the

---

[24] The film, which I have not yet seen, is said to be an indirect tribute to Apichatpong's parents, both doctors, who worked in a hospital in Khon Kaen, the "capital" of Isan, while he was growing up. However, I was able to view the banned scenes at an open meeting in May 2007, designed to rally filmmakers and film-lovers against the whole arbitrary system of censorship.

[25] Apichatpong informs me that the censors invited the Medical Council of Thailand and the Council of Buddhist Monks to a special private showing. These organizations are controlled by elderly conservatives, and are by no means representative. Apichatpong slyly wonders whether the Council of Buddhist Monks representatives had ever watched those popular local horror movies that feature monks running amok.

[26] In an unguarded moment, one of the censors, a scaly Thammasat University teacher who doubles as a henchman to "Sia Jiang" (see below), allowed himself to be interviewed on tape. His remarks showed that he had it in for Apichatpong, whom he said was "too big for his boots," "pretending to be a big international star," "running down religion," and "focusing on faggots."

first time any Thai filmmaker had not caved in, or attempted to bargain with, the censors.

One cannot be sure, but it is possible that the board might have acted differently prior to the September 2006 coup. It did not, after all, either censor or ban *Sat pralaat*. To be sure, it has long had double standards, such that foreign, especially Hollywood, films often circulate uncensored, despite their gory violence and fairly graphic sex, while Thai films have been much more strictly policed. But since the coup, censorship of the media has become much more intense, elaborate, and arbitrary. Furthermore, the coup leaders, facing their enemy Thaksin's populist nationalism, have felt it necessary to enforce (and reinforce) the traditional official nationalism, with its three icons, Monarchy, Buddhism, and Nation—a recipe for pharisaism, euphemism, and conformity. It is also possible, if not likely, that Apichatpong might earlier have acted differently, at least less brusquely; but maybe in 2007 he saw his own troubles as like those of many others whose freedom of expression was being repressed by the coup-makers and the state apparatus.

One could thus speak of an increased politicization. Though *Sut saneha* is ostensibly apolitical, the central male character is a poor, illegal migrant from Burma, who is warned by the two Thai women who protect and love him that he must pretend to be dumb so that his speech does not give him away. Such Burmese workers, fleeing poverty and interminable repression in their own country, have often been the victims of ruthless Thai employers, police, military men, and gangsters, and subject to social hostility. Without explicitly saying so, the film is on the side of the Burmese boy and his Thai friends. *Sat pralaat* is also seemingly apolitical, but this was the first Thai film that focused seriously and powerfully on the love between two men, and so broke with a long-standing official–national taboo.[27]

Hence, after rejecting the demands of the censors, Apichatpong, along with colleagues, friends, admirers, and activists, began, in May 2007, to organize a serious protest against the whole system of arbitrary censorship, demanding at the very least the establishment of a rational, clear, and even-handed rating-system for Thai (and foreign) films. (See Chalida Uabumrungjit's essay for the outcome of this campaign.)

Yet in some ways state censorship may be less insidious than that practiced by another, less visible, set of "viewers" who mostly generally share the censors' indifference to quality, but are deeply interested in commercial success. These are the Bangkok entrepreneurs who control, more or less successfully, financial backing for new films, own the cinemas and multiplexes of the country, and regulate the production and, especially, distribution of VCDs and DVDs. They are also people rich enough to have formidable connections within the state apparatus. Essentially we are speaking of a sometimes rivalrous cartel of three "family" commercial empires owned by … *luk jin!* This essay is not the place to go into much detail, since our focus is on Apichatpong and *Sat pralaat*. Suffice it to say that the "big enchilada" is the vain "Sia [Boss] Jiang," aka Jiang Sae Tae, aka Somsak Techaratanaprasert, who controls Sahamongkol Film International, a company that handles the production of local films and the import of popular foreign films. He also indirectly controls the SF chain of cinemas and multiplexes, which has wide influence through its power to

---

[27] It is a matter of public representation. At least two of Siam's post-World War II prime ministers have been widely known to prefer their own sex to the opposite, but the media never showed photographs of them with their lovers or referred directly to their sexual tastes.

decide what films will or will not be shown. It seems that early on Apichatpong approached "Boss Jiang" to get funds for his films. He must have been partly successful, since the Thai DVD and VCD of *Sut saneha* were produced by a distributor contracted to Sahamongkol. Apichatpong reports that the contract included a clause that any cuts required his consent, but, in fact, he was never consulted and the film was mangled. Busy preparing *Sat pralaat*, and feeling helpless, he let the mangled version go through. The authentic DVD, produced in Paris, has not been widely circulated in Siam. The final scene of the film never had a chance to be censored by the state, as private enterprise had already decisively intervened and deleted it.[28] Not surprisingly, Apichatpong and "Boss Jiang" fell out. This is why the only Thai filmmaker to have won a top prize (actually two!) at Cannes has never been included in the lavishly funded official delegations from Bangkok to the festival.[29] It is also probably the reason why *Sat pralaat* was never shown up-country, and shown only for three weeks, at one cinema, in Bangkok.

This fate of *Sat pralaat* cannot easily be explained by citing the actions of Sahamongkol alone, but only by considering, as well, his collusion with another component of the film cartel. This is the Major Cineplex Group, controlled by Vicha Poolvoralaks and his kinsmen, which owns the largest chain of multiplexes (perhaps 70 percent of all multiplexes in Thailand). Major is mainly a very powerful exhibition and distribution empire.

The last member of the cartel is GTH, a film production company created by a merger (compelled by the industry's financial problems) of the production houses Tai Entertainment and Hub Ho Hin into the integrated entertainment empire GMM Grammy, headed by "Ah Koo" Paiboon Damrongchaitham. GTH differs from the other members of the cartel in that its leader, Ah Koo, acting on good advice, has championed a number of talented young Thai directors who are using sophisticated technical methods, but primarily doing edgy mainstream films (for example, *Dek hor* [The Dorm, 2006] and *Beautiful Boxer*). Many of these films are quite good, as well as popular, yet they are nothing like Apichatpong's creations. It is interesting, however, that Ah Koo provided 25 percent of the budget for *Sat pralaat*—at the last minute—allowing it to be finished just in time for Cannes.[30] But GTH does not have the distributional power of Sahamongkol and Major, and so does not seem to have functioned as Apichatpong's censor.

In the end, the cartel probably matters more than the state board of censors because it operates out of the limelight and is rooted in huge, entrenched financial interests. Apichatpong's genius and reputation have enabled him to bypass the cartel at one level, by providing him with financial backers overseas, mainly in Western

---

[28] The Burmese man and the two women have escaped, for a time, into the jungle, where they happily bathe in a little stream, chat, and doze off. The man falls into a deep, exhausted slumber. The younger woman, his lover, watches him with a contented smile on her face, fishes his penis out of his shorts, and caresses it without waking him up.

[29] Since the time of writing this essay, Apichatpong has won the topmost prize at Cannes, the Palme d'Or, for *Uncle Boonmee Who Can Recall his Past Lives*.

[30] As usually happens when three large businesses merge, the leaders of GMM, Tai Entertainment, and Hub Ho Hin share seats on the new executive board and have brought some of their staff with them into the conglomerate's structure. Opposition to the daring of Ah Koo led him to create an autonomous company called Tifa to outflank this opposition. Alas, Tifa has recently been closed down.

Europe. But these backers can only help him make the films, not distribute them to his countrymen.

SELECTED FILMOGRAPHY

Room kat sat pralaat (Ganging Up on *Sat pralaat*, "Alongkot," 2004)
Saeng sattawat (Syndromes and a Century, Apichatpong Weerasethakul, 2006)
Sat pralaat (Tropical Malady, Apichatpong Weerasethakul, 2004)
Sut saneha (Blissfully Yours, Apichatpong Weerasethakul, 2002)

BILLBOARDS, STATUES, T-SHIRTS: REVOLVING IRONIES[1]

A few days ago, I took some foreign friends to tourist-ridden Kanchanaburi, and, as usual when I visit this very ordinary place, I asked our driver to stop at the hospital on one side of the broad street that bisects the town. I wanted, as always, to pay my respects to the blackened little statue of Colonel Phraya Phahon in the hospital's crowded parking lot. What surprised me this time was that two middle-aged women were on their knees, with deeply bowed heads, while making the offerings usually made to spirits or Buddha images. Phahon's pedestal was covered with many other quasi-religious objects. How could this have happened? Had the Colonel somehow become supernaturally beneficent? Is this why his image is attached to a chilly place of modern suffering, hope, despair, and uneasy thankfulness?

Statue of Colonel Phraya Phahon in Kanchanaburi province
Source: http://www.phahol.go.th/index.php/activity/211-2013-02-19-09-01-52

Colonel Phraya Phahon was born in Bangkok, but his wife was born and raised in the province of Kanchanaburi, to which he became very attached. When he became prime minister, he set up a paper factory there, using Kanchanaburi's vast forests to create jobs and cut the cost of paper (till then Siam depended on expensive

---

[1] "Billboards, Statues, T-shirts: Revolving Ironies" was originally published, in Thai, by the *Aan Journal*. See Benedict Anderson, "Paikosana, anusawari, seuyeud: Kwam yonyang wienwok," *Aan Journal* 4,1 (April–June 2012). Reprinted with permission.

imported paper). The local people were grateful for his efforts to develop the province's economy, took pride in him, gave his name to the first modern hospital there, and paid for his statue there after his death. But he is indelibly famous as the leader of the military–civilian alliance that bloodlessly overthrew the Thai absolute monarchy in June 1932, and as the country's first "commoner" prime minister from 1934–38. Under his benign rule, Siam acquired a constitution, a partially elective parliament, and a cluster of new laws engaging the population of the country as something new—"citizens." No scandal surrounds his prime ministership, his honesty has never been impugned, and he never killed anyone. He did not outstay his welcome, retired, and died when he was only fifty-two years old. A political leader with these progressive and system-changing achievements would normally be a "national hero." But, so far as I know, there is no monument to him in the capital, or anywhere else in the country. He survives iconically only in his home town.

Statue of Field Marshal Plaek Phibunsongkhram
Source: http://phetchabun-yaniga.blogspot.com/2012/01/phetchabun.html

His statue has its own purity. He was a short man in life, and remains so in his image. He wears a simple military uniform in the style of the 1930s, and his stance is calm and gentle, with no annoying ornaments and melodramatic poses. But he is not unique. Pridi Banomyong, the leader of Phahon's civilian partners, who had many achievements of his own in various ministerial posts, has a lone statue on the premises of Bangkok's Thammasat University, which he personally founded and directed during the late 1930s. Also calm, benign, and unpretentious. You could say he too has been demoted to a "local" status, admired only by Thammasat's students and some professors. Phahon's successor, Field Marshal Plaek Phibunsongkhram, prime minister from 1938 to 1943, and 1948 to 1957, has a solitary statue at the military base in provincial Lopburi, while the brutal General Phao, who turned the police into a serious rival with the military in the 1950s, has his own quiet statue inside the National Police Headquarters in Bangkok. It is as if "national heroes" or "great men and women" are difficult to find in sculpted form anywhere in the country. Moreover, one will rarely find any T-shirts inscribed with their names and faces.

A few years ago, I happened to be driven from Prajuab province (in the middle South) to the capital on the eve of a national election. The South is generally regarded as the stronghold of the Democrat Party, so I expected a massive billboard display along the entire route, glamorized faces of prominent leaders, promised new programs, etc. But, to my surprise, I saw almost nothing of the kind. There were huge numbers of billboards, indeed, but they were monopolized by representations of three powerful socio-economic forces. The closer I got to the capital, the more the billboards were dominated by the Real Estate conglomerates. Endless photographs of "for sale" luxurious mansions and condominiums, with glittering swimming pools, magnificent interiors, and grandiose gardens: but never a person. The buildings, brand new, are waiting for "you." The second cluster was more conspicuous in the provinces. The billboards were advertisements for magic amulets

Amulets advertised on Thai billboards
Sources: http://tamroiphrabuddhabat.com and www.pidthong.com

featuring grim-faced abbots or benign representations of the Buddha, and mass produced in dozens of different monasteries/temples. Prices of different amulets were on careful display, along with accessible websites and cell phone numbers for the crowd of buyers. But, generally speaking, the finally dominant billboards were reserved for pictures of the King, sometimes with the Queen, and less commonly with the most popular princess. If you were either ignorant or a bit crazy you might take these billboards as part of the electioneering process. However, I did not notice any royal or amulet T-shirts. On the trip to Kanchanaburi and back, I noticed that this billboard pattern has not changed at all.

It happens that every year I spend some time in Japan and in the Philippines, and I have tried to draw some comparisons, so as to decide whether the Thai pattern is something peculiarly unique, and if so, why. Last spring, I went with some old friends for a short holiday on the island of Shikoku, about which I knew little except that it once had a flourishing business in maritime piracy. Today there is even a nice Pirates Museum for local and foreign visitors. Looking for a few souvenirs along the southeastern coast, I was amazed by the number of T-shirts on sale featuring elegantly the features of Ryoma.

Royals on Thai billboards: the King
Source: http://2bangkok.com

Royals on Thai billboards: the Queen
Source: http://2bangkok.com

Ryoma is famous because of his role in the violent campaign of the 1860s to overthrow the ("national") Shogunate controlled for a quarter of a millennium by the Tokugawa lineage. He was fascinated by Western guns and typically went around wearing a belt with two of the legendary cowboy pistols produced in the United States. He was a prolific and gifted letter writer to his girlfriend and to his comrades, and these letters, published after his death, added to his fame. He was assassinated by the Shogunate's agents when still very young. Since the fall of the Shogunate is generally regarded as a key moment in Japanese history, and the beginning of the country's fabulous economic and military modernization, you might think that this romantic figure would be celebrated in Tokyo by a colossal statue. A national hero, for sure, I thought to myself. But there was no such statue. Then I discovered that in Northwestern Shikoku there were no representations of Ryoma at all, especially no T-shirts. Ryoma had become, at some level, a "local hero," even if a TV series on his life was a great hit.

A face towel featuring Ryoma. Source: http://www.bloomberg.com

In fact, Japan has all kinds of statues of prominent figures dating from the 1860s on, but they are socially and politically handled in the way that Pridi and Colonel Phahon have been. What Japan does not have is something like the Pantheon in Paris, which celebrates, collectively, a cluster of "great Frenchmen" like Voltaire and Rousseau, Victor Hugo and Zola, Jean Moulin and Jean Monnet. (The United States later followed suit, if clumsily, with the gigantic collective faces of George Washington, Thomas Jefferson, Abraham Lincoln, and Theodore Roosevelt at Mount Rushmore.) Why not? I think the answer is fairly obvious. "National heroes" are blocked by the Emperorship. Formally, all these heroes have the status of servants of the Tennos. Only the latter can represent Japan. The whole imperial system is based on the untouchable superiority of the sovereign, even if Japan is now a modern democracy. Any attempt to create a national Pantheon, with its multiple, collective distinction, could be regarded as a kind of gentle *lèse majesté*. But the emperors do not appear on billboards.

The Philippines seems to me to be the exact opposite of Siam. The country is unique in Southeast Asia for having no history of a powerful, domestic, dynastic state. No Spanish king ever came within ten thousand miles of Manila. Only paintings (very bad) were paraded once a year in the colonial capital. Up until the revolution started by Andres Bonifacio in 1996, public images were controlled by the all-powerful Catholic church: hence, the representation inside and outside churches of figures and scenes drawn from the Bible, and from Catholicism's obsession with the Virgin Mary and various post-Bible saints. Soon after Emilio Aguinaldo was chosen to be the president of an anticipated independent Republic, monuments in memory of the martyr and brilliant novelist, poet, and intellectual José Rizal began to be built. During the period of American colonization, the cultivation of secular saints (national heroes) began. In almost all Filipino towns today one will find statues dedicated to the "national heroes" of that revolutionary era. What is most striking is that these statues are not tied to locality—you can find statues of Rizal in places that the Father of the Nation never went. Other persons who sacrificed for the nation, if not as popular as Rizal, can be found in many townships. The key thing is that these monuments emerge from local decisions, and donations, not from the state. Every Filipino knows the names of Apolinario Mabini, Andres Bonifacio, Antonio Luna, Emilio Aguinaldo, and so on. Against this tide even the Catholic hierarchy had to bend: there is no "national" saint in the Philippines.

The Philippines Pantheon in Manila
Source: http://jesusabernardo.blogspot.com

Yet there were difficulties. During the early years of the American colonial regime, plans were drawn up for a Philippine Pantheon. This small Pantheon still exists in Manila, but it is a shell of what its designers anticipated. Over the years, families quietly removed the bones of some national heroes to their home towns. (The niches are now mostly filled with the toys, tin cans, and kitchen utensils of the caretakers who use the Pantheon as a kind of flat.) But the key thing is that these provincializations came from "below," not from the center of national political power. What one sees here is the collective logic of public imagery in republican institutions. As soon as one sees one hero, one is obliged to think immediately about others. Sukarno is unimaginable without Hatta, Gandhi without Nehru, U Nu without Aung San, Jefferson without Franklin, and vice versa.

In the later 1930s a kind of Thai Pantheon was actually created. A new "Buddhist" temple was built (in Bangkok) that was initially given the name of Democracy Temple. It had many unusual features, but the most significant was a "double chedi" (one inside the other), where the outer, circular walls were lined with niches for the ashes of the country's preeminent "commoner" citizens, while the inner chedi contained some relic of the Buddha. Hence, the temple's name was changed to Wat Phrasrimahatat (Lord Buddha's Relic Temple). Most of the ashes ended up being the remains of military men and sometimes their spouses, like Field Marshal Phibunsongkhram and his celebrated wife, La-iad. Conservative critics denounced the "modern" temple form as irreligious. No new ashes have entered these niches for a long time, with only one exception, when Phoonsuk Banomyong, devoted and loyal wife of Pridi Banomyong, passed away recently. The wat is not designated as a great gem for tourists to admire, and its main function is merely being the funeral home for officers of the Thai military. Today, it is a melancholy residue of another time, and without a future.

Interior of a *chedi* of "Democracy Temple," Bangkok
Source: www.manager.co.th

I have been watching billboards of the Philippines for a long time. They look to be totally different from those in Siam. The most striking aspect of the former is the almost total absence of the still very powerful Catholic hierarchy. The devastating attack of Luther on the Church's corruption has yet to be paralleled in Siam. The modern republican culture of the Philippines makes the brazen sale of "pardons," amulets, etc., really impossible at the national level. What makes the Philippine Church's position really difficult is, however, not the absence of a modern Luther. The deep enemy is a totally secular consumerist capitalism. Philippine billboards offer ample spaces for Real Estate, as well as claims of beneficence by ephemeral local politicians (this bridge was arranged by Congressman X or Senator Y), almost all with semi-criminal faces, not to speak of equally ephemeral claims to the same effect by short-term-limited presidents. But most of the billboards address consumers. In the 1990s, most of these billboards featured sexy, half-naked girls imploring women to buy brand-name bras, shampoos, lipsticks, perfumes, panties, gowns, powders, marital beds, and so on. After 2000 came the energetic counter from the other sex—almost naked, beautiful young men imploring men to buy minimalist underwear, deodorants, unbuttoned shirts, and super-tight jeans, as well as shampoos, perfumes, haircuts, cigars, and so on. There is almost nothing in current Filipino political culture that would seriously try to block the trend. The billboards are fine with everyone, at least so long as the models are understood to be genuine mestizos with "white"ish skins, American or Chinese faces, and so forth. They also have to be anonymous, i.e., not national-heroic. (The pity is only that Filipino T-shirts are just as blank, conformist, and witless as their Thai counterparts.)

Philippine billboards
Sources: http://carlosrull.com and newshopper.sulekha.com

In Thailand, one can detect the basic reason why Thai billboards do not reflect popular, "steamy" consumerist culture, even though no one thinks of Siam as a country of Puritans. It is a matter of juxtaposition. The iconography of the amulet industry is indicative. The core doctrine of classical Buddhism is that the sensory (including sensual) world is an illusion, the site of greed, sexual obsession, status-hunger, and other stupidities. This is why the advertisements almost always feature very old, cold-eyed abbots who seem to be near death. Beautiful images of the gentle Buddha confirm the rewards awaiting those who understand "illusion." The amulets themselves belong to the "underground" animist beliefs that underpin the classic tradition. For the right prices, one's amulets promise a gamut of non-illusionary aims—business triumphs, promotions, successful exams, sexual prowess, good luck, safety from criminals, etc. The advertisements are tactful about what exactly amulets can achieve. A useful compromise has been achieved. Then imagine the shock of the sudden appearance of advertisements featuring "killer" handsome male torsos selling deodorants, and half-naked, pretty women selling Vuitton bags and Chanel perfumes.

The same logical principle operates behind the barrage of decorous royalist ads. If one visits the National Museum in Bangkok, one will experience a technically skillful panorama of Siam's history. What strikes the casual visitor is that almost no one is mentioned by name except for five or six monarchs. The existing chronicles, however, indicate how precarious were the lives of polygamous rulers, many of whom were dethroned, assassinated, or expelled by their own relatives. The visitor will find no mention of poets, chroniclers, generals, philosophers, Buddhist saints, immigrants, film stars, and so on. It is as if nothing worthy of note was achieved unless it was engineered from on high. But the museum is monopolized space. Siam's streets are another matter. Nothing could be more jarring than royalty billboards intersecting with those featuring beautiful, ever-young, nameless commoner models along with shampoo.

Only smiling Real Estate slips smoothly along in the parade of public images in both Siam and the Philippines. It threatens no one, and its allure is attached to no persons.

Real estate billboards
Source: http://thailand-business-news.com

MUNDANE HISTORY/
JAO NOK KRAJOK[1]

Anocha Suwichakornpong's two titles for her internationally admired film already warn us that nothing in it is going to be straightforward. "Mundane" and "History" seem to be in a contradictory relationship, since the latter is a matter of continuing transformation, development, and surprises over the ages, while "mundane" usually means everyday life, full of constant repetitions leading nowhere in particular. But "mundane" is also derived from the Latin word for the world or the universe. As we shall see, the film firmly links everyday human repetitions with those of the cosmos. *Nok krajok* seems simple enough at first, meaning "sparrow," the most mundane of all wild birds. But it is also used slangily (mostly among males) as a mildly derogative insult. If one calls an acquaintance *Ai krajok*, it means he is "useless, hopeless, a nobody, a good-for-nothing." The up-to-date Thai dictionary offers *Nok krajok liang mai cheuang*, meaning someone who is disloyal or untamable, backed by the idea that you can feed a sparrow but it will never become a reliable pet. One title thus foreshadows the links between everyday repetitions in human life, like birth and death, and the grand cycles of the cosmos. The other title looks forward to individual rebelliousness, responsibility, and some kind of freedom.

The opening story line, such as it is, pivots on the endless repetitions in the everyday life of a household consisting of Khun Thanin, a widowed bourgeois professor, Ake, his crippled son, Khun Somjai, the housekeeper, and Kaew, the Isan cook. The chilly Thanin, with his expressionless face, says only a few repetitive words, and every day leaves the house for hours to attend unlikely meetings on campus. Somjai is an intelligent women who looked after Ake when he was a child, tries to manage the household's everyday cycle of meals, cleaning, and laundering as best she can, but there is an intimation that after Thanin was widowed, she became the man's mistress but no longer excites him. Kaew at one point says that she is thinking of getting another job, but it doesn't seem too likely. Ake, a sullen, intelligent young man, is the victim of an unexplained accident in which he lost the ability to stand or walk. Most of the time he therefore lies in bed, without any hope of a normal life, let alone a fine career and a happy family of his own. It's clear that he loathes his father and usually refuses to talk to him, but exactly why is never explained. He is the film's would-be sparrow.

But also from the start the monotony is constantly broken and in some places replaced by suspense through Anocha's ingenious handling of the visual images. The most important, I think, is her zigzagging use of time, so that the watcher often

[1] "Mundane History/*Jao nok krajok*" was originally published, in Thai, by the *Aan Journal*. See Benedict Anderson, "Jao Nokkrajok/Mundane History," *Aan Journal* 4,4 (April–June 2013). Reprinted with permission.

can't tell whether the time of Scene A follows Scene G or vice versa, though at some level they feel connected. Almost as significant is her manner of keeping scenes very short and never "fully finished," so that almost all are enigmatic, with so many questions that are not directly answered. It is not that we are waiting for violence, confessions, tears, or intrigues, which we soon feel will never transpire. The suspense is perfectly attached to the tedium.

Khun Thanin alone at the table

Pun, Kaew, Kaew's young relative, and Khun Somjai together at the table

The implied monotony of the grand house is changed almost immediately with the arrival of Pun, a strong and thoughtful man born in Phrae, but successfully trained as a male nurse at the University of Khon Kaen. From now on, it is he who handles the medicine for Ake, as well as washing and cleaning him up, feeding him, handling the wheelchair, carrying him up and down stairs, keeping him company, and, perhaps, giving him the strength not to despair of his life. We never know whether Pun had a predecessor. At first he does not intend to stay long. He says to his wife (girlfriend?) on the telephone that the house is so beautiful, but the people in it are "so soulless." But eventually he tells Kaew in the downstairs kitchen that now he likes the place and will stay on.

The two men gradually get to know each other, and then even like one another. But one visible outcome is that Ake refuses ever to have dinner with his father in the second floor dining room. When Somjai tells him that his uncle and aunt are waiting to come up to see him, the lad says icily "Just tell them I'm asleep and that goes for any other visitors." When Somjai protests, he brutally says "You can go." Now Pun and Ake are alone together. The male nurse tries quietly to break through Ake's painful obsession with himself by saying wistfully that when he was young he wanted to be a newspaper reporter, then a professional photographer after trying to be a writer, but he says nothing about his adult life. Ake responds that he also wanted to be a writer, then took courses to become a film director. Pun goes on to say that his father absconded when he was two years old, while his mother wasn't very nice; she was strict with him, and gave all her love to his baby sister. He has no family (saying nothing about his girlfriend). He seems to be trying to get Ake to see that other people have damaged families, aborted dreams, and a lot of loneliness.

The relationship between the pair has an unexpected side to it. Early on, while Ake is having dinner in bed and sees that Pun is watching over him, the lad says irritably "Aren't you going to feed me?" Knowing that the lad can perfectly well feed himself, Pun stands silent. Ake throws a kind of tantrum by hurling his spoon to the floor, and then commanding "Feed me!" (But we don't see Pun doing anything of the kind.) Later he tells Pun that he has Googled him, and found four entries, all about his male nurse diploma in Khon Kaen. It becomes obvious that Ake enjoys being carried in the arms of Pun, especially when they go down to the garden: he throws his arms around Pun's neck and lays his happy head on the nurse's chest. One afternoon there is a sudden downpour while Ake and Pun are in the garden. Ake refuses to get back into the house. Pun takes the bulk of the rain and is soaking wet by the time they get upstairs together. Suddenly Ake tells him that he looks like a waterlogged duck, and starts to sing a children's song about wet ducks. Pun parries calmly by replying "What nursery are you in?"

Ake is now almost never alone, with one exception. Anocha shows him in his bathtub trying to masturbate, and in a rage of frustration when he cannot get the smallest erection. Finally there is a powerful enigmatic moment—when Pun finds Ake with a heavily bandaged right hand, he simply removes the bloody bandage, replacing it with a clean one. What perhaps explains this scene comes later on in the film, when we see Somjai quietly reminding Ake that she took care of him as a child, urging him to come to terms with his condition, and finally asking him to realize that his father has suffered a lot too. Ake says nothing, but we know he loathes his father, and the scene abruptly ends. But it is almost certain that he "must then have" broken the silence by ferociously crushing the glass on the table with his right hand, and that it is Somjai who bandaged it.

Ake in the bathtub

Almost everything mentioned in the paragraph above—tantrums, silly nursery rhymes, childish ordering people around, and the happiness of being carried in someone's arms—suggests that what Ake misses above all is his deceased mother. Anocha makes sure that, with one odd exception, no one mentions her, let alone says anything significant about her. Near the start of the film there is a brief "downstairs" would-be-gossipy supper attended by the "staff"—Khun Somjai, Kaew, Kaew's amiable dumb nephew, and Pun. Kaew says that Ake's mother had a long, drawn-out death, adding "every human being has his or her karma." Kaew also talks about Khun Thanin's constant absences. An upset Somjai tells everyone to shut up, and orders Pun to go upstairs to attend to Ake.

Perhaps halfway through the film we feel that Ake has found a kind of mother in Pun: always kind, forgiving, loving in a parental way, and willing to join in nursery rhyme jokes. Male nurses seem usually to be a kind of oddity. The traditional ideology of hospitals says that men are doctors and women nurses. In the minds of many patients, nurses are kind, warm, and patient, while doctors are chilly, busy, and even ruthless. For a long time, the function of male nurses has only been to handle jobs that require great physical strength—mainly moving the bodies of patients unable to walk to operating tables, hospital beds, stretchers, and so on. Pun, away from any hospital, performs the work of both genders, and does it perfectly: he is patient, tactful, warm, as well as very strong. Early in the film, there are a few discreet few minutes during which Pun cleans up Ake in his bed, meaning he cleans the young man's behind and probably also his genitals.

Many male patients feel embarrassed and humiliated when female nurses briskly deal with their dirty rectums and smelly testicles. But mother is always an exception for the child. This is why Ake makes no fuss at all when his as-it-were-mother removes his pajamas. Of course, Pun is also felt as a good older brother, and in some ways a good father too. He is the exact opposite of Thanin: the good father, Ake imagines, that he never had.

It's at this point that *Mundane History* moves sharply away from the narrative. We see something new in the relationship between the men when we find them stretched out together on their backs in the large garden. It is as if they have become somehow equal in their affection for each other. But Pun is also a kind of useful elder-brother philosopher. He says that when he was a boy he was sure the earth was flat. It took many years before he could change his mind and accept that it is round. "It is so hard to change one's basic beliefs." He also talks about whether it is possible to live without a past. The future is always unknown, so one has to live life day by day.

Then we hear a calm male voice (it might just be Pun's, but we can't be sure) talking about the birth and especially the death of stars. When small stars finally lose the hydrogen that keeps them going, they shrivel and decay into white dwarves. Big stars, in the same circumstances, eventually explode and vanish from sight. For a few minutes we simply watch a big star's beautiful calm sphere turning into a frightful boiling sea of reddish gases, and finally watch its death by terrifying explosions.

After this section is over, there follows an enigmatic series of juxtapositions. 1. Images of a healthy Ake hopping downstairs to open the gate for his father's car. 2. Pun praying at a waterside temple (furnished with mysterious, large, ugly statues of tigers). Pun follows Thai Buddhist traditions, buying a caged pair of *nok krajok* and then setting them free. 3. A meditative look at the pet turtles in a cage-like aquarium

Pun with caged *nok krajok*, before he releases the birds

by Ake's bed. 4. Three almost empty rooms, bathed in a dark orange light, with miniature pyramids and neoliths, symbols of the remotest stages of human history, on the floors. (They are part of Bangkok's generally ignored planetarium.) 5. Pun and Ake are stretched out next to each other in the garden. Pun asks, with great calm, "What kind of accident did you have?" Neither Ake nor Anocha provide any answer. 6. Fast images of some kind of (mob?) demonstration laid transparently on top of one another.   Immediately, and finally, the scene shifts to a hospital room, where an unconscious woman is giving birth by caesarian section, attended by a group of surgeons and nurses. We don't really see the specialists' faces, just their busy hands and fingers. They are trying to pull an infant girl out of the mother's body. She is covered with sticky blood and is screaming at the top of her voice, while her little hands try to fend off the attentions of the nurses washing her clean. Meanwhile a doctor is sawing through the umbilical cord that for nine months has kept the two so tightly together. Finis.

How does one begin to "make sense" of *Nok krajok*, which, like most of the best films, is a complex interweaving of different motifs and riddles?

Without the explosion of a giant star and a screaming, bloodied baby girl, it would not be difficult to think of *Mundane History* as a political allegory along two lines. Non-Thai viewers, especially those who know little and care less about Siam, are likely to see in the film a Thai version of the venerable theme of a decaying, impotent bourgeoisie. As we have noted, Pun memorably counterposes the "beautiful mansion" against its "soulless" inhabitants. Money is no problem. Thanin has enough to pay the servants decently, and lets them eat the food that they prefer. He pays for Pun to work round the clock as Ake's nurse. He is an at-least third-generation bourgeois, a professor and intellectual, but there is no sign that he does anything useful or original. He is responsible for the endless dreariness of his household since he holds himself apart from the others. His crippled son could also be described as an allegorical representative of a dead-end, spoilt, self-pitying younger bourgeois generation. Opposed to these two men are the warm, working-class Kaew and Pun, without whose contributions the whole mansion would fall apart.

For Thai viewers, however, the film can appear an allegory of the decline of the Thai monarchy over the past decade. Taking a cue from the title (*The King Never Smiles*) of a recent banned biography by an American journalist,[2] Anocha and her tall, thin, skilled actor (Paramej Noiam) make Thanin an instantly recognizable double for the ruler. He too never smiles, and his chilly, aloof, and expressionless face mirrors the flat photos on millions of royal billboards across the country. Sullen Ake could then be interpreted as a symbol of a younger generation of alienated, self-obsessed royals with nowhere to go as the popular movement for serious democratization becomes a powerful political force. But no one in the film says anything remotely "present political." Anocha is not in the least apolitical, and the film was made during and after the months in which the "royalist" right-wing Yellow Shirts (PAD, People's Alliance for Democracy) were pushing for a military coup to overthrow the populist government of Thaksin Shinawat. For Thai viewers, there are two very short and separate PAD-related scenes. In the first, Thanin stands silent on the mansion's second-floor open-air patio, which could be taken as a symbol of the throne. On the soundtrack one can hear far away a favorite PAD song. In the second, we are shown brief, layered, fast-moving images of PAD supporters, which are like the unconnected views a traveler sees looking through the window of an express train. The traveler thinks—if at all—so what? My feeling is that these two

---

[2] Paul M. Handley, *The King Never Smiles: A Biography of Thailand's Bhumibol Adulyadej* (New Haven, CT: Yale University Press, 2006).

political–allegorical elements in Anocha's film are not enough to marginalize her deeper preoccupations.

Perhaps more indicative of the film's concerns are the number of Buddhist signals. Anocha juxtaposes Ake's turtles, swimming round and round in the bedside aquarium, with the caged sparrows that Pun liberates when praying at a temple. Nothing in the universe, even gigantic stars, can avoid the cycle of birth and death. Watching the screaming baby being born, one may remember an old adage which says that at the moment we are born we are already sentenced to death. One could think of Pun, the moral center of the film, as the Good Buddhist, selfless, humble, loving, thoughtful for others, uncomplaining, and in a manner of speaking living day by day, for death can come at any moment. Does he hope that he can find a way to liberate his human sparrow? What would liberation mean?

Khun Thanin on the second-floor patio

But I believe that, at the deepest level, *Nok krajok* is less about eternal cosmic cycles than about the history of our times. My impression is that Anocha is carrying out an "investigation" of what it is like to live day by day, these days, as a (Thai) male. If one walks around in Bangkok or up country, one rarely sees a woman or a girl doing nothing. But one is accustomed to the sight of males doing nothing—they hang out together, drinking and smoking listlessly, staring at nothing in particular, as if waiting for something to happen that will probably never happen. If drunk enough, they often boast coarsely and dishonestly about the "who cares" nameless women they claim to have fucked. Angst maybe, not the existential kind of ennui that we find in Baudelaire's poems or the *skuchnost* that pervades the great nineteenth-century Russian novels and plays.

Years ago, I idly asked an old Thai friend of mine how he would explain the recent demographic explosion of visible male homosexuals in a society whose written history barely mentions them. After thinking for a while, he said that the main reason is that girls and women have changed so much. More and more, they have entered the labor market on a big scale; they have their own businesses; they get elected; they become doctors, judges, newspeople, professors, and, of course, TV celebs; they have started to use the language of males; they discipline the children; they drive their own cars; and so on. Men don't like competing with women, so they often retreat into the company of other men, whom they understand very well. Sex with other men often seems to be "easier," less ritualized, freer of family responsibilities, more promiscuous, less expensive ...

Intuitively, he was onto something, but only at a tangent. According to a report published recently by the *Bangkok Post*, over the past decade the number of monks and novices has sensationally dropped from 6,000,000 to 1,500,000. One can explain this change in many ways, but one obvious reason is the decline of the respect that this all-male institution traditionally commanded. It is well-known that in the better universities girls have become the majority in faculties that twenty years ago were basically only for boys. (Political science is a fascinating example of this trend, not least because it is the gateway to careers in the powerful Ministry of the Interior.) In the bureaucracy and in the big corporations, women have acquired positions that make them the superiors and/or commanders of many males. The traditional male–female division of labor in rural society is inevitably weakened by urbanization and industrial advances. Television plays its own part. In comedies, fathers are usually dumb, old-fashioned, incompetent, and, in a friendly way, irresponsible. In telenovelas, the key figures are often girls and mothers (who understand each other even when they scream their heads off), not fathers and sons, who are rarely very close. In pop music, the trend is "boy bands" (not "bands") for the pleasure of women and girls. Medicine also plays a peculiar part. It is today quite possible for a woman, married or not, to become pregnant through what we can call artificial insemination. Like various domestic male animals, men can "donate" their sperm, first to doctors, and through them to a woman. Normally, neither the man nor the woman is permitted to know anything substantial about the other, so there is nothing in the process that makes the male a father through traditional marital sexual intercourse. She is a mother-to-be, he is merely a "donor." And her husband— if she has one??

Unless I am badly mistaken, Anocha is fascinated about contemporary angst among males, and here she has perhaps borrowed from Turgenev's nineteenth-century masterpiece, *Fathers and Sons*. Fatherhood is basically a social–political office, while motherhood is a biological experience. The Gospel according to Saint Matthew provides the reader with a long chain of begettings, from Abraham to Jesus, with only one woman named, and she is so "honored" only because she isn't a Jew. (Really, only two or three minutes in bed can make one a begetter—if only one were completely sure?) The role of fathers in Siam was created mainly to secure authority over the children, and especially over boys. They provided for the family's basic needs, punished, often brutally, their sons' waywardnesses, trained them in male skills, social positions, argot, manners, and religious doctrines. The office of traditional fatherhood sometimes looks like monarchy in diminutive form: authoritarian, aloof, and lifelong. But at the same time, because political, fatherhood is competitive vis-à-vis sons in a way that sharply contrasts with the relations between mothers and daughters. It is interesting to note that the naming and ranking of intrafamily crime works politically too. The worst crime (and the commonest in ruling circles) is parricide, followed by fratricide, perhaps matricide (rare), but there is no technical word for murder of sons by fathers (which may be not a crime at all, depending on eras and the circumstances). Children, especially male children, were often regarded as belongings or assets in the economic sense of the word. So to speak, the more the merrier.

But we know historically that both little and gigantic monarchies were beginning to be unstable during the nineteenth century (in Europe) and the twentieth century (elsewhere) with the onset of industrialization, popular nationalism, and democratization. Secular schooling, usually managed by the state, took boys (later girls) away from the little monarchies for a substantial part of their pre-adult lives, with two decisive changes. Starting with the growing bourgeoisies, children stopped being assets (making money for the family) and became debits, with the result that families, which had been big, began to become much smaller. Secondly, schools were the social-knowledge machines, tied to science, technology, and non-father disciplines, which shaped the first generations of youngsters who knew more than Father, not least about the doctrines of permanent progress, nationalism, citizenship, law, and invention. The clear signs of this "sons overcome fathers" appear with the abrupt development of political organizations (mostly nationalist) in whose names Youth and/or Young were central. Young Italy, Young Ireland, and so forth in Europe. By the turn of the twentieth century, the same thing happened in different parts of the non-European colonized zones: Young Vietnam, Young Burma, Young Java, Young Islam, Young Egypt, Young Turkey, and others. (It is striking that the countries with strong surviving monarchies did not produce such movements. There was no Young Thai, no Young Japan, no Young Brunei, no Young Nepal.) All these organizations and movements were originally created by young males in high schools and universities. (This is one reason why early communist and socialist parties were often led by men in their twenties, not fifties, and post-World War II independent states were ruled by men in their thirties, not sixties.) Youngness was formally a kind of accusation against "Father" as much as against the colonial regimes. Fathers were hopelessly "old" and often ignorant and collaborationist. It's needless to add that these young heroes, once in power, fought hard to be Fathers for the next forty to fifty years, and gradually lost popular trust. One can be seriously Young only for a short time. What then? By the end of the twentieth century came a second major generational break created not by new forms of schools, but by new technologies, and with increasing speed. We can see this clearly today in the development of rebellious youngsters who have outstripped "fathers" by their command of the intricacies of computer manipulation, and the complexities of the World Wide Web. But will the youngsters eventually use their skills to become, some time later, electronic Dads?

Mundane History is about three males, with two women at the margins. The gaping hole is the dead mother/wife. But Anocha is not interested in this dead woman, she is always thinking about a father and son who can't or won't communicate. Their language is silence. Thanin responsibly pays for services and goods to satisfy his son's physical needs as a proper bourgeois father should, but what then? If one sets aside the idea that Thanin sits in allegorically for the monarch, one sees something deeper: pain. We will remember how Somjai begs Ake to understand that his father suffers too, though she doesn't say why. In the few scenes where the father and son are together, Ake is completely hostile, and humiliates Thanin—with rudeness and silence—in front of the servants. Thanin does not hit back, and stoically accepts his son's hatred, and then disappears from the melancholy home as often as he can. The pain is surely guilt for something undescribed, but it's also his complete failure to be a father. Stoicism is his only option.

Into this cul-de-sac appears an unexpected possible savior: Ai Pun, who has no father that he can remember. The beauty of Pun is that he can be a mother (also elder brother, nurse, and perhaps even low-volt Dad) to a young man who is absolutely not his DNA son. So their ultimate connection is not competitive or generationally driven. Men are at their best when they don't think of themselves economically or politically in the stupid sense of these words. The brief utopian moments in the film are unforgettable: 1. Pun, alone, frees the *nok krajok* from the cage. Be free, live free while you can, and if you try, you birds owe me nothing—and death is always at your door. 2. Pun and Ake lie comradely together on the garden's grass. Ake says nothing. Pun talks about forgetting the past, living the day today because the end can come at any time. (*Nota bene*: There is no trace at all of anything erotic.) How can one best live as a man? Anocha calls her film *Jao nok krajok* to signal something that the rest of the film shows: "caged men." The unwritten text in this wonderful film is the anxiety, fragility, and perhaps, in the end, attachment/violence inside the ranks of those millions of human beings who don't remember being born, don't know when they will die, and ... can't give birth to babies.

SOUTHEAST ASIA PROGRAM PUBLICATIONS
Cornell University

Studies on Southeast Asia

Number 64 *Slow Anthropology: Negotiating Difference with the Iu Mien*, Hjorleifur Jonsson. 2014. ISBN 978-0-87727-764-4 (pb.)

Number 63 *Exploration and Irony in Studies of Siam over Forty Years*, Benedict R. O'G. Anderson. 2014. ISBN 978-0-87727-763-7 (pb.)

Number 62 *Ties that Bind: Cultural Identity, Class, and Law in Vietnam's Labor Resistance*, Trần Ngọc Angie. 2013. ISBN 978-0-87727-762-0 (pb.)

Number 61 *A Mountain of Difference: The Lumad in Early Colonial Mindanao*, Oona Paredes. 2013. ISBN 978-0-87727-761-3 (pb.)

Number 60 *The* Kim Vân Kieu *of Nguyen Du (1765–1820)*, trans. Vladislav Zhukov. 2013. ISBN 978-0-87727-760-6 (pb.)

Number 59 *The Politics of Timor-Leste: Democratic Consolidation after Intervention*, ed. Michael Leach and Damien Kingsbury. 2013. ISBN 978-0-87727-759-0 (pb.)

Number 58 *The Spirit of Things: Materiality and Religious Diversity in Southeast Asia*, ed. Julius Bautista. 2012. ISBN 970-0-87727-758-3 (pb.)

Number 57 *Demographic Change in Southeast Asia: Recent Histories and Future Directions*, ed. Lindy Williams and Michael Philip Guest. 2012. ISBN 978-0-87727-757-6 (pb.)

Number 56 *Modern and Contemporary Southeast Asian Art: An Anthology*, ed. Nora A. Taylor and Boreth Ly. 2012. ISBN 978-0-87727-756-9 (pb.)

Number 55 *Glimpses of Freedom: Independent Cinema in Southeast Asia*, ed. May Adadol Ingawanij and Benjamin McKay. 2012. ISBN 978-0-87727-755-2 (pb.)

Number 54 *Student Activism in Malaysia: Crucible, Mirror, Sideshow*, Meredith L. Weiss. 2011. ISBN 978-0-87727-754-5 (pb.)

Number 53 *Political Authority and Provincial Identity in Thailand: The Making of Banharn-buri*, Yoshinori Nishizaki. 2011. ISBN 978-0-87727-753-8 (pb.)

Number 52 *Vietnam and the West: New Approaches*, ed. Wynn Wilcox. 2010. ISBN 978-0-87727-752-1 (pb.)

Number 51 *Cultures at War: The Cold War and Cultural Expression in Southeast Asia*, ed. Tony Day and Maya H. T. Liem. 2010. ISBN 978-0-87727-751-4 (pb.)

Number 50 *State of Authority: The State in Society in Indonesia*, ed. Gerry van Klinken and Joshua Barker. 2009. ISBN 978-0-87727-750-7 (pb.)

Number 49 *Phan Châu Trinh and His Political Writings*, Phan Châu Trinh, ed. and trans. Vinh Sinh. 2009. ISBN 978-0-87727-749-1 (pb.)

Number 48 *Dependent Communities: Aid and Politics in Cambodia and East Timor*, Caroline Hughes. 2009. ISBN 978-0-87727-748-4 (pb.)

Number 47 *A Man Like Him: Portrait of the Burmese Journalist, Journal Kyaw U Chit Maung*, Journal Kyaw Ma Ma Lay, trans. Ma Thanegi, 2008. ISBN 978-0-87727-747-7 (pb.)

Number 46   *At the Edge of the Forest: Essays on Cambodia, History, and Narrative in Honor of David Chandler*, ed. Anne Ruth Hansen and Judy Ledgerwood. 2008. ISBN 978-0-87727-746-0 (pb).

Number 45   *Conflict, Violence, and Displacement in Indonesia*, ed. Eva-Lotta E. Hedman. 2008. ISBN 978-0-87727-745-3 (pb).

Number 44   *Friends and Exiles: A Memoir of the Nutmeg Isles and the Indonesian Nationalist Movement*, Des Alwi, ed. Barbara S. Harvey. 2008. ISBN 978-0-877277-44-6 (pb).

Number 43   *Early Southeast Asia: Selected Essays*, O. W. Wolters, ed. Craig J. Reynolds. 2008. 255 pp. ISBN 978-0-877277-43-9 (pb).

Number 42   *Thailand: The Politics of Despotic Paternalism* (revised edition), Thak Chaloemtiarana. 2007. 284 pp. ISBN 0-8772-7742-7 (pb).

Number 41   *Views of Seventeenth-Century Vietnam: Christoforo Borri on Cochinchina and Samuel Baron on Tonkin*, ed. Olga Dror and K. W. Taylor. 2006. 290 pp. ISBN 0-8772-7741-9 (pb).

Number 40   *Laskar Jihad: Islam, Militancy, and the Quest for Identity in Post-New Order Indonesia*, Noorhaidi Hasan. 2006. 266 pp. ISBN 0-877277-40-0 (pb).

Number 39   *The Indonesian Supreme Court: A Study of Institutional Collapse*, Sebastiaan Pompe. 2005. 494 pp. ISBN 0-877277-38-9 (pb).

Number 38   *Spirited Politics: Religion and Public Life in Contemporary Southeast Asia*, ed. Andrew C. Willford and Kenneth M. George. 2005. 210 pp. ISBN 0-87727-737-0.

Number 37   *Sumatran Sultanate and Colonial State: Jambi and the Rise of Dutch Imperialism, 1830-1907*, Elsbeth Locher-Scholten, trans. Beverley Jackson. 2004. 332 pp. ISBN 0-87727-736-2.

Number 36   *Southeast Asia over Three Generations: Essays Presented to Benedict R. O'G. Anderson*, ed. James T. Siegel and Audrey R. Kahin. 2003. 398 pp. ISBN 0-87727-735-4.

Number 35   *Nationalism and Revolution in Indonesia*, George McTurnan Kahin, intro. Benedict R. O'G. Anderson (reprinted from 1952 edition, Cornell University Press, with permission). 2003. 530 pp. ISBN 0-87727-734-6.

Number 34   *Golddiggers, Farmers, and Traders in the "Chinese Districts" of West Kalimantan, Indonesia*, Mary Somers Heidhues. 2003. 316 pp. ISBN 0-87727-733-8.

Number 33   *Opusculum de Sectis apud Sinenses et Tunkinenses (A Small Treatise on the Sects among the Chinese and Tonkinese): A Study of Religion in China and North Vietnam in the Eighteenth Century*, Father Adriano de St. Thecla, trans. Olga Dror, with Mariya Berezovska. 2002. 363 pp. ISBN 0-87727-732-X.

Number 32   *Fear and Sanctuary: Burmese Refugees in Thailand*, Hazel J. Lang. 2002. 204 pp. ISBN 0-87727-731-1.

Number 31   *Modern Dreams: An Inquiry into Power, Cultural Production, and the Cityscape in Contemporary Urban Penang, Malaysia*, Beng-Lan Goh. 2002. 225 pp. ISBN 0-87727-730-3.

Number 30   *Violence and the State in Suharto's Indonesia*, ed. Benedict R. O'G. Anderson. 2001. Second printing, 2002. 247 pp. ISBN 0-87727-729-X.

Number 29   *Studies in Southeast Asian Art: Essays in Honor of Stanley J. O'Connor*, ed. Nora A. Taylor. 2000. 243 pp. Illustrations. ISBN 0-87727-728-1.

Number 28   *The Hadrami Awakening: Community and Identity in the Netherlands East Indies, 1900-1942*, Natalie Mobini-Kesheh. 1999. 174 pp. ISBN 0-87727-727-3.

Number 27   *Tales from Djakarta: Caricatures of Circumstances and their Human Beings*, Pramoedya Ananta Toer. 1999. 145 pp. ISBN 0-87727-726-5.

Number 26   *History, Culture, and Region in Southeast Asian Perspectives*, rev. ed., O. W. Wolters. 1999. Second printing, 2004. 275 pp. ISBN 0-87727-725-7.

Number 25   *Figures of Criminality in Indonesia, the Philippines, and Colonial Vietnam*, ed. Vicente L. Rafael. 1999. 259 pp. ISBN 0-87727-724-9.

Number 24   *Paths to Conflagration: Fifty Years of Diplomacy and Warfare in Laos, Thailand, and Vietnam, 1778-1828*, Mayoury Ngaosyvathn and Pheuiphanh Ngaosyvathn. 1998. 268 pp. ISBN 0-87727-723-0.

Number 23   *Nguyễn Cochinchina: Southern Vietnam in the Seventeenth and Eighteenth Centuries*, Li Tana. 1998. Second printing, 2002. 194 pp. ISBN 0-87727-722-2.

Number 22   *Young Heroes: The Indonesian Family in Politics*, Saya S. Shiraishi. 1997. 183 pp. ISBN 0-87727-721-4.

Number 21   *Interpreting Development: Capitalism, Democracy, and the Middle Class in Thailand*, John Girling. 1996. 95 pp. ISBN 0-87727-720-6.

Number 20   *Making Indonesia*, ed. Daniel S. Lev, Ruth McVey. 1996. 201 pp. ISBN 0-87727-719-2.

Number 19   *Essays into Vietnamese Pasts*, ed. K. W. Taylor, John K. Whitmore. 1995. 288 pp. ISBN 0-87727-718-4.

Number 18   *In the Land of Lady White Blood: Southern Thailand and the Meaning of History*, Lorraine M. Gesick. 1995. 106 pp. ISBN 0-87727-717-6.

Number 17   *The Vernacular Press and the Emergence of Modern Indonesian Consciousness*, Ahmat Adam. 1995. 220 pp. ISBN 0-87727-716-8.

Number 16   *The Nan Chronicle*, trans., ed. David K. Wyatt. 1994. 158 pp. ISBN 0-87727-715-X.

Number 15   *Selective Judicial Competence: The Cirebon-Priangan Legal Administration, 1680–1792*, Mason C. Hoadley. 1994. 185 pp. ISBN 0-87727-714-1.

Number 14   *Sjahrir: Politics and Exile in Indonesia*, Rudolf Mrázek. 1994. 536 pp. ISBN 0-87727-713-3.

Number 13   *Fair Land Sarawak: Some Recollections of an Expatriate Officer*, Alastair Morrison. 1993. 196 pp. ISBN 0-87727-712-5.

Number 12   *Fields from the Sea: Chinese Junk Trade with Siam during the Late Eighteenth and Early Nineteenth Centuries*, Jennifer Cushman. 1993. 206 pp. ISBN 0-87727-711-7.

Number 11   *Money, Markets, and Trade in Early Southeast Asia: The Development of Indigenous Monetary Systems to AD 1400*, Robert S. Wicks. 1992. 2nd printing 1996. 354 pp., 78 tables, illus., maps. ISBN 0-87727-710-9.

Number 10   *Tai Ahoms and the Stars: Three Ritual Texts to Ward Off Danger*, trans., ed. B. J. Terwiel, Ranoo Wichasin. 1992. 170 pp. ISBN 0-87727-709-5.

Number 9   *Southeast Asian Capitalists,* ed. Ruth McVey. 1992. 2nd printing 1993. 220 pp. ISBN 0-87727-708-7.

Number 8   *The Politics of Colonial Exploitation: Java, the Dutch, and the Cultivation System,* Cornelis Fasseur, ed. R. E. Elson, trans. R. E. Elson, Ary Kraal. 1992. 2nd printing 1994. 266 pp. ISBN 0-87727-707-9.

Number 7   *A Malay Frontier: Unity and Duality in a Sumatran Kingdom,* Jane Drakard. 1990. 2nd printing 2003. 215 pp. ISBN 0-87727-706-0.

Number 6   *Trends in Khmer Art,* Jean Boisselier, ed. Natasha Eilenberg, trans. Natasha Eilenberg, Melvin Elliott. 1989. 124 pp., 24 plates. ISBN 0-87727-705-2.

Number 5   *Southeast Asian Ephemeris: Solar and Planetary Positions, A.D. 638–2000,* J. C. Eade. 1989. 175 pp. ISBN 0-87727-704-4.

Number 3   *Thai Radical Discourse: The Real Face of Thai Feudalism Today,* Craig J. Reynolds. 1987. 2nd printing 1994. 186 pp. ISBN 0-87727-702-8.

Number 1   *The Symbolism of the Stupa,* Adrian Snodgrass. 1985. Revised with index, 1988. 3rd printing 1998. 469 pp. ISBN 0-87727-700-1.

SEAP Series

Number 23   *Possessed by the Spirits: Mediumship in Contemporary Vietnamese Communities.* 2006. 186 pp. ISBN 0-877271-41-0 (pb).

Number 22   *The Industry of Marrying Europeans,* Vũ Trọng Phụng, trans. Thúy Tranviet. 2006. 66 pp. ISBN 0-877271-40-2 (pb).

Number 21   *Securing a Place: Small-Scale Artisans in Modern Indonesia,* Elizabeth Morrell. 2005. 220 pp. ISBN 0-877271-39-9.

Number 20   *Southern Vietnam under the Reign of Minh Mạng (1820-1841): Central Policies and Local Response,* Choi Byung Wook. 2004. 226pp. ISBN 0-0-877271-40-2.

Number 19   *Gender, Household, State: Đổi Mới in Việt Nam,* ed. Jayne Werner and Danièle Bélanger. 2002. 151 pp. ISBN 0-87727-137-2.

Number 18   *Culture and Power in Traditional Siamese Government,* Neil A. Englehart. 2001. 130 pp. ISBN 0-87727-135-6.

Number 17   *Gangsters, Democracy, and the State,* ed. Carl A. Trocki. 1998. Second printing, 2002. 94 pp. ISBN 0-87727-134-8.

Number 16   *Cutting across the Lands: An Annotated Bibliography on Natural Resource Management and Community Development in Indonesia, the Philippines, and Malaysia,* ed. Eveline Ferretti. 1997. 329 pp. ISBN 0-87727-133-X.

Number 15   *The Revolution Falters: The Left in Philippine Politics after 1986,* ed. Patricio N. Abinales. 1996. Second printing, 2002. 182 pp. ISBN 0-87727-132-1.

Number 14   *Being Kammu: My Village, My Life,* Damrong Tayanin. 1994. 138 pp., 22 tables, illus., maps. ISBN 0-87727-130-5.

Number 13   *The American War in Vietnam,* ed. Jayne Werner, David Hunt. 1993. 132 pp. ISBN 0-87727-131-3.

Number 12   *The Voice of Young Burma,* Aye Kyaw. 1993. 92 pp. ISBN 0-87727-129-1.

Number 11   *The Political Legacy of Aung San*, ed. Josef Silverstein. Revised edition 1993. 169 pp. ISBN 0-87727-128-3.

Number 10   *Studies on Vietnamese Language and Literature: A Preliminary Bibliography*, Nguyen Dinh Tham. 1992. 227 pp. ISBN 0-87727-127-5.

Number 8   *From PKI to the Comintern, 1924–1941: The Apprenticeship of the Malayan Communist Party*, Cheah Boon Kheng. 1992. 147 pp. ISBN 0-87727-125-9.

Number 7   *Intellectual Property and US Relations with Indonesia, Malaysia, Singapore, and Thailand*, Elisabeth Uphoff. 1991. 67 pp. ISBN 0-87727-124-0.

Cornell Modern Indonesia Project Publications

Number 76   *Producing Indonesia: The State of the Field of Indonesian Studies*, ed. Eric Tagliacozzo. 2014. ISBN 978-0-87727-302-8 (pb.)

Other CMIP titles available at http://cmip.library.cornell.edu

Copublished Titles

The Ambiguous Allure of the West: Traces of the Colonial in Thailand, ed. Rachel V. Harrison and Peter A. Jackson. Copublished with Hong Kong University Press. 2010. ISBN 978-0-87727-608-1 (pb.)

The Many Ways of Being Muslim: Fiction by Muslim Filipinos, ed. Coeli Barry. Copublished with Anvil Publishing, Inc., the Philippines. 2008. ISBN 978-0-87727-605-0 (pb.)

Language Texts

INDONESIAN

Beginning Indonesian through Self-Instruction, John U. Wolff, Dédé Oetomo, Daniel Fietkiewicz. 3rd revised edition 1992. Vol. 1. 115 pp. ISBN 0-87727-529-7. Vol. 2. 434 pp. ISBN 0-87727-530-0. Vol. 3. 473 pp. ISBN 0-87727-531-9.

Indonesian Readings, John U. Wolff. 1978. 4th printing 1992. 480 pp. ISBN 0-87727-517-3

Indonesian Conversations, John U. Wolff. 1978. 3rd printing 1991. 297 pp. ISBN 0-87727-516-5

Formal Indonesian, John U. Wolff. 2nd revised edition 1986. 446 pp. ISBN 0-87727-515-7

TAGALOG

Pilipino through Self-Instruction, John U. Wolff, Maria Theresa C. Centeno, Der-Hwa V. Rau. 1991. Vol. 1. 342 pp. ISBN 0-87727—525-4. Vol. 2., revised 2005, 378 pp. ISBN 0-87727-526-2. Vol 3., revised 2005, 431 pp. ISBN 0-87727-527-0. Vol. 4. 306 pp. ISBN 0-87727-528-9.

THAI

A. U. A. Language Center Thai Course, J. Marvin Brown. Originally published by the American University Alumni Association Language Center, 1974. Reissued by Cornell Southeast Asia Program, 1991, 1992. Book 1. 267 pp. ISBN 0-87727-506-8. Book 2. 288 pp. ISBN 0-87727-507-6. Book 3. 247 pp. ISBN 0-87727-508-4.

A. U. A. Language Center Thai Course, Reading and Writing Text (mostly reading), 1979. Reissued 1997. 164 pp. ISBN 0-87727-511-4.

A. U. A. Language Center Thai Course, Reading and Writing Workbook (mostly writing), 1979. Reissued 1997. 99 pp. ISBN 0-87727-512-2.

KHMER

Cambodian System of Writing and Beginning Reader, Franklin E. Huffman. Originally published by Yale University Press, 1970. Reissued by Cornell Southeast Asia Program, 4th printing 2002. 365 pp. ISBN 0-300-01314-0.

Modern Spoken Cambodian, Franklin E. Huffman, assist. Charan Promchan, Chhom-Rak Thong Lambert. Originally published by Yale University Press, 1970. Reissued by Cornell Southeast Asia Program, 3rd printing 1991. 451 pp. ISBN 0-300-01316-7.

Intermediate Cambodian Reader, ed. Franklin E. Huffman, assist. Im Proum. Originally published by Yale University Press, 1972. Reissued by Cornell Southeast Asia Program, 1988. 499 pp. ISBN 0-300-01552-6.

Cambodian Literary Reader and Glossary, Franklin E. Huffman, Im Proum. Originally published by Yale University Press, 1977. Reissued by Cornell Southeast Asia Program, 1988. 494 pp. ISBN 0-300-02069-4.

HMONG

White Hmong-English Dictionary, Ernest E. Heimbach. 1969. 8th printing, 2002. 523 pp. ISBN 0-87727-075-9.

VIETNAMESE

Intermediate Spoken Vietnamese, Franklin E. Huffman, Tran Trong Hai. 1980. 3rd printing 1994. ISBN 0-87727-500-9.

Proto-Austronesian Phonology with Glossary, John U. Wolff, 2 volumes, 2011. ISBN vol. I, 978-0-87727-532-9. ISBN vol. II, 978-0-87727-533-6.

To order, please contact:
Mail:
Cornell University Press Services
750 Cascadilla Street
PO Box 6525
Ithaca, NY 14851 USA
        E-mail: orderbook@cupserv.org
Phone/Fax, Monday–Friday, 8 am – 5 pm (Eastern US):
Phone: 607 277 2211 or 800 666 2211 (US, Canada)
Fax: 607 277 6292 or 800 688 2877 (US, Canada)

Order through our online bookstore at:
SEAP.einaudi.cornell.edu/publications

Milton Keynes UK
Ingram Content Group UK Ltd.
UKHW010155260924
448856UK00007B/212